By Andrew Tobias

The Funny Money Game

Fire and Ice

The Only Investment Guide You'll Ever Need

Getting By on $100,000 a Year (and Other Sad Tales)

The Invisible Bankers

Money Angles

The Only Other *Investment Guide You'll Ever Need*

The Only *OTHER* INVESTMENT GUIDE

You'll Ever Need

ANDREW TOBIAS

SIMON AND SCHUSTER
New York London Toronto Sydney Tokyo

Published by Simon and Schuster
A Division of Simon & Schuster, Inc.
Simon & Schuster Building
Rockefeller Center
1230 Avenue of the Americas
New York, NY 10020

SIMON AND SCHUSTER and colophon are registered trademarks
of Simon & Schuster, Inc.

Designed by Irving Perkins Associates, Inc.
Manufactured in the United States of America

BOMC offers recordings and compact discs, cassettes
and records. For information and catalog write to
BOMR, Camp Hill, PA 17012.

Library of Congress Cataloging-in-Publication Data

Tobias, Andrew P.
The only other investment guide you'll ever need.

Includes index.
1. Investments. 2. Finance, Personal.
I. Title.
HG4521.T6   1987   332.6'78   87-20494
                                    ISBN 0-671-64166-2

Portions of this book have appeared in and are
adapted from *Playboy, Parade,* and *AdWeek.*

CONTENTS

From annuities and baseball cards to timberland, unit trusts, and zero coupon convertible bonds.

The Only OTHER Investment Guide You'll Ever Need?

This is not a revision of *The Only Investment Guide You'll Ever Need*. We already did that *(STILL The Only Investment Guide You'll Ever Need)*—twice. First, in 1983, for changes in the rules on IRAs, among other things, and then again at the end of 1986 to take account of the new tax law.

So if you're just looking for the same old principles of personal finance, go ahead. Read the other book. But if you want to find out what's happened since then, if you want to hold your own at *today's* cocktail parties, around *today's* water coolers, well, there's just nothing for it: skip this month's donation to Save the Children (they're kids—they'll manage), and buy this book.*

Let's face it. In the 10 years since that old book was written, the world has spun into high gear. Back then, checking accounts paid no interest, savings bonds were a joke, auto loans ran three years, and trading volume on the New York Stock Exchange averaged 25 million shares a day. (The Dow fell four points "on light volume," newscasters will say today, when 140 million shares have traded hands.) Back then, about three people had ever heard of personal computers (two of them named Jobs and Wozniak), the largest mutual fund family offered a choice of 15 dif-

---

*"Give a man a fish and you feed him for a day. Teach him to do risk arbitrage and you'll feed his entire village."

—Anonymous

7

ferent funds (today: 92), and $10,000 spread among the 10 mutual funds I recommended in that book was worth just $10,000. Today it would be worth $55,000 (versus $38,000, invested in the Standard & Poor's 500 average, or $17,000, in a savings account). There were no cash management accounts, no home equity loans, no salary reduction plans, no universal life, no single-premium life, no index options, no program trading, no frequent-flier miles (the true currency of the eighties), no zero coupon bonds, no leveraged buyouts, no master limited partnerships, no global shift toward free-market economics, no gargantuan trade and budget deficits, no automatic teller networks, no Financial News Network—not even a Home Shopping Network. (How did anyone ever *buy* anything?)

The top federal income tax bracket was 70%.

The basics of personal finance haven't changed much—they never do. And there are still just a relatively few commonsense things you need to know about your money.* But the welter of investment choices and the thicket of jargon and pitches have grown a great deal more dense. Perhaps this book can be your machete.

It is divided into three parts. In the first—Home Economics—I will argue that you must take responsibility for your own affairs (Chapter 1: Trust No One) and that you really ought to have a plan (Chapter 2: Do It for Mom). I will take your time to consider the financial high points of things like your home, your kids, your car, your credit cards, your taxes, your insurance, and your retirement fund. Even so, I will try not to bore you to tears.

In the second part—Investing—I will explore the very best way to make money from the stock market (be a broker); the importance of minimizing not just commission costs but "spreads" (which can be far more important); a broad strategy for dealing with uncertain financial times—are financial times ever anything but uncertain?—and any number of systems for beating the market, including a few that may actually work. In the final

*That was the rationale of the first book: not that it was the only investment guide that was any *good*; just that, sadly, reading book after book about money won't increase your return—but could tempt you to plunge where you shouldn't.

chapters reside a variety of even more adventuresome ways to put your money to work, including several deals I myself have invested in purely for your amusement (though that was not my goal at the time).

Part III is an alphabetical survey of investment alternatives ranging from antiques and annuities through comic books and closed-end funds (including one managed by the famed John Templeton organization that you may be able to buy for 80 cents on the dollar), to junk bonds, tax certificates, vulture funds, and zero coupon convertibles.

Those of you to whom such things are old hat I hope will find in this book an afternoon's entertainment and perhaps comforting confirmation of your already good sense.

Those of you employed on Wall Street or in the sale of insurance or the provision of legal services—please ignore the parts where I say terrible things about you. I don't mean them about *you*, just about a few of your colleagues.

Those of you ordinarily numbed by things financial I hope will come away realizing that you *can* understand what's important to know about your money—or, if you have none, come away with the feeling that it's altogether possible to get some.

PART I

Home Economics

There is no dignity quite so impressive,
and no independence quite so important,
as living within your means.
—Calvin Coolidge

Chapter 1

TRUST NO ONE

Taking Responsibility for Your Own Affairs

Let's start with an easy one.

"If you or anyone you know is over fifty, I *urge* you to get pencil and paper ready."

So begin the celebrity life insurance commercials you may have seen on TV. Dick Van Dyke does them. Ed McMahon does them. Even Gavin MacLeod—good ol' Murray on the *Mary Tyler Moore Show*—does them.

Murray, Murray, *Mur*ray.

But the plans sound good, don't they? No matter how bad your health, *you cannot be turned down* for this "top quality, big dollar" protection. Yet amazing as it seems—well, this is why I told you to get your pencil and paper ready—Murray's plan costs just $5 a month. And—get this!—your premiums are guaranteed never to rise as you get older.

Says Murray: "I can't tell you what a relief it is to know that we won't be a burden on our children." Here the kids thought they stood to inherit a pretty penny—Murray did go on to captain the *Loveboat*, after all—but had it not been for this insurance,

13

they'd have been left with nothing but the funeral bill. *Thank heavens for this insurance.*

If you're 50, Murray says, just $5 a month buys you $10,000 in protection.

Catch #1: If you die of an illness, your heirs get $2800, not $10,000. The bulk of the insurance benefit is for *accidental* death only. Yet accidents are a minor cause of death among older people. (Dick Van Dyke's pitch calls them "one of the leading causes of death for people over forty-five." But actually, fewer than 3% of deaths among people over 45 are caused by accidents. So more than 97% of the time the payoff would be $2800, not $10,000.)

It's true, you can't be turned down for this coverage; but— Catch #2—only after you've paid premiums for two years are you actually covered. Die of an illness before then, and your heirs get nothing but a refund of the premiums you've paid.

True, too, your rates are guaranteed not to rise (well, sort of); but—Catch #3—as you get older, your coverage falls. Say you pay $5 a month, month after month, for 25 years. Then, at 75, having paid in a total of $1500, you have a heart attack and die. This policy pays your heirs a grand total of $225. Period. (Die after age 79 and they get no benefit at all.) This is what Murray endorses as BIG DOLLAR protection. He can't tell you what a relief it is to know that $225 will be there when his loved ones need it.

If at age 79 you died not of an illness but, say, hang-gliding into a utility pole, your heirs would get an extra $775, except that—Catch #4—death while hang-gliding doesn't qualify for the accidental death bonus. Neither does death in a war (declared or undeclared), in a private plane, by suicide, surgery, or while intoxicated, if intoxication caused the accident. (If you were merely three sheets to the wind in the bar car of your commuter train when it derailed and flew off a cliff, you'd be okay.)

Catch #5: Your rates are guaranteed never to rise *only so long as the insurance company doesn't raise them.* If it decides everybody should pay $6 a month instead of $5, or to cancel all the policies altogether because it's not making money on them, the company is free to do so.

Catch #6: Five bucks a month is the least you can pay; but this is portrayed as *such* a good deal for "folks like us," as Murray puts it—you know, warm, bald guys who make $80,000 an epi-sode (Gavin MacLeod's peak pay in 1984)—that many folks sign up for the full $40 a month's worth, to cover both them and their spouses four times over. Five dollars a month is nothing. But $40 a month, in the budgets of many older Americans—$480 a year —is a hefty sum.

The pitchmen freely acknowledge they're paid to endorse these insurance plans, but Dick Van Dyke says, in his follow-up letter: "P.S. I'm sure you know I would never speak out for anything I didn't personally believe in." Gavin MacLeod, in *his* P.S., writes: "I want you to know I would never speak out for anything I didn't believe in with my whole heart." The cash Continental American Life paid him to endorse this plan has nothing to do with it.*

Trust no one. It kills me to say that, and I'll admit there are exceptions—you can trust Superman, you can trust Dan Rather (you can trust me, of course)—but the list is shorter than you think. I mean, my God: if you can't trust *Murray* . . .

Here is an ad for the Oppenheimer Special Fund. Oppenheimer is no slouch of an investment firm, and this is its *special* fund. In fact, says the ad, this fund has appreciated at a rate of 21.5% a year for the last 10 years. Compare *that* with what your local bank is paying.

You're smart enough to know performance like that can't nec-essarily be repeated (if only you had thought to invest 10 years ago!). And you imagine, given that they're trying pretty hard to sell this to you, that there may be a sales commission involved (there is: only $4575 of the $5000 you were thinking of investing actually goes to work for you—the rest is an immediate loss). But never mind that. We're talking about 21.5% annual growth— enough, if it continued for another two decades, to turn a single $2000 IRA contribution into $90,000!

You are all set to send in your money, when you come across

---

*MacLeod and Van Dyke were both reportedly paid $25,000 to make the television commercials, plus a commission on each toll-free call the commercials produce. An executive close to the arrangement estimates the final take for each man to be between $100,000 and $200,000.

Jane Bryant Quinn's column in *Newsweek*. She has studied the prospectus—you could have studied it, too, but you would have been a rare investor if you did—and she has noticed that "the big gains that Oppenheimer packs into its alluring yield of 21.5% came long ago. Between 1974 and 1980, share values rose an average of 39% a year. But zigzag performance from 1980 to 1984 brought an average annual loss of 4%."

No place in the ad do you see anything about an average annual loss of 4%.

Maybe the fund will regain its touch, Quinn concludes, "but its ad (and similar ads for other funds) would lead you to think it has been making a lot of money lately, which is not the case."

In fact, in the great stock markets of 1985 and 1986, the Oppenheimer Special Fund did manage gains of 16.8% and 15.1% (before allowing for the sales commission). But that performance placed the fund in the bottom fifth of the mutual funds ranked by Lipper Analytical Services in 1985; in the middle fifth in 1986.

Trust no one. You've got to take responsibility for your own affairs.

Many people wish they could turn the whole mess over to someone else. Widows particularly express this wish, having in some cases been made to feel over many years of marriage that they can't possibly understand anything having to do with money. But the folks who do understand money, while many have your best interests at heart, have their own interests at heart, too. You have to take responsibility for your own money because no one cares about it as much as you. That doesn't mean you can't rely on a variety of experts to help—a good accountant, a good mutual fund manager, perhaps a good Realtor or insurance agent, financial planner or attorney. But ultimately it's you who are in charge.

If you don't understand what you're investing in, or haven't formed a broad spending/borrowing/saving/insuring/investing plan yourself, it's unlikely things will work out terribly well. (Most people wind up with nothing, says financial adviser Venita Van Caspel, "not because they plan to fail, but because they fail to plan.") What's more, you *can* do it. The simple investments are very often the best. And that goes, too, for the simple loans, the simple insurance, and the simple financial plans.

It's not enough to respond to advertising headlines or the salesperson's enthusiasm or the lavishly illustrated brochure. You've got to read between the lines—or at least read the prospectus. And since you won't—most prospecti are unreadable—you've got to stick to sensible investments recommended by competent, disinterested parties. Not competent *or* disinterested, competent *and* disinterested—which certainly leaves out Murray, may very likely leave out tips from your hair stylist, and may even leave out advice from your accountant or financial planner, who could be getting a commission for steering you into a particular deal.

If only you had access to an expert you could *trust*. Someone who did know how to read a prospectus.

With that in mind, pour yourself a beer and get out your letter opener, for what we have here—delivered by hand to our door—is a fat manila envelope from nothing less than U.S. Trust, the United States Trust Company, one of the oldest, classiest, most exclusive banks in the country. ("When you do something very well," its ads say, "you simply cannot do it for everyone.")

Inside is everything you'll need to evaluate and sign up for the Samson Properties 1985-A Drilling Program. U.S. Trust describes Samson 1985-A as "a quality oil and gas investment with relatively moderate risk, inherent tax benefits, and the potential for significant upside economic gains." (As opposed, one presumes, to downside economic gains.)

The bank's cover letter outlines the deal. With it, in your envelope, come a colorful Samson sales brochure, a deadly 165-page Samson prospectus, a huge U.S. Trust business reply envelope for your signed papers, and a form you sign agreeing to pay the bank a 5% "advisory fee" for bringing the deal to your attention.

(There is already a 7.5% sales commission built into the deal, but the bank can't touch it—it's illegal for banks to sell securities like these—so, instead, it charges this 5% advisory fee. The bank's not *selling* anything—merely recommending that you buy it and enclosing all the papers you need to sign to do so.)

By paying the "advisory fee," you are in effect getting the deal at 105% of retail. You could avoid the fee by purchasing Samson units directly through a stockbroker, but when you deal with a classy bank—this is not a bank that's out hawking car loans—you should show a little class yourself.

Participations in Samson 1985-A run $25,000 and up. Much of that money will go toward the drilling of development wells—the kind of wells you drill in proven fields, even if they won't make you a fortune—and 90% or more of what you invest will be deductible in 1985. (The tax law on oil deals has been substantially tightened since 1985, of course, but either way, what really matters in an oil deal is how much oil you produce. Tax deductions are peachy, but not if you never get your money back. How rich could you get giving everything to the Red Cross?)

THESE ARE SPECULATIVE SECURITIES AND INVOLVE A HIGH DEGREE OF RISK, cautions the front page of the prospectus. The SEC makes 'em say stuff like that. The bank prefers to describe it as "relatively moderate risk." And, as only clients with net worths of $1 million or incomes of $200,000 are advised to participate, it's true. What's an extra $25,000 or $50,000 to somebody like that?

Even so, as a potential investor you might reasonably want to know whether you'll make any money investing in Samson. And you have a choice. You can read the three-page analysis from the bank. You can read the colorful six-page Samson brochure. Or you can read the 165-page prospectus.

I know most of you would lunge for the prospectus, but let's start with the colorful brochure.

Under the heading PRIOR PROGRAM PERFORMANCE, the brochure explains that by mid-1984, "Samson's 1973–1981 Programs had distributed cash equal to 127% of total cash invested" and would distribute a further 226% over the life of those programs.

The brochure says you shouldn't count on future programs *all* doing so well, but, hey, 127% and 226%—that's like three and a half times your money! Plus, U.S. Trust likes the program, and Samson must be getting more experienced each year, and drilling costs are really low these days, and boy, could I ever use the tax deduction—where do I sign?

At least that was my reaction.

The brochure does say, "These figures assume an equal investment in each of the programs offered from 1973 through 1981," but that sounds innocuous enough.

So much for the brochure.

Now let me tell you how to read an oil-and-gas prospectus:

1. Find the table of contents.
2. Find the page that shows the driller's track record, titled "Prior Performance" or "Prior Activities."
3. Look for the column that shows how much actual cash investors in past deals have received.
4. Compare that with how much they actually invested.
5. End of story.

Says one prominent tax accountant: "If their average program isn't paying back in three or four years, forget it."

In Tulsa-based Samson's case, it turns out that its very first program, a teeny-tiny deal in 1973 that involved a total of just $325,000 and 11 investors, has paid off like gangbusters. But all its subsequent programs, ranging from 3 to 30 times as big, have had less spectacular results.

(Funny how often that first deal, which helps to sell all subsequent deals, is a lot more successful than the rest.)

So, in the first place, if you don't assume "an equal investment in each of the programs," but assume instead the amounts that were actually invested, the return on those 1973–1981 programs by mid-1984 would have been not 127% (all your money back and then some), but 45%.

Of the nearly $30 million that investors handed Samson in 1981 (not to mention the $70 million in 1982, 1983, and the first part of 1984) less than $1 million had been paid back by September 30, 1984.

Of the three 1980 deals—one private, two public—one had paid back 74% by September 30, 1984, two had paid back 17% and 9% respectively. Guess which one was the private deal.

And understand, these numbers are not return *on* investment (with luck, that comes later), they're return *of* investment.

If there were a cynic in the room—and I trust there's not—he might suggest that Samson raised $100 million in drilling investments from 1981 through 1984, and millions more in 1985, on the strength of one crummy little $325,000 program it had drilled ten years earlier.

In fact, as it turns out, *that first deal wasn't drilled by Samson at all*. It was drilled by May Petroleum. Samson merely purchased the producing wells at two-dollar-a-barrel-era oil prices and kept pumping as oil prices shot sky-high, apparently realizing that it had the makings of a great brochure.

Having said all this, it's important to be clear that there are many drilling companies whose records are at least as uninspired (anybody else out there in a Buckeye deal?) and that Samson's 1973–1981 programs still have a lot of hydrocarbons in the ground. The brochure says that those programs are projected to return yet a further 226% of investors' money.

Still, I wondered, what were these projections based on? What was Samson figuring, and U.S. Trust apparently buying, as a reasonable projection for the price of that oil still in the ground?

Right there on page 78, paragraph 3, is your answer, plain as day. The 226% return yet to come is based not only on the fabulous results of that first teeny-tiny program Samson didn't drill, but also on the assumption that oil will continue (continue?) to sell for $29.50 a barrel through 1986 (it actually dropped to $10 at one point) and then climb, over the following sixteen years, to $75. ("It should be noted," notes the prospectus, "that no consideration has been given to recent price declines.")

Ho-kay. Now that you've listened to all my carping—exactly the kind of negative attitude that did *not* make this country great —if you still want to pony up $26,250 for a $25,000 unit in Samson 1985-A, and you've got diamonds and a dinner jacket, I'll put you in touch with U.S. Trust. One of the nice things about going through the bank (and it actually is a *very* fine bank, which I actually owe a *lot* of money) is that you get the benefit of its independent analysis.

"In addition to the information contained in the enclosed Offering Prospectus, supplied by [Samson]," writes the bank in its cover letter, "certain other facts should be made known to you."

Oh, boy, I thought: the dirt.

"In particular, our analysis has established [Samson's competence and its track record]."

Whereupon, under "Track Record," the bank's summary simply restates the assertion of Samson's brochure: "Through June 30, 1984," the bank writes unquestioningly, "Samson's 1973–1981 programs have distributed cash equal to 127% of total cash invested and had estimated future cash distributions equal to 226% of cash invested."

Somebody at U.S. Trust should have read the prospectus.

Yet if you can't blindly rely on U.S. Trust in such matters— truly one of the finest fiduciary institutions in the country—on whom can you blindly rely?

No one.

There are two ways to look at your money: from street level, crushed on all sides by a mob of loudly competing alternatives; or from the balcony.

Come on up to the balcony. You won't get rich up here (you won't get rich down there, either), but you'll breathe easier and avoid the pickpockets. Up here, you'll focus on the big decisions and develop a financial strategy—nothing fancy—that makes sense for you.

For most of us, especially younger people who haven't accumulated much in the way of assets, here's the broad outline of that strategy: Spend a little less than you earn and put the difference someplace safe. You knew that. But do you do that?

What's hard about managing your money isn't understanding the intricacies of high finance or taxation, it's developing good habits. Thrift. Industry. Patience.

Chapter 2

DO IT FOR MOM
Making a Budget Really Means Making a Plan

"I walked home to save bus fare."
"Gee, you could have saved a lot more by not taking a taxi."
—Old joke

Now don't get angry; what we're going to do in this chapter is make a budget. It's as much my fault as yours you don't have one (well, you don't, do you?), because, like you, I've always thought it was too childish to discuss.

What has recently dawned on me, however (your mom called, if you must know, and frankly, she's worried sick about the way you handle money), is that not only have you not made a budget, you're not entirely sure, really, how to do it. Oh, you know how to do it. Any idiot can do it. But should it be a weekly budget? Monthly? What about taxes? How should you handle expenses versus investments?

This chapter is important, because it's not just a budget you'll end up with, it's an overall plan. Admittedly, if you're rich to begin with or frugal by nature—if money clings to you like a wet undergarment—you can probably skip all this. But if like many successful people you have trouble making ends meet, let alone overlap, listen up.

First, get a pencil and a yellow legal pad. Next, tell your secretary to hold your calls. If you are a secretary, get a smaller legal pad. If you neither are nor have a secretary—if you've got a man's job, like driving a truck or operating a crane—do this at home, in your favorite chair, late at night, when no one can see you. (Real men make bets, not budgets.) With the ball game *off*.

No, no, no, no. Not next week. Now.

If you have a significant other, sit him or her down, too, and work on this together.

#1. TALLY YOUR NET WORTH

Okay. First thing you do, tot up everything you own, subtract everything you owe, and that's your net worth.

In other words, before you even start to make the budget, take a few minutes to see where you stand. Down the left side of the first sheet of your yellow legal pad, list all your assets and their approximate value—the house, the car, the savings account. Now, on the right side, list all your debts—the mortgage and car loan and credit card balances. Which list totals more?

If you own more than you owe, you have a positive net worth. You're already three steps ahead of the game.

If you have a negative net worth—you owe more than you own—you can see why your mother placed that call. (What's that? You say your mom's been dead for six years? You think just because she's dead she's not worried?)

Subtract what you owe from what you own and write the total at the bottom of the page. MY NET WORTH: _____.

#2. SET GOALS

Where would you like to be a year from now? "Out of debt" might be an appropriate goal. And two years from now? "Out of debt with $2000 in an IRA and $2500 in the bank and a stereo system that will wake up the dead." (At which point, over the din, you can gloat to your mom that there was nothing to worry about in the first place, O she of little faith.) And five years from now? "A net worth of $60,000 headed for half a million."

It is to reach these goals that you make your budget. Write them down on the second page of your yellow legal pad. Don't make them too aggressive. Try to set goals that, after going back and forth with your budget for a while, you secretly think you'll be able to exceed. If you aim too high, you'll never feel you're doing well enough.

You can still have unwritten goals and hopes and dreams—by all means!—but don't make them part of your official financial plan. Think of them (and not too often, if you can help it) as icing on the cake. Sure you want a Porsche. Everybody seems to want one (not me—I want to be invisible and to fly). But it's really nuts to want one so much you're unhappy you don't have one.

#3. FIGURE YOUR ANNUAL EARNINGS

At the top of the third yellow page, list all your sources of annual income: your take-home pay (multiply your paycheck by the 12, 24, 26, or 52 times a year you receive it), payments from Grand-dad's trust (and what a grand old dad he was), the $20 a week you pick up reffing Little League, dividends, and so on.

Note that for most folks, it's not a long list. "Take-home pay: $28,400." End of list.

Note also:

• Precision is not the goal. Ballpark estimates are fine.
• When in doubt, estimate low. That way, any surprises are likely to be pleasant ones.

#4. TAKE A FIRST PASS AT YOUR EXPENSES

This is like naming all the states. If you picture the map and start with Maine, gradually working your way south and west, you will come up with 43 states. Then you'll remember Arkansas (if you're from Arkansas, you'll remember Delaware) and a few others and get to 47. The last three are murder, though you know them perfectly well (Nebraska—of course! Alabama!), and you may even have to sneak a look at the map to find them.

So it goes with budget categories. You'll quickly come up with headings to cover most of your expenditures, although with budget categories, unlike states, there are no preset boundaries. You might have one broad category for Entertainment or several narrower categories all summing to it: Barhopping, Dinners, Movies, Records, Video Rentals, Books and Magazines, Theatrical and Sporting Events, Bingo. Whatever makes sense for you.

Nor is there a specific number of budget items the way there's a specific number of states, so you won't know with quite the same certainty whether you've missed any. You'll *think* you've thought of everything, just as, until you count up your list of states, you think you've hit them all. But of course you have not. (Gasoline —of course! Lawn Care!)

I could make it easy for you by listing 50 sample categories, but this is your budget, not mine. I am merely your mom's last best hope of saving you from homelessness. The ranks of the formerly-middle-class homeless are reportedly exploding (one budget category, accordingly: Charity! Of course!), and homelessness is not something we think you'd be good at.

So list your own budget categories; but if you get stuck, sneak a look at the map—last year's checkbook and credit card statements. Under what headings would last year's expenditures have fallen? (Miscellaneous! Of course!)

Next to each category, estimate what you currently spend. If you haven't any idea what you currently spend—well, all the more reason to be going through this exercise. Two nights out a week at $75 apiece for dinner ($45) and a movie ($10) and gas and parking or cabfare ($10) plus a little nightcap ($10) on the way home? That's $7800 a year.

Some categories, like this one, are best thought of in weekly terms and multiplied by 52. Your rent or mortgage payments and electric bill are naturally thought of in monthly amounts and multiplied by 12. Your semiannual trips to the dentist are multiplied by two—but don't include them at all if you're reimbursed for dental care by insurance. Reimbursable expenditures don't affect your financial plan, so ignore them.

Ignore, too, the items that are automatically taken out of your pay, because it was only your net take-home pay that you listed as income, above. Or, if you prefer, list your *gross* pay as income and list each of the deductions—taxes, health insurance, and so on—as an expense item. Any approach you're comfortable with is fine as long as it is logical.

Don't include Credit Cards as a budget category. Only the annual credit card fee itself and, more important, credit card interest ought to be budget items. The rest—the clothing and dinners and such you charge to the cards—should go into categories like "clothing" and "dinners."

On your first pass, jot down both the annual expenditure and the way you figured it ("$75 twice a week = $7800"). Make no effort to economize. When in doubt, estimate high. Round up. Your auto insurance runs $875? Call it $1000.

Leave for the end of your list those "expenditures" that aren't really expenditures at all: investments. The $2000 you voluntarily contribute to an IRA is not like the $2000 you blow on a weekend in Tangiers. It's cash that merely moves from your front pocket to your back pocket. Similarly, spending $40,000 on àn Oriental rug, if it's really worth $40,000 (as the ones that fly clearly are), isn't spending money at all. It's merely shifting funds from one investment, like a savings account, to another, like a rug. (If the rug would fetch only $25,000 were you immediately to resell it, then you have, in effect, invested $25,000 in a rug and spent $15,000 on your living room.)

If you buy a new car every four years, for cash, don't budget zero for the first three and then $12,000 for the fourth; budget $3000 a year (plus maintenance, plus insurance). If you buy it on time, as most people do but with the help of this exercise you may someday not have to, just budget your monthly payments.

If you own your home, include an allowance for maintenance and repairs even though you can't be sure what might need fixing or when. If you budget $1500 a year, planning to repaint, but the roof starts to leak—well, this year you might patch the roof and, if funds are scarce, hold off repainting until next year.

#5. TAKE A SECOND PASS AT YOUR EXPENSES

What have you forgotten? Clothes? Furniture? Appliances?

Inevitably you'll think of other things as you go along, but that's why you do this in pencil. Your eraser should be a crumbly stump by the time we're done. There should be eraser-rim crease marks across your yellow pad.

#6. REFINE YOUR PLAN

Add up your expenditures, not counting things that are really investments, like IRA contributions. How does what you expect to shell out compare with what you expect to rake in?

Ideally, you're raking more than you're shelling, and by enough to meet the goals you've set for yourself on the second page of this legal pad. Usually, though, you're not.

What's the shortfall? How far is your anticipated income from covering all your anticipated expenses plus whatever you wanted to set aside to meet your goal for next year? Are you living a $50,000 life-style on a $40,000 income?

You have three ways to narrow the gap:

1. Spend less.
2. Earn more.
3. Set less aggressive goals.

Go back over your budget and, without being unrealistic, see what you can trim. ("There are several ways to apportion family income," counseled Robert Benchley, "all of them unsatisfactory.") How about buying a hibachi for $30 (not one of those ridiculous $159 gas grills that take all weekend to assemble) and converting some of your $75 nights out to $17 evenings of barbecued chicken ($15 with the briquettes, Chablis, and salad) and James Bond ($2 at the video store)?

How about shopping around for cheaper auto insurance (or at least trimming that $1000 ballpark estimate we used to the $875 you actually pay)? Before, shopping for the best price on auto insurance was a chore you never got around to. Now it's still a chore, but a chore that's part of a grand plan.

How about not smoking, and saving $900 a year on cigarettes and life insurance premiums and cold medicine and automobile repairs (smokers have far more accidents than nonsmokers)?

How about asking your doctor to prescribe diazepam for $16 instead of Valium for $33 (diazepam *is* Valium) and using the 69-cent shaving cream instead of the $2.39 shaving cream (shaving cream *is* shaving cream) and buying in bulk when items are cheap and on sale? Buying staples this way instead of one at a time at the convenience store can stretch $1000 to buy $1400 of the very same items you would have bought throughout the course of the year anyway. That's a 40% tax-free return on your $1000 investment, plus you save trips to the store and never run out.

These are repugnant notions to someone of your breeding, but even the British nobility have had to economize, auctioning off the odd heirloom. It's actually worse for them, because they're living a little less well each year, with no end in sight. You, on the other hand, are merely making temporary, voluntary sacrifices in order to pole-vault into an entirely new, more comfortable and secure economic stratum. You're not buying cheaper shaving cream when you buy cheaper shaving cream—you're getting out of debt and into mutual funds. You're not waiting until after 11:00 P.M. to call when you wait till after 11:00 to call—you're taking control of your future. (Better still, let them call you.) Even your sex will be better—yes, it will—because with money in the bank and a clear view of your future, you'll feel better about yourself.

So first trim your budget.

But don't trim it unrealistically. Don't set yourself up to fail.

Next, if you're a man, trim your hair. ("And tuck in your shirt," advises your mom. "Look at you!") You can have your hair cut every three weeks at $25 a clip—$425 a year—or you can get one of those stainless-steel razor-blade hair-trimming doohickies Brookstone and others sell for $11.95 and save, over five years, $2125 plus maybe 100 hours of getting to, sitting in, and returning from the barber's chair. Or have it cut professionally a few times a year and trim it yourself the rest. (Brookstone: Peterborough, NH 03458.)

#7. REFINE IT SOME MORE

If your expenditures and goals for saving still exceed your income, think about increasing your income.

Sadly, this often involves doing more work. But if you don't already work two jobs or live rent free by acting as super for your building or drive a cab on weekends or wait tables or type term papers—and if you want to achieve your goals and work less hard in the future—you should consider it. For one thing, you'll earn more money. For another, you'll spend less. You'll be too busy and tired to spend.

If you can't get or don't want more work, take yet another pass through your expenses—but a radical one this time. You could, for example, move to a cheaper home. You could give up skiing for jogging, take in a roommate, or put the kids up for adoption.

Your other choice is simply to set less aggressive goals.

Round and round you go, juggling income, expenses, and goals, brushing eraser nubble to all corners of your kitchen table, until you arrive at an earning-spending-saving plan that adds up.

The process itself is useful. It helps you set priorities. It helps you see where your finances are headed and, if you like, head them somewhere else. What's involved here, really, is taking control of your life.

By estimating your income low and your expenses high, you set yourself up to succeed. That makes your budget a game that's fun to play instead of a constant burden of guilt and discouragement you'll soon abandon.

(Speaking of discouragement, if you've got three small kids, don't be discouraged that you're unable to save much. For many, it's only before the kids are born and after they've graduated that any serious saving is possible. But even just funding an IRA as they're growing up, while it's not easy, can put you $250,000 or $500,000 ahead of the game in your later years. So try to set *something* aside.)

In setting your goals, spend a little time thinking about the things you have (like your health, and a $359 25-inch Sharp color TV with remote control) and not just the things you don't (eternal youth and a $2995 36-inch Matsushita).

#8. BLOW $5 ON A BUDGET BOOK

Once you've settled on a plan, buy a simple budget book at any stationery store to track your progress, or devise a record-keeping system of your own. It doesn't much matter what method you choose, so long as you use it.

Nor need you wait until January to start. The government budgets on a fiscal year; so can you. Most budget books are set up to record 12 months' expenditures but let you fill in the names of the months. The first can be October just as easily as January.

If the stationery stores are closed as you read this—or you want to get off to a good start by saving $5 on a budget book—use the rest of your legal pad. You'll want a separate sheet for each of your budget headings and then one summary sheet to track your monthly progress with the whole lot of them.

Here's how you might go about setting it up:

• Number each individual sheet—the one for Automobile Expenses and so on—from 1 through 31 down the left side of the page (plus a last line for totals) and from 1 through 12 across the top—a column for each of the next 12 months. When you spend $35 on a new tie (are you out of your mind?), enter $35 on the sheet you've labeled Clothing, under the proper month and on the line for today's date. If there's room, you might even write a tiny note to remind you: YSL tie.

• At the end of each month, go through those pages and add up the month's expenditures in each category. Then take the totals and enter them on a single summary sheet.

• Down the left margin of that summary sheet list your income and expense headings; to the right set up 15 columns. (Okay, so tape two pages together. This is not my problem.) The first shows your annual targets. The second divides those same targets by 12—your monthly targets. (For some items—Christmas Gifts—you'd just leave this second column blank or make a little note to yourself, like "all Dec.")

• The next 12 columns of the summary sheet you'll fill in with totals from the individual budget sheets as you complete each of the next 12 months.

• The final column is for summing the previous 12: your year-end total. For Clothing it might read $2135. (Three custom-made suits and that stupid tie.) How does that compare with the target you began with?

#9. KEEP TRACK OF WHAT YOU SPEND—OR CHOOSE AN ALTOGETHER DIFFERENT SYSTEM

Before you go to bed each night, enter the day's expenditures on the appropriate budget pages. To help remember what you spent, save your receipts and carry a three-by-five card in your wallet with one of those stubby eraserless pencils.

Is all this too tedious for words? Fine. See if I care that your mother is beside herself with worry.

You can facilitate matters by buying a preprinted budget book, as I've said. Or you can rocket your finances into orbit by computerizing them (of course, for this you'll need a computer, and for that you'll need $1200). Or you can *forget all this nonsense and contrive another system altogether:*

Step #1: Destroy all your credit cards.

Step #2: Deposit the first 20% of each future paycheck in one or more investment accounts that you never, ever touch (the "don't-touch-it budget," as budget counselor Betty Madden calls it).

Step #3: Put the remaining 80% in a single checking account and make do, no matter what, with the balance in that account. Forget budgeting and record keeping. If you're hungry but there's nothing left in the account, eat leaves. If the rent's due but there's nothing left in the account, sleep in the street. If your car breaks down and you can't get to work until you repair it, sleep in a street near your work.

It's an unconventional financial discipline, but better than the Visa budget system most people use. Under that system, Visa tells you exactly what you can afford to spend (your available credit) and exactly how much to pay each month (your minimum monthly payment), all the while collecting 15% or 20% for its trouble.

#10. GIVE YOURSELF A BREAK

If you do take the time to plan your financial future and to track your progress as it unfolds, don't be slavish about it. Who cares if you forget to jot down every last expense? Who cares if you go over budget from time to time? The idea isn't to account for every penny (although it could be an intriguing experiment for three months to see exactly where the money goes). The idea is to spend less than you earn each year, get out of debt, and build a secure, comfortable future.

The trick is to live a little beneath your means. Sounds glamorous, no? Okay, no. But if, earning $23,000 a year, you can force yourself to live as if you were earning $18,000 or $20,000 (people do, you know); or if, earning $140,000, you can live as if you were making $115,000—your life in the long run will be far more secure and, soon, more comfortable to boot. Your money begins to work for you, your savings swell, and you can pay for things with cash. The other way, living a bit above your means, you get deeper and deeper into hock, and life costs an extra 18% in finance charges. One way you're motivated by the carrot (saving up in great anticipation of whatever it is you're saving up for), the other way by the stick (having to pay for it—even though it wound up raining the whole time you were there).*

Living beneath your means is tough. (Living *within* your means is tough!) Making a game of it helps. Seeing it as a challenge helps. "Paying yourself first" helps (direct the first 10% or 15% of every paycheck to a savings account or mutual fund). But tough as it is, as you begin to see results, it gets easier. And if you want to get ahead of the game, you're more likely to succeed this way than by buying lottery tickets each week, hoping to win big.

One way or another, the future will come. With a little planning, you can have a say in how it looks. Even the difference between coming out just $500 ahead each year rather than $500

---

*"I bought a dress on the installment plan [runs the old ditty]. The reason, of course, was to please a man. The dress is worn, the man is gone—but the dang installments go on and on."

behind is the difference, for a 25-year-old who earns 8% after tax on his savings or borrows at 12%, between having $57,000 at age 55—or owing $120,000.

Think of your budget not as your albatross, but as your secret weapon.

Chapter 3

DON'T LEAVE HOME WITHOUT IT

Borrowing: When and How to Use Credit

> "I have no idea how much my interest rate is," says Suzanne Carver, a Chicago housewife, as she paws through her purse to check her card. "It doesn't say on here. Well, as long as I can buy things with it, who cares?"
> —*The Wall Street Journal,*
> March 19, 1987

Just because you have a secret weapon doesn't mean you'll never be in debt. Even rich people have debts. Managing that debt wisely can save you lots of money. More than that, how you structure your debt is a major aspect of your overall financial plan.

YOUR CREDIT CARDS

The simplest, safest, most sensible way to earn 18% on your money, tax-free and risk free—is to pay off your 18% credit cards. Not having to pay 18% is as good as *earning* 18%. This is truer than ever now that consumer interest is slated to be only

40% deductible in 1988, 20% deductible in 1989, and just 10% deductible (truly more trouble than it's worth to calculate) in 1990.

Pay off your credit cards!

But have you ever noticed how hard that is to do—I mean, even if you have the money and can afford to? If you call the credit card company and ask how much you owe, *they won't tell you*. They'll say they don't know.

They know your minimum payment, your last payment, your Social Security number, and your mother's maiden name—they know what you had for breakfast—but they haven't the faintest idea what you'd have to pay to stop the accrual of interest charges.

Well, of course not. If you were borrowing money at 5% and lending it out at 19.8%, would you want it paid back?

The minute you stick that plastic card into the instant teller machine for a $20 cash advance, you start paying interest on that $20—and on your other $823 in current charges, even though you pay your bill the minute it arrives. *Beware the cash advance.* Beware, too, those checkbooks they send with your name and address already printed on the checks and an invitation from your credit card company to use them any way you want. Pay an unexpected repair bill, they suggest, or the baby-sitter or your taxes— it's just so easy! What's unclear to some people is that the minute you use one of those checks, or at least the minute the check is presented for payment, you begin paying interest on it *and all your other charges*, even if you're the type who always pays within the 25-day grace period.

Because that's just it. As an interest-free convenience, paid promptly, credit cards are great. As a means of borrowing, they should be a last resort. (Okay, a pawnshop should be your *last* resort. Pawnshops in some states charge interest at annual rates of 200% or more.)

I carry just one card. It makes for less bill paying, simpler record keeping, and if I ever lose my wallet—which is unlikely, because I keep it chained to my leg—I'll have just one lost card to report: the American Express card.

You may think I've chosen the American Express card so I can blind busboys with the reflection from my platinum card, but I don't have a platinum card. With it, American Express has secured a permanent place in the marketing pantheon, selling tens of thousands of its customers, for an extra $200 or so annual membership fee on top of what the green or gold cards cost— *nothing*. Nothing! That bold stroke alone could eventually add a dime to Amexco's annual earnings and thus half a billion dollars to its market value.

Well, then, perhaps I favor the American Express card for its optional flight insurance? (For just $4 a ticket, they'll pay your heirs an extra $250,000 if your plane should land head first.) But no, you're more likely to be hit by lightning than to die on a scheduled domestic flight, so your premium dollars go 5 or 10 cents to insurance, 90 or 95 cents to American Express's brilliant marketing.

I stick with American Express because of the letter it sent me. I don't read everything Amex sends (there being only 24 hours in the day), but I read this because, though bulk rate, it was marked IMPORTANT NEWS INSIDE, PLEASE READ IMMEDIATELY.

It developed that while Amex has yet to adopt a suggestion I once gave it for 75-cent-a-check restaurant insurance (believe me, more people choke to death in restaurants than die on United to Chicago), Amex is now providing free baggage insurance.

And not just penny-ante baggage insurance. We're talking— free—up to $500 on bags you check and up to $1250 for carry-ons. It's this latter that's really such a breakthrough because, up to now, if an airline misrouted one of your carry-on bags, it took absolutely no responsibility for losing it. Never mind that it was under the seat in front of you when you took off from Chicago but in Guadalajara when you landed in Des Moines. Your loss.

But now American Express, free, just for your having used its card to charge your tickets, is willing to step up to the plate and take that risk—with certain exceptions. (Well, what do you want from free insurance?) Leave your hat, coat, or umbrella on the plane? Too bad. Lose your $400 pair of astigmatic contact lenses? Tough. Airline folder drop out of your jacket pocket with the remaining legs of your trip around the world? Sorry. Pack away some cash in your gym bag? Should have used traveler's checks.

Neither are you covered for "silverware, plants, bedding, motorcycles, boats, cars, or other conveyances"—*I'm not making this up*—that you may have carried onto the plane. (And you wonder why those darn coat racks are always full?)

Some things are covered. These include raincoats packed away in the belly of the plane (but not those carried on) and computers, jewelry—now we're talking!—sporting equipment—yes!—cameras—yes!—tape recorders—yes!—but all this up to a combined maximum of $250.

I know what you're thinking. You're thinking, Gee, how can American Express give away the store like this? How can it afford to provide free baggage insurance? What must such a thing cost?

It costs 29 cents per cardholder per year. That's what Amex pays Fireman's Fund for the insurance. Of course, since Amex *owns* a good chunk of Fireman's Fund, and Fireman's Fund is presumably charging more than it expects to have to pay out in claims (this is how you make money selling baggage insurance), the true cost to Amex may be lower still.

Give everybody an extra dime's worth of baggage insurance, heralded with full-page ads and direct mail, and, at the same time, raise the annual membership fee $10.

A few years ago Amex was giving the Statue of Liberty a penny—a full penny—every time you used your card. Personally, I was blown away. I said to myself, How can they afford to do that?

All I can say is, *I* never leave home without it, and you shouldn't, either.*

---

*Unless you prefer Sears' Discover card, which gives you a $15 cash rebate on your first $3000 in annual charges and 1% on all additional charges; or the Eastern, Continental, or American Airlines MasterCards that give you a frequent-flier mile, arguably worth a penny or two, for every dollar that you charge. So long as you're sure to pay these off each month to avoid their obscene finance charges, using one of them as your primary credit card is an easy way to get something for nothing. You will also build a credit history, if you haven't already. Building a sterling record with American Express counts for nothing, because Amex does not release credit information.

FINANCING YOUR CAR

Automobile financing has come a long way since GMAC loaned its first customer $1300 to purchase a 1919 Chevy. In those days, down payments were high, and the loans ran ten months. Today, the average term is around 48 months. Yet the word on auto financing remains the same: Don't. If you can afford to, pay cash. Financing, even more than power windows or air, is an expensive option.

Not everybody *can* afford to pay cash, needless to say, which is why (a) the rich get richer and why (b) you should consider—I'm just saying consider, I'm not telling you how to run your life—a less expensive car. I know driving up to the Rotary Club ball in a previously owned Pinto is not the most impressive thing you may ever do, but it can save a ton of money. The overall savings, in purchase price, insurance, financing, operating costs, and maintenance as compared with something fancy and new, could mean as much to you, after tax, as a $5000-a-year raise. And you can always say your good car is in the shop ("Those Jaguar mechanics are just *so* slow," you can say) or, in a pinch, you could probably borrow your teenager's car.

No? You're not buying this? You think a $16,000 car will move you along the highway of happiness faster than a $4500 clunker traveling at the same speed? All right, borrow—but borrow as little as possible at the lowest rate you can find for the shortest period of time. This is even more true now that the interest deduction is being phased out (and now that, with the higher standard deduction, you're less likely to be itemizing anyway).

It's a fundamental of personal finance: Only borrow money if you have to (they're not lending it to you out of the goodness of their hearts) or if you can invest it at a higher rate, after tax, than you're being charged. It only makes sense to borrow at 11% (say) if you have a risk-free way to invest it, after tax, at 12%.

What's more, the promotional rates available from time to time are not always entirely what they seem. A Toyota dealer I spoke with was offering 6.5% financing on any car in inventory and 5.5% on trucks—but, when pressed, admitted you could get a better price if you paid cash. Don't let an attractive interest rate distract you from an unattractive price. And don't feel you have to borrow through the dealer. Banks and credit unions, among others, often offer more attractive rates. (See page 204, "Credit Unions," for information on one credit union that's easy to join.)

When interest rates are "on sale" and unprofitable to the dealer, it doesn't hurt, in negotiating for the best-possible price, to let him know you'll be paying cash. When rates are the profitable add-on they normally are, it doesn't hurt to let the dealer assume you'll finance. If you're really a skunk, you could feign interest in his various insurance options as well—but don't buy! Dealer-arranged accident insurance can often be bought cheaper off the lot; extended warranty plans are rarely as good a bet for the buyer as for the dealer; and credit life insurance, which pays off the loan balance if you die, is in most cases a good deal only for the terminally ill.

(Credit life on an $8000 48-month loan cost $336.51 at one large sunbelt bank—plus $88.77 in interest for financing *it*. The total comes to $425.28 for what averages out to little more than $4000 of coverage over four years—$8000 at the outset, declining to zero as the loan balance declines. For the same money, almost anyone under 55 can get 5 to 25 times as much annual renewable term insurance.)

Leasing, meanwhile, requires the least cash down—but the most over the long run, because you are paying to finance the entire car and building no equity. At the end of the lease you don't own a paid-up used car; you own nothing and have to start all over again.

FINANCING (OR REFINANCING) YOUR HOME

As popular as automobile leasing has become, the hot new way to finance your car—and just about everything else—is the home equity loan. As you doubtless know, this is a line of credit secured by your home, which you may draw upon and pay back, in full or in part, as often as you like. It's like a giant credit card, only it carries a much lower interest rate and gives you 20 or 30 years to repay. What's more, because it's a mortgage, the interest remains deductible under the new law so long as you haven't borrowed more than you originally spent for the house, plus improvements. (Even then it's deductible if you can show that the extra borrowing went to pay for education or medical care, or if you took out the loan before August 16, 1986.)

Whenever you want to "charge" something, just pay for it with a check from your home-equity-loan checkbook. Citibank, for one, perhaps confusing you for Brazil, requires not a penny of repayment—just interest—for the first 10 years and then gives you 20 years to pay off the loan.

The advantages are compelling. So are the dangers. Many people already have trouble handling credit cards. Imagine the trouble they could have with one the size of a house! And what sense is there taking out a 30-year loan to pay for a 6-year automobile (or a quick trip to Key West)? With nothing forcing you to pay off the loan over the life of the car, it's quite possible you won't. When it comes time to buy a new one, you'll just go deeper into debt.

Instead of owning your home free and clear at retirement, you could find yourself mortgaged to the hilt and unable to make the payments. Or you could run into trouble much sooner, because these loans are tied to the general level of interest rates. If rates shoot up, you might be hard-pressed to meet the new, higher payments. Bye-bye home.

Home equity loans are convenient, inexpensive, and deductible. But they put a much greater burden of self-discipline on the borrower.

If you do opt for one, seek a lender offering "no points" and minimal up-front fees, as in today's hotly competitive environment some do.* That saves a chunk of cash, and you'll have lost less if you ever decide to sell the house, drop the credit line, or replace it with another somewhere else.

---

*Points are service fees a lender will charge up front to make the loan (and to make some money). Each point is 1% of the loan, so three points on a $100,000 loan equals $3000, cash, that you have to pay to borrow the $100,000. On a mortgage taken to buy your own home, points are currently deductible as an interest expense *if you pay them separately* (but not if they are subtracted from the loan proceeds). But when refinancing, or when mortgaging a home you

• • •

But wait. Why are we talking about your second mortgage (which a home equity loan typically is) before we've talked about your first? And why are we talking about any of this before you decide whether it's better to buy a place or simply to rent?

On the issue of owning or renting, I offer the following thoughts. First, life is not a business. If you want to own a home and can afford to, that may be reason enough to buy. Second, though: There's no shame in renting, particularly at times when the prices of homes in your area seem to have lost touch with reality, or when the cost of renting is kept artificially low by dumb but well-intentioned rent-control laws like New York's, or when you're likely to be moving every couple of years. (In that event, you pay an extra 6% in real estate commissions each time you sell; and you forfeit the points and other closing costs you incurred taking out your mortgage. Those "transaction costs" can eat deeply into the profit you might otherwise have made on the home.) It's also nice not to have to worry about the roof or the septic tank.

True, money paid in rent is money down the drain, while money paid on a mortgage builds equity and affords a tax deduction. But with a 30-year loan, the equity builds so slowly in the early years as to be all but negligible. And the tax deductions are not magic; they merely cut your taxes. The question is whether they cut your taxes by enough to make owning a place cheaper than renting one. If even after figuring the tax savings it costs more to own than rent, as it generally does when you figure everything in, you have to decide whether the extra expense of ownership is justified by (a) your greater enjoyment and (b) the potential for appreciation.

If you do buy—a home is a terrific inflation hedge, apart from everything else—you face three primary decisions: how much of

_____

originally bought for cash (which, oddly, is also considered a refinancing), or when purchasing investment properties, points must be amortized over the life of the loan—$3000 in points on a 30-year loan would be deductible at the rate of just $100 a year (with the balance deducted if you paid the loan off early).

the purchase price to borrow, whether to take a 15-year or 30-year loan, and whether to go for a fixed- or adjustable-rate mortgage. Here are three strategies that make sense under different circumstances.

Strategy #1—Don't Borrow At All

This could be wise, for example, if mortgage rates were very high and you had lots of money sitting in securities that were earning less than the mortgage would cost. Why pay 9% to borrow (after figuring the tax advantages) if you've got a ton of money earning just 6% after tax someplace else?* There *is* a reason you might want to do this, which I'll come to in a minute (strategy #3); but on the face of it, anyway, you are losing 3% a year, after tax, on every dollar you so borrow. On a $100,000 mortgage, that would be a waste of $3000 a year—plus the points and fees you pay to take out the mortgage (and the wasted time and effort applying for it).

Another reason to buy for cash is that it may help to knock several thousand dollars off the purchase price. Offering cash counts for a lot in most real estate negotiations.

So when you can afford to, and the cost of borrowing is high, it may make sense to borrow nothing at all.

Strategy #2—Borrow As Little As Possible for the Shortest Time Possible

If it costs you more to borrow than you can earn on your savings —as it usually does—then there's lots to be said for borrowing no more than you have to. Why buy more of something—in this case, mortgage money—than you need (particularly now that home equity loans have lowered the cost of second mortgages, should you ever find you didn't borrow enough)?

What's more, borrowing for 15 years instead of 30 adds surprisingly little to your monthly payment—$859.68 versus

---

*What matters in financial decisions isn't what something costs or earns before tax—it's what you're left paying, or receiving, after tax. Taxes cut the true return on most investments, and tax savings cut the true cost of deductible expenses—*if* you have enough deductions to make it worthwhile to itemize. More on how to figure this in chapter 5.

$702.06 on a 10%, $80,000 loan—yet cuts the number of payments in half. You may also knock an extra quarter point or more off the interest rate, plus a full point or more off the closing costs that the bank charges.

(If you don't qualify for a 15-year loan because the payments are higher than the bank thinks you can handle, take out a 30-year loan but make occasional prepayments to accomplish the same thing. Sending in an extra $2750 at the end of the first year, say, when you get your bonus, shortens the aforementioned 30-year loan by five years! Just check with your bank first to be sure there are no prepayment penalties.)

With a 15-year loan, you might even be able to arrange things so that the mortgage payments stop before the tuition payments start.

Going this route is a sound form of forced savings. After 15 years you've paid off, and thus in effect saved up, $80,000. After 15 years with the 30-year loan, you've paid off—saved up— only $14,668.*

Okay, 15 years. But that still leaves you to choose between a fixed- or an adjustable-rate mortgage.

Take a fixed-rate mortgage if interest rates are low—lock in those low rates.

Take an adjustable-rate mortgage if rates are high.

But how low is low? And, for that matter, how adjustable is adjustable?

If the rates and fees for both types of mortgages were the same, you'd generally prefer a fixed-rate loan. It eliminates your risk. Even if you have to pay a little more, it may well be worth it.

But if the adjustable-rate loan is *substantially* cheaper, and if it has caps on how much it can rise in any one year and over the life of the loan, it may well be a better deal than its fixed-rate competitor. This is especially true if you don't plan to keep it long—if

*A more recent innovation than the 15-year mortgage is the fortnightly payment. Some banks now offer the option of deducting half your monthly payment from your checking or savings account every two weeks. By so doing, you make 26 half-monthly payments a year—13 months' worth instead of 12—and thereby shorten what would otherwise have been a 30-year mortgage by more than 10 years.

your career requires that you move every few years. Unless the fixed-rate were assumable, as few are anymore, why pay extra to lock in an interest rate for 30 years if you'll be paying it for only 4 or 5?

So there's actually a lot to be said for a "well-capped" adjustable-rate loan. There's also a lot to be said for the new "convertible" adjustable-rate mortgages some banks offer, which give you the option of locking in a fixed rate after a specified number of years, if interest rates have fallen. But adjustable-rate loans can be deceptive, so be careful. The low initial rate is often just a promotion. Far more important is what the rate will be after the first adjustment. You needn't get caught up in the details of which interest-rate measure the loan is tied to (though beware indices that the bank itself controls). Just ask your lender what rate you'd be charged after the first adjustment if, hypothetically, that adjustment were made today. Roughly speaking, *that's* where the loan is starting out, not the come-on rate; and *that's* the number to look at in comparing alternatives.

Beware, too, adjustable-rate loans that are capped—but only as to your monthly payments. With these, any excess above the cap may actually be tacked on as additional principal you owe, meaning either that your monthly payment will stay high long after other interest rates have come back down, or that additional monthly payments will be added onto the back end of the loan. What started as a 30-year loan could conceivably become a 34-year loan.

There are so many variations in points, rates, market conditions, and your own personal circumstances that it's hard to come up with simple rules of thumb. But here's one: *If you can't afford the higher fixed-rate loan, you can't afford the house.* That isn't to say you shouldn't take the adjustable loan. But your reason for taking it shouldn't be that without its low initial rate you couldn't afford the house.

Strategy #3—Borrow All You Can for 30 Years, Fixed

The idea isn't to buy more house than you can afford (nor to do this when interest rates are high), but simply to snag a great deal:

with a 30-year fixed-rate loan, the lender is on the hook to you for 30 years, while you're barely on the hook at all. If rates zoom, you're protected. If rates plunge, you simply pay off the loan and refinance at the lower rate. Your only penalty for refinancing, ordinarily, is a new set of closing costs. It's an enviable position to be in and sometimes worth the extra cost of the fixed-rate loan, especially if you think you might own the property a long time.

This is why a wealthy investor might want to lock in a 9% rate even though he could pay for the property with cash that was currently earning only 6%. By keeping his cash free for other things, he'd be in a position to profit if rates went sky-high.

Ironically, it's the wealthy who should sometimes take the 30- rather than the 15-year loan—not as a way to make the home affordable, but simply as a financial strategy. If *they* move after a few years, they don't have to sell the home to pay for their next one—they can simply rent it out and continue to keep the bank on the hook for 30 years at what might by then have become a bargain rate.

The rest of us—who may have to stretch to make the monthly payments—are generally better off with the 15-year loan. It builds equity much, much faster. And it's often cheaper.

Should You Refinance an Existing Mortgage? The Points-Versus-Interest-Rate Trade-Off

If it weren't for points and closing costs, it would make sense to refinance a fixed-rate loan every time mortgage rates dropped a quarter of a point. That's in effect what an adjustable-rate mortgage does—except that it can ratchet up as well as down.

The trade-off is between a lower interest rate or lower points. That's often the trade-off, too, in trying to decide between two otherwise similar mortgages.

You don't have to read what follows. Your own instincts and common sense will probably be more than adequate to make a reasonable choice in such matters. But give the next few paragraphs a shot, if you've come this far (hey, they make sense to me), because they introduce the notion of your "discount rate," and that may help you think more clearly about money.

In comparing a 9.5% loan that charges 2.5 points with a 10% loan that charges none, the crucial question, naturally, is how long you'll hold the mortgage. In this example, the 10% loan costs less at first, because there are no points to pay. But after a few years, the saving on the basic rate of the 9.5% loan may more than outweigh the 2.5 points you had to pay up front to get it.

Just how long it takes for the 9.5% loan to pay off its up-front fees and overtake the 10% loan depends on your personal "discount rate."* The higher your discount rate, the longer it takes for the 9.5% loan to make sense.** In this example, if your discount rate were zero—meaning you'd happily give up $1 today if you were merely promised $1 back a year from now (you fool!)— then the break-even would come after just five years. Each year you'd pick up half a point of interest (9.5% versus 10%) and after five have completely erased the extra 2.5 points you had to pay to get the 9.5% loan.

But if, like most humans, your discount rate is 5% or 10% or 20% or 50% (depending on how desperate you are for cash now)—meaning that you'd give up $1 now only if you were guaranteed $1.05 or $1.10 or $1.20 or $1.50 a year from now— then it would take a lot longer for the 9.5% loan to justify the extra 2.5 points you had to pay to get it. In fact, it might never catch up at all.

Your discount rate is essentially what you figure money is worth to you, after tax—that is, the best rate at which you could put some to work. Maybe it's 20% if you haven't yet paid off some 20% credit card loans; maybe it's 5%, if that's what you

---

*It also depends on whether the points and fees are immediately deductible. If they are, they cost less (after tax) than if they're not—so they're less of a burden on the 9.5% loan and can be recouped more quickly. In the example that follows, I assume that both the points and the mortgage interest are fully deductible.

**To some people, a bird in the hand is worth two in the bush. To others, it's worth four in the bush or eight in the bush or a hundred. This is how Aesop and his bankers thought about discounted cash flow ("thrush flew," as it was known). Now there are pocket calculators, birds come vacuum-packed in oven-stuffer pouches (don't they?), and the whole concept has become more refined.

expect from your investments, after tax; maybe it's 200% if you've been borrowing from the guys with the baseball bats. The higher it is, the more painful it is to part with those extra 2.5 points up front.

If your discount rate is 20%, then you have to figure that the 2.5 points you save by taking the 10% mortgage could itself be appreciating at 20%—half a point a year. Well, then, the 9.5% loan will *never* catch up to the 10% loan, in your eyes, because each year you gain half a point on the interest rate (9.5% versus 10%)—but lose the half point by which your 2.5 points could have been growing.

No one "sets" your discount rate; it's just a way of quantifying the cost to you, personally, of tying up money you could otherwise spend or invest. To a man one sandwich away from starvation, his "discount rate," if he had only $2 in the world and a sound mind for finance, would be infinite.

For most people, the break-even in this example would come after seven or eight years. So if you expected to keep the mortgage forever, you'd pay the extra points and go with the 9.5% loan. But if you expected to move in a few years or refinance, the 10% mortgage would make more sense.

Typically, it's not worth the hassle and cost to refinance until you can chop at least 1% or 2% off your interest rate. By choosing an adjustable-rate mortgage when rates are high, all this "refinancing" happens automatically, without points or fees, as the rates eventually fall. Once they've fallen low enough, you might want to go to the expense of locking them in by switching to a fixed-rate loan.

OTHER WAYS TO BORROW

You can borrow cheaply and conveniently against the value of the securities in your brokerage account, either by asking your broker to mail you a check or, if you've set up a checking account with your broker, writing the check yourself.

You can borrow conveniently but less cheaply by linking a revolving credit line to your checking account, which lets you overdraw your account without penalty, turning it into a sort of credit card.

You can borrow in certain circumstances from your company-sponsored profit-sharing or retirement fund—check with the personnel department. (If you own your own business, you may still be able to borrow from your profit-sharing plan, but be sure to check and double-check the negatives very carefully before you do. You don't want to trigger a "premature distribution" or expose the fund's assets to creditors.)

You can borrow from friends or relatives and have them make you feel like *dirt*. Oh, they won't *say* anything, but they'll sound ever so slightly . . . superior . . . from then on. You know. Like on *Dallas*.

You can borrow from the seller. If it's an $800 vacuum cleaner you've bought (well, this is no ordinary vacuum cleaner; you can also use it to spray paint your home, blow dry your hair, dust the crops), it's called "buying on the installment plan," and it's usually as close to usury as you can get. If it's a home you've bought, it's called "making the seller take back a mortgage," and if he's as anxious to sell his home as I think he is, you're likely to be able to negotiate an attractive rate.

Or you can borrow against the cash value in your life insurance policy. Insurance! Now there's an idea. Before we get to the good stuff, like stock market systems and wildcat wells, I suppose we ought to talk about insurance.

Chapter 4

FIRE AND LIFE
Insurance: Buying It Right

You've got to have insurance. Ben Franklin thought so. Winston Churchill thought so. ("If I had my way, I would write the word 'insurance' over the door of every cottage and upon the blotting book of every public man.") But you don't have to overpay for it.

INSURING YOUR HOME

Homeowners' insurance is easy to buy because there are just a few set "forms" of coverage all the companies offer, with unintelligible names like "HO-2" (for most homeowners), "HO-4" (for renters), and "HO-6" (for condominium owners). Your agent can explain.

Call State Farm and GEICO to get quotes over the phone and then call your local independent agent. If it costs just a few dollars more to deal with a friendly local agent, it may be worth it. But first be sure you're getting a competitive price.

• Be sure to have enough coverage. If your home isn't insured for at least 80% of its replacement cost, even partial losses won't be fully covered.

• Be sure to ask what the policy covers and what it doesn't. If it's one of the growing minority of policies that are now written in English, *read* it.

• Be sure to add $1 million in liability insurance (in case David Rockefeller slips on your stoop)—in most cases, the extra coverage costs less than a good dinner. This may not be strictly necessary if you have no assets to protect anyway—"You can't get blood from a stone, David," you can tell Rockefeller when he demands compensation for his pain and suffering—but it's a courtesy to your neighbors and guests. Should the Christmas tree decorations you wired electrocute them as they go to hang an angel, you can tell their stunned relatives not to worry—that financially, anyway, they're in good hands.

• Be sure to consider paying a little more for "replacement cost coverage," which will buy you a new stereo if yours is stolen. Ordinarily, you are covered only for "actual cash value," which technically means the cost of the stereo when you first bought it (which might be a lot less than it would cost now) minus depreciation—though not all insurers will drive such a hard bargain.

• Be sure to have any valuables listed in a schedule attached to your policy if you want them to be covered—things like jewelry, antiques, silverware, furs, and your stamp collection.

• Be sure to ascertain what you'd save in premiums each year by opting for the highest deductible. It's not the little risks you want to pay the insurer to protect you against, it's the big ones. Indeed, you might not file a small claim even if you were covered for it, what with the hassle involved and the not entirely unfounded fear that the insurer would raise your rates when it came time to renew or decline to renew altogether.

If by shouldering an extra $500 in risk you'd save only $15 a year, as through the quirks of insurance pricing is sometimes the case, common sense tells you to pay the extra $15. But if you'd save $100 or $200—that's a bet you might take.

It used to be that uninsured casualty losses were largely tax deductible. For someone in the 50% tax bracket, that meant the federal government already bore almost half any uninsured risk for free. Now, however, tax brackets are lower; and in any event, uninsured casualty losses are deductible only to the extent that they total more than 10% of your adjusted gross income (having first reduced each loss by $100). In other words, they're almost never tax deductible at all. The argument for high deductibles still makes sense in many situations; but with Uncle Sam no longer sharing the risk, it's less compelling than before.

• If you live near a lot of water, or what could be a lot of water once in a rare while, buy federal flood insurance (through any local insurance agent). Bear in mind that, unlike most coverage, which can be "bound" immediately when you call, with flood insurance you've got to pay the year's premium five days in advance; and you can only cancel the policy in midyear if you sell the house—not because hurricane season has passed. (The government isn't *that* dumb.)

• A toll-free number for information on federal flood insurance: 800-638-6620; on federal crime insurance (burglary): 800-638-8780.

• If you have a business-related computer setup at home, your homeowners' or renters' policy probably won't cover it without a special endorsement. Ask your insurance agent for a quote on coverage and/or call Safeware at 800-848-3469 (614-262-0559 in Ohio).

• If you have lots of valuable art, one of the companies to call for a quote is Chubb Insurance, which does well serving the well-to-do (phone 212-483-8888 for the name of a local agent). They'll handle your Rolls and polo ponies, too. Test their quote against the best your current insurance agent has to offer. You could probably do better still if you shopped further, but you're rich. Why bother?

INSURING YOUR CAR

Same thing. Shop around. Check the deductibles. Don't pay extra for medical coverage if you already have good health insurance; don't skimp on liability insurance if you have assets to protect; don't bother with collision coverage for a beat-up old car. Call GEICO, State Farm, and the Automobile Association of America, if you're a member, for competitive quotes, which they can give you over the phone, to be sure you're not paying too much. If you live in California and have an excellent driving record, call Twentieth Century Insurance (213-704-3000). If you know anyone insured by Amica Mutual, ask to be recommended for coverage (Amica won't accept applications without a referral). If you have served in the military (or, in some states, even if you haven't), get a quote from USAA in San Antonio (800-531-8080).

INSURING YOUR RENTAL CAR

The rental car companies are becoming increasingly desperate to get you to sign up for what they call "the insurance," which typically adds $9 or more to each day's rental and many millions to their bottom line.

Without "the insurance" you used to be liable for only the first $500 of damage to the car. Then they raised it to $1000 and then to $3000. Now some of the auto rental companies put you at risk for *all* the damage you do to their cars, which forces an awful lot of people to sign up. Before you do, however, remember that $9 a day is the equivalent of $3285 a year—and that it only covers damage to the rental car. You were already covered for theft and liability. The actual value of the $9 daily coverage they're selling is more like 50 cents.

In any event, your own auto insurance policy may already cover you for rental car damage. Check before you leave for your trip. Also, many credit card issuers have begun offering free rental car insurance as an inducement to use their cards, particularly their premium gold cards. If yours doesn't, keep an eye out for an offer from one that does.

INSURING YOUR UMBRELLA

For about $100 you can get a policy that protects you for up to $1 million in personal liability if, blinded by the rain and hunched under your umbrella, you accidentally ram into someone at top speed, sending him or her hurtling into oncoming traffic.

An umbrella liability policy covers just about any noncriminal activity you might be sued for that's not related to your business or profession. If someone drowns in your pool, you're covered. If someone sues you for malpractice, you're not.

You're unlikely ever to file a claim; but if you have assets to protect, you need this supplementary coverage.

(Note that many policies pick up where your auto liability coverage leaves off *only to the extent you already carry "250/500" protection*—$250,000 per person, $500,000 each occurrence. If you had an accident and carried just "10/20" in liability coverage, you could be liable for up to $480,000 yourself before your umbrella policy kicked in.)

INSURING YOUR REFRIGERATOR

"Oh, and incidentally," says the salesperson casually as he's writing up your order, "we're offering twenty percent off on our complete in-home five-year parts-and-labor warranty."

To which you should reply, in your best Church Lady tone: "Oh, isn't that special!"

You could get lucky on one of these deals and have your refrigerator break down three times one year, but most of the time you'll come out ahead taking the risk yourself.

INSURING YOUR HEALTH

Group health insurance at work is the best; Blue Cross/Blue Shield is generally second best. If you're young and healthy, your insurance agent may be able to find you something better (Blue Cross doesn't take age into account in setting rates). If you're over 55, you automatically qualify for group coverage arranged by the American Association of Retired Persons (1909 K St. N.W., Washington, D.C. 20049).

In considering other policies, ask what proportion of the premiums collected is actually used to pay claims. If the figure isn't readily available, in writing, there may be a reason. With Blue Cross and most group plans, more than 90% of the premiums collected go to pay claims. Many mail-order plans pay out 50% or less.

INSURING AGAINST DISABILITY

Disability insurance is often important but always expensive, particularly if you go with a policy that defines disability as the inability to do your regular work (as opposed to *any* work).

You may already be covered by disability insurance at work, by workers' compensation insurance if you're injured on the job, and by Social Security benefits, which currently average in excess of $6000 a year and can exceed $17,000 if you are married with dependent children. For details, check with your personnel department and with the local Social Security office.

If you buy a policy on your own—and too many people who should never seem to get around to doing it—one way to cut the cost is to choose a high deductible. With disability insurance, this is measured in time, not dollars. Coverage that kicks in only after the first six or twelve months of disability will be much less expensive than coverage that kicks in the moment your ski's binding fails to release. A 44-year-old stockbroker (who'd obviously get a lower rate than a 44-year-old lion tamer) would pay the Northwestern Mutual $2824 annually for a policy that promised $3500 a month in disability benefits if those benefits began a month after the disability occurred, but just $2198 if payments began after two months, $1865 if they began after three months, or $1641 if they began after six. The expectation is that even the most inept skier will be back at his desk after six months.

A crucial point in choosing a policy is how disability is defined. Ask to read the policy before you make this investment. Insurers are notoriously resistant to honoring disability claims as opposed, say, to death claims, because disability claims are much easier to fake.

INSURING YOUR LIFE

You could make a career out of trying to find the best-possible life insurance policy, just as hundreds of thousands of people have made careers out of trying to sell it to you; but the simplest way to buy life insurance is often also the best: First determine how much you need (page 58). Then shop by phone for the cheapest coverage you can find—renewable term insurance. Buy it and be done with it.

Term insurance is plain vanilla insurance. It builds no cash value—it's not an investment—but it has three advantages. First, you don't need to be an expert to shop for it; policies are relatively easy to understand and compare. Second, it's cheap—the only way many families can afford the coverage they need. Third, you're not locked in to it. There's no penalty if you should ever want to drop the policy or switch to a better one.

The disadvantage is that it becomes very expensive as you grow older (when you really *might* die). So it's important to take what you save by buying this cheap insurance in your twenties and thirties and forties and fifties and invest it. Otherwise, though your kids will be grown and able to fend for themselves, your spouse and aged parents might be left with nothing but Social Security.

Investment-oriented life insurance products like whole life *force* you to save. They make you pay $1500 instead of $300 in the early years so that, as the amount of coverage your $1500 can buy shrinks, the savings you've built up through the policy expands to take its place. (It's not usually described this way, but that's what's happening.) The problem is, 20% or 25% of the people who commit to these expensive plans, with good intentions, let them lapse after just a year or two and lose much of the excess they paid in.

Investment-oriented life insurance products are not necessarily bad deals. But if life insurance is what you're after, you needn't multiply the cost and complication fivefold by committing to a lifelong savings plan. Buy term insurance and invest the difference—in an IRA, in tax-free municipal bonds, in mutual funds, in paying down the mortgage on your home. When the insurance salesman tells you that only 2% of the people who buy term insurance policies ever collect anything—as if that proves it's a waste of money—ask him what proportion of the people who buy fire insurance ever collect anything, and whether, as a result, he believes people shouldn't insure against fire.

To find a good term insurance policy you could start by calling InsuranceQuote (800-972-1104; 602-345-7241 collect in Arizona) and SelectQuote (800-343-1985). After asking some questions, each will mail you descriptions of five different policies, complete with prices for the next 20 years, that are represented as being among the best buys available. If you buy, these brokers get a commission; otherwise, the service is free. Both deal only with A plus- and A-rated insurers; both have service representatives to help answer your questions and guide your applications through to acceptance. Although their ads make it sound as if they do a computer search of hundreds of insurers' rate tables to find you the lowest-possible prices, it's not quite that dramatic. Select-Quote has relationships with about 20 insurers that offer low-priced term insurance products and does a computer search of those to come up with five illustrations for you; InsuranceQuote has relationships with 80. Even so, either one is likely to find you a good value and offer some good advice; neither one will hound you with phone calls or junk mail.

Also call USAA Life at 800-531-8000 (512-498-8000 in Texas).

And call your local independent insurance agent. Especially if you're looking for substantial coverage—several hundred thousand dollars or more—he or she may be able to find you highly competitive rates.

If you live or work in New York, Massachusetts, or Connecticut, call your local savings bank and ask about savings bank life insurance. The rates are even lower than they seem, because the printed rates are likely to be reduced by dividends (This will be true of term insurance policies offered by many mutual insurers.)

If you're looking for a small amount of coverage (anything under $100,000), call Savers Life at 800-223-7608 (212-753-6531 in New York) and compare their rates with others you may be considering.

By making these calls you may not find the absolute lowest rates available—even if they were all entirely comparable, which they are not—but you should come close enough to know you've gotten a good deal.

Note that one $200,000 policy costs much, much less than four $50,000 policies. Don't buy credit life policies that cover only the $11,000 balance on your auto loan or mortgage insurance policies that cover only the outstanding balance on your mortgage. It's almost always cheaper to buy one large all-purpose policy.

Beware policies whose rate structures look great but can rise if the insurer needs to raise them. And beware policies with incredibly low first-year rates—but sharply higher rates thereafter. (You can outsmart those by switching from policy to policy each year; but where really large coverage is involved, some insurers have begun keeping track of, and declining to write insurance for, policy switchers.)

If you're hardy, you may choose to take a calculated risk with a "reversionary" term policy. It offers rock-bottom rates for those in good health but requires requalification every five years or so. If your health deteriorates, they'll still insure you—but at a significantly higher rate. (Of course, you're always free to seek a better rate elsewhere.)

A strong proponent of term insurance, the A. L. Williams Company, deserves special mention. Founded just ten years ago by an ex–high school football coach, it employs more salespeople and sells more life insurance than any other company in America, including the Prudential. Several hundred thousand people have sold for A. L. Williams at one time or another (mostly part-time), all pitching cheap term insurance to the dismay of the traditional insurance industry. The paradox is that because of the cost of spreading its message—that sales force—A. L. Williams doesn't always offer the cheapest insurance. There's been much debate over A. L. Williams and some of its more agile ploys,* but suffice it to say that you should stick with annual renewable term insurance and buy the cheapest policy you can find.

As for the whole life policy you already own, if it pays divi-

---

*Here's one. It's always rankled A. L. Williams that the company it represents, MILICO, has received a not-so-hot B+ rating from A. M. Best & Co., the arbiter of financial strength among insurers. So in 1986, according to Joseph M. Belth, nationally known life insurance professor and industry gadfly, the company obtained and began publicizing an A+ rating from Standard & Poor's. What the publicity fails to mention is that A+ is not S&P's highest rating— AAA is, followed by AA. Of the 33 life insurers Standard & Poor's has rated (which it does only upon request, for $15,000), all but A. L. Williams and one other were rated AAA.

dends (and you need insurance), you shouldn't necessarily drop it. You've already paid the sales charge; dropping it won't get that money back. Contact your agent or the company and determine the rate of interest being credited to your cash value. If it's decent, keep it—as an investment—and cover any additional insurance needs you may have with inexpensive term insurance.

HOW MUCH INSURANCE DO YOU NEED?

Enough to replace you, financially, if you die. Take out a pad and pencil and estimate what your family would need if you died this afternoon. Then pass the pad to your spouse and let him or her see how much coverage *he* needs. A typical calculation goes as follows:

1. *How much of your annual income would your heirs need to replace if you died?* For most families, this number falls somewhere around 75% of your annual take-home pay. (Remember: they'd no longer have to feed or clothe you or buy you the cigarettes that did you in in the first place.)

   If you take home no pay, but merely do 80 hours a week of cooking, cleaning, day caring, and shopping, estimate the cost of your replacement.

2. *Subtract the annual Social Security benefits your family could expect to receive.* For a widow or widower at 62, benefits are currently around $6000 to $8000 a year; for a widow or widower caring for one child, they range from $10,000 or so to upward of $18,000; for a widow or widower caring for two or more children, from $12,000 upward of $20,000—all this scheduled to keep pace with inflation and at least half tax free. Exact benefits depend on how high your earnings had been while alive and when you entered the system. (Perversely, the widow of a 23-year-old gets more than the widow of a man who'd been paying into the system for decades.)

3. The difference between numbers 1 and 2 above—if there is a difference— is the *annual income gap* you'll want life insurance to make up. But for how long? This depends on

the ages of your children and spouse, whether you'd expect your spouse to remarry—that sort of thing. *Choose a time period from the table below and multiply the annual income gap by the figure on the right.* The result is an amount of insurance that should last the number of years you require and keep up with inflation.

	Multiply by:*
5 years	4.7
10 years	9
15 years	12
20 years	15
25 years	18
30 years	20
50 years	26

Say you earn $45,000 a year and take home $31,000. You figure your heirs could make do with $25,000, of which Social Security would kick in $15,000 until the children are grown. To provide an additional $10,000 for 20 years, you'd multiply $10,000 by 15—$150,000.

4. *To this number add a lump sum* as a cushion for funeral expenses, grief-induced family illnesses, the payment of worrisome debts—at least half a year's salary and in no event less than $15,000.

Now you have a grand total of your insurance needs. But wait!

5. *Subtract whatever assets you've amassed* such as savings accounts, stocks, bonds, and retirement accounts (including whatever you'd be entitled to from work). Subtract still more if there's a wealthy and loving grandparent in the picture who would want to help out or whose wealth would eventually pass on to the family. And subtract the value of the group life insurance you have at work—but make a mental note that you may have to replace it if you switch

---

*This assumes your heirs could invest the proceeds to earn 3% after taxes and inflation. If you think they could earn more, you'd need less insurance—but you're probably not being realistic.

jobs, and that in the event of a long terminal illness that forces you from your job, you will have to promptly exercise your (very expensive) option of continuing the policy on your own.

6. *Round up to the nearest $25,000 or $50,000*—and there's your answer.

HOW MUCH INSURANCE DO YOUR CHILDREN NEED?

Until they have dependents: none.

LIFE INSURANCE INVESTMENT PRODUCTS

Term insurance is just insurance. What insurers would really like to sell you are *investments* that—oh, yes, incidentally, offer some life insurance. Whole life, universal life, variable life, single premium deferred annuities and single premium life—you'll find information on each in part III. Their advantage is that the money you save under the umbrella of an insurance policy is sheltered from taxes until you withdraw it.

The new tax law has left these products relatively unscathed, but you may wish to steer clear anyway. One reason is the sales fee that, however it's folded into the price of the product, is like the load on a mutual fund. And there are other problems:

• Many of these savings plans provide a mediocre rate of return.

• It's nearly impossible for most families to afford as much whole life as they need when they need life insurance most ($300 may buy a young parent $200,000 of term insurance but just $25,000 of whole life).

• The penalty for early withdrawal from a whole life plan—for letting the policy lapse after just a few years—is *enormous*.

• There's no easy way for you to tell a good whole life plan from a bad one, in part because it mixes two things together, insurance and savings. What you really want to know is, assuming a good low rate for the insurance portion of your policy, what rate of interest will you be paid on the savings portion? This is hard to find out. Just because a salesman promises something, or a computer spits out an illustration showing how your money will compound or the premiums you're required to pay will vanish— doesn't mean you can count on it. A company may always have lived up to its illustrated benefits in the past—it was easy for insurers to fulfill their modest promises in an era of ever-rising interest rates (and longevity). Lately, however, insurers have been making bolder promises at the start of an era where the general level of interest rates may *not* keep rising (and where mortality statistics, in light of AIDS, may turn grim). It's easy to meet illustrations based on 6% compounded growth when interest rates are rising into double digits. It won't be easy to meet double-digit illustrations if the general level of interest rates falls back into single digits.

"It is questionable whether policy illustrations were valid 20 years ago," writes Charles E. Rohm, senior vice-president of Principal Mutual Life in Des Moines. "They definitely are not valid today." What's more, he points out, the policy offering the highest return on your money may be backed by the riskiest investments, like junk bonds. But consumers are not given that information.

It's not that investment-oriented insurance products aren't worth a look (or at least, in part III, a peak); just that, once you do start looking, and form a personal relationship, however fleeting or superficial, with a friendly professional eager for your business, you may soon have invested too much time to want to simply write it off, let alone go through the unpleasantness of rejecting the salesperson. So you buy. This is not a good reason to lock yourself in to a major financial decision.

Chapter 5

HEAVY LEVY
Planning for Taxes, Tuition, Retirement, and the Hereafter

*What's so fair about eliminating the interest deduction on your
first car but not on your second home?*
—Murray Weidenbaum

Believe it or not, a single, self-employed New Yorker earning
$29,000 in 1988 will be in the 59.7% tax bracket. If she earned
an extra $1000, 59.7% of it—$597—would be due in taxes.*

Point #1—the new low tax brackets may not *totally* wipe out
the underground economy, at least not in New York City.
Plumbers may still ask to be paid in cash (no, it's not because

*Two hundred eighty dollars in federal income tax (the famous 28% bracket
everyone talks about), $150.20 in Social Security tax, $83.75 in New York State
income tax, $43 in New York City income tax, and, because she is self-em-
ployed, $40 in a thing called the New York City "unincorporated business tax."

they think your check will bounce), and you may still have to bite your lip knowing they not only make twice the hourly wage you do, but, like as not, don't report it.

Point #2—it's still important to understand your tax bracket.

Your tax bracket is *not* how much tax you pay on average (on *average,* the woman in this example would be paying about 38% of her income in taxes—$11,000) but how much you pay on the margin—on the last few dollars you earn. Because it is on the margin that financial decisions are made.

How much would I actually get to keep—after tax—if I gave up my Saturdays to work overtime? What does a mortgage really cost me, after tax, if I can deduct the interest?

What matters in financial decisions is how you come out *after* taxes. What matters is how much you get to keep. You need not know your tax bracket down to the last digit, but you should know it in broad strokes—and easily can, as you'll see.

Chances are, you're not in the 59.7% tax bracket. Three factors keep you from its clutches.

• First, if you live in a no- or a low-income-tax state, your combined tax bracket won't be anything like 59.7%. Florida, Texas, Washington, Nevada, South Dakota, Alaska, and Wyoming currently levy no income tax. Connecticut, New Hampshire, and Tennessee tax only investment income. Had she lived in one of these states, our single, self-employed New Yorker would have been in more like the 43% than the 59.7% tax bracket.

• Second, if you're not self-employed, the Social Security tax bite is only 7.51%, not 15.02%.* And whether self-employed or not, it stops biting altogether when your 1988 income exceeds $45,000 or so. (The ceiling rises each year. It was $7800 in 1971.) So if both you and your spouse earn more than that, nei-

---

*Your 7.51% contribution is matched by your employer for a total of 15.02%. In 1990, the rate goes to 7.65% for employees, 15.3% for the self-employed.

ther one of you need take Social Security tax into account in figuring your tax bracket.*

(Actually, Social Security tax can be ignored in most financial decisions anyway. It's levied only on earned income, not investment income, so it doesn't affect the yield on a stock or a bond; and, like a resistant strain of mosquito, it's immune to deductions like mortgage interest and charitable donations that lower your income tax, so it doesn't affect their true cost.)

• Third, if you itemize, local income tax lowers your federal tax. If the self-employed New Yorker had been an itemizer, 28% of her local income taxes would have been absorbed by Uncle Sam, knocking her bracket down from 59.7% to 55%.

But one effect of the new tax law (which, given Congress's boundless energy, will doubtless soon be "the old tax law") is that fewer taxpayers will find it worthwhile to itemize. Fewer deductions are allowed; and the standard deduction you get to take if you *don't* itemize has jumped—to $3000 in 1988 if you're single (up from $2540) and to $5000 if you file jointly (up from $3760).

This suggests an obvious tax-saving strategy for the many who will find that their deductions each year don't quite, or just barely, exceed the standard deduction: bunch them every *second* year.

Before considering the broader implications of the tax law and its impact on the way you save for your children's educations and for retirement, take a minute to review this strategy.

*Of course, if you do earn enough to escape further Social Security tax payments, you probably also earn enough to suffer the 5% surcharge, which raises from 28% to 33% the federal tax on income between $43,150 and $89,560 (for single taxpayers) or between $71,960 and $149,250 (joint). Only when you exceed these levels of income do you soar, relatively unfettered, into the stratosphere of low tax brackets (until Congress decides to raise them).

If it seems odd that a single, self-employed Texan earning $1 million a year would be in the 28% tax bracket but that one who earned $60,000 would be in the 33% bracket (because of the surcharge) while one who earned $30,000 would be in the 43% bracket (because of Social Security tax)—two points are worth noting. First, life is unfair. Second, the millionaire would still be paying vastly more in total tax ($287,000 or so) than either of the others ($21,000 and $10,000, respectively), even though he or she might consume no more—or perhaps less—in the way of government services.

THE STRATEGY

Instead of taking $5500 in deductions each year, say—all but $500 of which you and your spouse could have had anyway beginning in 1988 by filing jointly and taking the standard deduction—plan to itemize in 1989 and 1991 but *not* in 1988 or 1990. Come December 1988, hold off giving to charity and paying local taxes, if you're allowed to, until January 1989. Then, 11 months later, still in 1989, make your donations and pay your local taxes. By doubling up every second year this way you'll get the $5000 standard deduction half the years, but perhaps $7500 the other half. Net net: you save several hundred dollars in taxes every second year—and with less work, because you only have to itemize half as often.

Even if you're a heavy itemizer, there's a corollary strategy that applies to all those miscellaneous deductions that used to be fully deductible, such as unreimbursed business expenses, investment advisory fees, professional journals, education expenses related to advancing in your job, and the cost of preparing your tax return. Now they're deductible only to the extent they exceed 2% of your adjusted gross income. So if you normally spend $1000 a year on these things but have adjusted gross income of $50,000, they won't save you a dime. Bunch them into every second year, however, and at least some of the deduction may be preserved.

Whether it's really worth the effort to plan in this detail—and whether the IRS will go along with some of your more creative bunching—is open to question. Undeniably, though, if you're planning two major medical expenditures—a $3500 tummy tuck and $4500 of cosmetic bonding—it would be better to have them both done the same year than to be tucked in December and bonded in January. Each year's unreimbursed medical expenses are deductible only to the extent they exceed 7.5% of your adjusted gross income. On $50,000 in adjusted gross income, only nonreimbursed medical bills over $3750 would be deductible. So having the two operations in separate years would yield a total deduction of $750 (nothing from the tuck, $750 from the bonding), versus $4250 if you did them both the same year.

THE BROADER IMPLICATIONS

1. Semisimplification

The new tax law, for all its wild complication, actually does simplify things for many people. By raising the personal exemption and standard deduction, it removes millions of taxpayers from the tax rolls and relieves millions more of the chore of itemizing their deductions. An element of fairness is lost—the nonitemizer with $1800 in charitable donations gets the same standard deduction as the nonitemizer who gave nothing—but it reduces paperwork.

At the other end of the spectrum, for high-income taxpayers who invested in tax shelters and rent their vacation homes part of the year, it adds lots of complications in the short run. But by reducing the top federal tax bracket from 70% as recently as 1979 (how quickly we forget), and from 50% in 1986, to just 33%—or just 28% if you're making really big bucks (and if Congress doesn't have a change of heart)—it gives high-income individuals far less incentive to bend themselves into contortions trying to beat it.

"You wanna know the best tax shelter of all?" more than one professional concluded back when the rate was 50%. "Just pay your taxes." Now, with the rate down dramatically, more and more high-income individuals will be saying that. And that will simplify their financial lives. Why risk a dollar to save 28 cents in taxes?

The old advice was always, Never invest in a deal purely for its tax benefits. Examine it as an *economic* deal. Would it be worth the risk even if it provided no tax benefits?

That advice stands. The difference is that now, with lower tax brackets, more of us will actually take it.

2. A More Rational Economy

With fewer deals being done to avoid taxes, our economic resources should wind up being allocated a little more efficiently.

3. Less Incentive to Borrow

With the deduction for consumer interest being rapidly phased out (just 40% deductible in 1988, 20% in 1989, and

10% in 1990), there's less reason than ever to borrow when you can pay cash.

4. More Incentive to Save

Most people will be in lower tax brackets than they were before, which means they'll get to keep more of their interest and dividends. To a top-bracket individual, $1000 of interest was worth just $500 in 1986; it's slated to be worth $720 in 1988.

5. Lower Interest Rates

With less incentive to borrow, the demand for money will slacken a bit. With more incentive to save, the supply of money will increase a bit. Less demand and more supply means the price of money—interest rates—will be lower than would otherwise have been the case. Rates may shoot up, but probably not as high as they otherwise might have. And when they fall, they may fall a little farther than they otherwise would have.

Other things being equal (not that they ever are), lower interest rates make for a healthier economy.

6. Less Incentive to Take Risk

In 1986, three-fifths of any long-term gain was exempt from taxation. There was a strong tax incentive to take risk in hope of long-term capital gain.

In 1988, none of a long-term capital gain is exempt from tax, so a dollar of treasury bond interest is just as good, after tax, as a dollar of long-term gain (better, actually, because the treasury bond interest is exempt from state income tax).

There will still be an incentive to take risk: over time, on average, risky investments outperform safe ones. (The marketplace in effect "pays" you to take that risk.) But on the margin, the new tax law will shift money out of risky investments into safer ones and will shift investor preferences from low-yielding growth-oriented stocks to more mature companies paying higher dividends.

Other things being equal, less risk taking makes for a less dynamic economy.

7. **Increased Importance of Local Taxes**

With federal tax brackets so much lower for high-income individuals, the local income taxes that once seemed relatively small—and that were 50% absorbed by the deduction against federal taxes anyway—will now constitute a significantly larger share of the total tax bite. No one is going to move from Wisconsin to Florida just to cut his taxes, or from New York to Connecticut or from Massachusetts to New Hampshire. But the new tax law magnifies the attraction of low-tax states and threatens the long-term health of higher-tax states.

8. **Still No Tax on Not Spending**

For most readers, a penny saved—not spent—remains nearly as good as two pennies earned. You can become $1000 richer by earning $2000 and paying half, or nearly half, to the government. (A Miami millionaire need earn only an extra $1389 to keep $1000; our self-employed New Yorker must earn $2480.) Or you can become $1000 richer by not spending it.

There are three broad ways of doing that. Some involve real sacrifice (not eating), some involve perceived sacrifice (not eating at expensive restaurants), and some—my favorite—involve little or no sacrifice at all (eating things you would have anyway, only bought on sale). As I argued in chapter 2, the average family can make $1000 stretch to buy $1400 of the very same staples it would have bought in the course of the year anyway—tuna fish and shaving cream and table wine and bathroom tissue—by buying these items in bulk when they're on sale. That's a $400 saving on a $1000 "investment"—a 40% tax-free return.

If you have trouble living up to the budget you set in chapter 2, it might help to start thinking in terms of what things really cost. That Mitsubishi TV only appears to cost $819. If you're in the 40% tax bracket, you have to *earn* an extra $1365 to pay for it. Seeing it this way could increase your enthusiasm for the $400 Zenith, which may be virtually as good, anyway.

9. Or on Not Selling

The tax on long-term capital gains does jump under the new law—but only if you sell. If you own an asset that's appreciated a lot, but that may continue to, there's a stronger incentive than ever not to sell and incur the tax—particularly if you believe Congress may one day lower it. Also, under current law (which there is some thought in Congress of changing), you can escape the capital gains tax altogether by holding your appreciated asset until the bitter end. Under current law, it will be passed on to your heirs not at its original low cost, but at its value as of the time of your demise.

YOUR KIDS

The best financial advice, of course, is not to have any. But if you've already ignored that—and I hope you have—the traditional advice has to do with saving for their educations. Under the new tax law, many of the devices people established to shift income from their high tax brackets to their kids' low brackets have been thrown out, at least for children under 14.* But the first $500 in investment income a child under 14 earns escapes tax, and the next $500 is taxed at his or her low tax bracket (beyond that, it's taxed at the parents' rate). So it still may make sense to give several thousand dollars to each of your children, if you can afford to, through a custodial account at a bank, brokerage firm, or mutual fund. Any one of these institutions will have the forms for setting up such an account, which you can then administer on behalf of your child.

Just how much to give and in what form naturally varies from

---

*Even if they hadn't been, there's this conundrum: If your child shows up at the financial aid office with $20,000 in the bank, she may not get the same scholarship she'd have been granted if she were penniless and you had used that money instead, say, to build up equity in your house. What you save in taxes you could lose, in full or in part, in financial aid. Of course if you're an anesthesiologist making $150,000 a year, no financial aid would have been forthcoming anyway, so there's nothing to lose.

situation to situation. But if you are in the 40% tax bracket (33% federal and 7% state, say) and your child is in the 0% or 15% tax bracket, there's an obvious advantage to having interest, dividends, and capital gains taxed at his or her lower rate.

Say you split $5000 between two infant twins, and it grew by 11% a year for 18 years in a mutual fund. At first, no tax would be due and then, as the funds grew, only a little, leaving the twins with $30,000. That same $5000 invested under *your* name would grow by only 6.6% after tax (if you were in the 40% tax bracket for most of those 18 years), leaving you with not quite $16,000.

You come out nearly $15,000 ahead on a $5000 investment, just by arranging your finances a little differently. With triplets, it's even more dramatic.

Of course, once you give money to your children, it's theirs. But they can't spend it on something stupid until they're 18 or 21, depending on the state.

For an infant, shares in a no-load mutual fund might be an appropriate investment. Infants have a long time horizon, and over long periods of time stocks outperform safer investments. Or, if the market seems high, you might first invest in a no-load bond fund, planning to switch a portion of the funds into stocks when the market's lower.

As your child's fortune swells to the point where it throws off more than $1000 a year before he or she turns 14, you might invest part of it in tax-free municipal bonds or low-yielding growth stocks, or else in U.S. savings bonds, which allow you to defer tax on the interest they accrue. At age 14, investment income in any amount is taxed at your child's low rate, so any time thereafter you could declare the accrued interest on these bonds and see it lightly taxed.

Once your child turns 14, you can give her as much money as you want (subject to gift tax limitations) and still have the income it throws off taxed at his or her lower rate.

If you were about to sell stock in which you had a $15,000 profit, using what was left after tax to pay tuition, you could give

HOW TO CALCULATE YOUR TAX BRACKET

Step #1. Enter the approximate income you expect this year. It doesn't have to be precise—none of this has to be precise. "Oh, about forty grand, same as last year," will do just fine.

Gross Income: _____

Step #2. Subtract the standard deduction ($3000 if you file singly in 1988, $5000 if you file jointly) or else a rough guess at the itemized deductions you'll be allowed.

Deductions: – _____

Step #3. Subtract any deductible IRA or Keogh contributions you plan. And subtract $2000 for each member of the family, yourself included. (The personal exemption is pegged at $1950 in 1988 and $2000 in 1989.)

Exclusions and Exemptions: – _____

Step #4. Subtract anything else I've left out, like the allowable portion of tax shelter losses.

Adjustments: – _____

Your Approximate Net Taxable Income: = _____

Step #5. Based on this approximate taxable income, find your federal tax bracket below:

If your taxable income is . . .		. . . this is your 1988 tax
Single	Joint	bracket
up to–$17,850	up to $29,750	15%
$17,850–43,149	$29,750–71,900	28%
$43,149–89,560	$71,900–149,250	33%
over $89,560	over $149,250	28%

Federal Tax Bracket: _____

Step #6. Add your Social Security tax rate. On 1988 income up to an estimated $45,300, it is 7.51%—or 15.02% if you have income from self-employment. Above that, for each spouse, it is *zero*.

Social Security Tax: + _____

Step #7. Check last year's state income tax form to see the tax rate on income like yours, and, if you itemize your deductions, shave it by 15% or 28% or 33% (the portion Uncle Sam absorbs by virtue of the deduction). Or find your state in the table on the next page and assume, as I have, that you are in your state's top bracket.

Local Income Tax: + _____

Step #8. Add #5–#7. This is your tax bracket, at least when it comes to knowing how much of an extra $1000 in earnings you'd get to keep. For most financial decisions, you can ignore the Social Security portion, because that tax is not due on investment income, or reduced by deductions.

Your Tax Bracket: = _____

YOUR LOCAL INCOME TAX BRACKET*

	If your federal bracket is:				*Income Threshold*
	Nonitemizers	*15%*	*28%*	*33%*	
Alabama	5	4.3	3.6	3.3	$ 3000/$6000
Alaska	0	0	0	0	—
Arizona	8	6.8	5.8	5.3	$ 7000/$14,000
Arkansas	6	5.1	4.3	4	$ 25,000
California	11	9.4	7.9	7.3	$ 29,000/$58,000
Colorado	8	6.8	5.8	5.3	$ 14,000
Connecticut	0	0	0	0	—
Divs. & Int.	12	10.2	8.6	8	$100,000
Capital Gains	2.8	2.4	2	1.8	—
Delaware	8.8	7.5	6.3	5.9	$ 40,000
D.C.	11	9.4	7.9	7.3	$ 25,000
Florida	0	0	0	0	—
Georgia	6	5.1	4.3	4	$ 7000/$10,000
Hawaii	11	9.4	7.9	7.3	$ 31,000/$61,000
Idaho	7.5	6.4	5.4	5	$ 5000
Illinois	2.5	2.1	1.8	1.7	—
Indiana	3	2.6	2.2	2	—
Iowa	13	11	9.4	8.7	$ 77,000
Kansas	9	7.7	6.5	6	$ 25,000
Kentucky	6	5.1	4.3	4	$ 8000
Louisiana	6	5.1	4.3	4	$ 50,000
Maine	10	8.5	7.2	6.7	$ 25,000/$50,000
Maryland	5	4.3	3.6	3.3	$ 3000
Massachusetts	5	4.3	3.6	3.3	—
Investment Income	10	8.5	7.2	6.7	—
Michigan	4.6	3.9	3.4	3.1	—
Minnesota	8	6.8	5.8	5.3	$ 13,000/$19,000
Mississippi	5	4.3	3.6	3.3	$ 10,000
Missouri	6	5.1	4.3	4	$ 9000
Montana	11	9.4	7.9	7.3	$ 46,000
Nebraska	19% of federal	2.4	3.8	4.2	—
Nevada	0	0	0	0	—
New Hampshire	0	0	0	0	
Investment Income	5	4.3	3.6	3.3	—
New Jersey	3.5	3	2.5	2.3	$ 50,000
New Mexico	8.5	7.2	6.1	5.7	$ 42,000/$64,000

| | If your federal bracket is: | | | | |
	Nonitemizers	15%	28%	33%	Threshold
New York ('88)	8.4	7.1	6	5.6	$ 17,000/$34,000
New York City	12.7	10.8	9.1	8.5	$ 25,000/$34,000
Self-Employed	16.7	14.2	12	11.1	$ 25,000/$34,000
North Carolina	7	6	5	4.7	$ 10,000
North Dakota	10.5% of federal	1.5	2.1	2.3	—
Ohio	6.9	5.9	5	4.6	$100,000
Oklahoma	6	5.1	4.3	4	$ 1250/$2500
Oregon	10	8.5	7.2	6.7	$ 5000
Pennsylvania	2.1	1.8	1.5	1.4	—
Rhode Island	22.6% of federal	2.9	4.6	5	—
South Carolina	7	6	5	4.7	$ 13,000
South Dakota	0	0	0	0	—
Tennessee	0	0	0	0	
Investment Income	6	5.1	4.8	4	—
Texas	0	0	0	0	—
Utah	7.8	6.6	5.6	5.2	$ 3750/$7500
Vermont	24% of federal	3.1	4.8	5.2	—
Virginia	5.75	4.9	4.1	3.8	$ 12,000
Washington	0	0	0	0	—
West Virginia	6.5	5.5	4.8	4.4	$ 60,000/$120,000
Wisconsin	7.9	6.7	5.7	5.2	$ 30,000/$40,000
Wyoming	0	0	0	0	—

*This table assumes you are in the top local tax bracket, which in most states is an easy distinction to achieve. It applies to 1987 taxable income in excess of the amounts shown in the right-hand column. (Where two amounts are shown, the first is for taxpayers filing singly.)

your child the stock instead and let her sell it. If she were 14 or older, the gain would be taxed at her lower tax bracket, saving, in this example, $2000 or $3000 in taxes. Just be sure the gift is legally completed before the sale is made. Also, be aware that gifts over $10,000 a year to any one recipient—$20,000 a year if made jointly—may be subject to gift tax. (It is the donor, not the donee, who pays gift tax.)

Whatever your child's age, *earned* income is taxed at her low bracket. So if you run your own business or are self-employed, here's another way to shift income from your tax bracket to hers: Hire her to help. As long as the work is legitimate and the pay is not out of line, you will have a valid business deduction. (If you're self-employed, this deduction could lower your Social Security tax as well.) Your child will have to pay income tax, but at a low rate. And if she's under 21 and working for her mother's or father's unincorporated business, she won't have to pay Social Security.

If you really want to get the power of compound interest working for her early, you could encourage her to shelter part or all her earnings in an IRA. Set aside $750 in an IRA at age 14, 15, and 16, and at 65 (if your child can imagine such a thing, which she surely can't), compounding at 10%, it will be worth well over a quarter of a million dollars. Should she be able to compound those three little IRA contributions at 12%—$650,000.

Here's a good way to pay for your kids' education: Get your parents to do it. Whatever they pay will escape gift tax (gifts for medical or education expenses are exempt); will lower the value of their estate when it comes time to pay inheritance tax; and will subject neither you nor your children to income tax.

Another offbeat but interesting alternative is to sign up for one of the prepaid tuition plans colleges have begun to offer—see page 233.

But enough of the details. Two broader aspects of kiddie finance bear mentioning—the money habits your kids pick up from you and the guidance you give them in managing their principal asset. After all, it would be nice if, in your old age, they could provide you with some financial security instead of your having to continue to provide it for them.

It's easy to suggest that you pass along a healthy respect for money and saving. I don't claim to know how to do it, but I suspect that setting a good example couldn't hurt. It may also help to pay them a regular allowance and enough for small chores so that, with a budget of their own, they can be responsible for all the basic nonessentials (movies, Mars bars, *Mad* magazine, Mother's Day gifts).

As for their principal asset, it is, of course, their careers. Now I know they're your kids, not mine, but I have something to say to them. In asking you to pass it along, I also ask that you pick the right moment, so that it really makes an impression.

A few minutes before daybreak would be good. Your kids are peacefully asleep in the next room or in their dorm rooms at school. Wake them up! Shake them or phone them or pound the table a few times to make sure they're really listening. Then tell them not to go to law school. Lawyers are great, tell them, but we have too many lawyers. Investment bankers are great, tell them, but at the rate we're going, investment bankers will merely preside over the orderly sale of America to our better-educated, better-organized friends abroad. (It's becoming a cliché: the Japanese have one-thirtieth as many lawyers as we do, but four times as many engineers. While we're litigating over how to split up the pie, they're figuring out how to make it bigger.)

Science, tell them. Math! Physics! Biology! Medicine! Chemistry! Metallurgy! Genetics! Lasers! Computers! Optics! Engineering! Oceanography! Adhesives!

Are they looking at you like you're crazy? Never mind. What's so exciting and challenging about the next 50 years aren't the advances that will come in divorce law. It's the incredible scientific progress that will make or break mankind.

Science, kids—and ample incentives for the technologically literate, never fear. You can have that Porsche *and* expand the frontiers of progress.

If your child is hopelessly devoid of all mechanical or scientific aptitude, so be it. Let him go to law school. Otherwise, at least don't encourage him or her by offering to pay for it.

YOUR RETIREMENT

It would break my heart to see you become a bag lady.* Standing between you and that fate are, first, if you're a man, your sex, but then, too, these five broad areas of potential support:

*Bag ladies don't buy books.

1. Social Security. By one name or another, it will almost surely still be there. As today, it will provide no more than a bare-existence safety net—which is really all it was ever intended to do. It was not intended as a national retirement plan but as a welfare scheme for those who had failed to provide for their own needs. Most of today's retirees are getting far more from Social Security than they contributed, even after allowing for the interest their contributions could have earned. (The maximum contribution for a wage earner in 1963 was $174, compared with $3400 today.)

Today there are approximately three workers contributing to the system for each retiree; in 20 or 30 years there may be only two. But that doesn't mean the system will collapse, only that the benefits may be even a little less lavish than they are today.

Benefits may not entirely keep pace with inflation (in the seventies, they outstripped inflation, which is one reason the system was thrown into crisis); they may become fully subject to tax (with the not unreasonable result that Mrs. DuPont, who really doesn't need the money, would wind up giving a larger part of her benefits back); and the age at which full benefits may be claimed may be nudged a year or two farther into the future (because we are living a lot longer than we did when the system was first designed).

But the safety net will be there. For the next few decades, in fact, the retirement fund will be running a huge surplus. The government will try to spend that surplus on much-needed weapon systems and tobacco subsidies; we future retirees will argue that it should be invested in treasury bonds for our future retirement; some compromise will be reached.

In figuring your benefits, you should assume they'll be almost what they'd be (adjusted for inflation) if you retired today: $6000 to $9000, if you've been reasonably well employed over the years. Add 50% to that rough range if your spouse is also of retirement age. And double it if he or she, like you, has been paying into the Social Security system at a rapid clip.

(For a free layman's sketch of the wildly complicated formula by which benefits are calculated—believe me, you don't want more than a sketch—phone your local Social Security office and ask to be sent *Estimating Your Social Security Retirement Check*. To see whether you've been credited with the contributions you've made to the system, ask also for form #7004.)

2. Your pension and profit-sharing plans at work. Visit the personnel office to understand what those benefits might be worth if you left the company or when you retire. If you tell the personnel manager you're developing a personal financial plan, he's likely to be impressed rather than annoyed by your questions.
3. The tax-sheltered retirement plans you control yourself—an IRA, a Keogh plan, a 401(k) or 403(b) salary reduction plan.
4. The assets you've amassed outside the benefit of any such shelters, and inheritances you may receive.
5. Your kids—so be nice.

IRAs, SEPs, KEOGH AND SALARY REDUCTION PLANS

If your employer offers a salary reduction plan, grab it. If it's one of those that kicks in 50 cents or a dollar for each dollar you contribute, sell your mother-in-law into slavery if you have to, but contribute every penny you're allowed to.

If you earn income from self-employment, whether full time or on the side, sock away 20% of it each year (up to a maximum of $30,000) in a Keogh plan. You can establish a Keogh with virtually any bank, brokerage firm, or mutual fund—and may, even if you are also covered by a retirement plan at work. But before you do, ask about the advantages and disadvantages of establishing a simplified employee pension plan (SEP) instead. A SEP is a giant IRA that currently permits contributions of 13% of your net earnings from self-employment up to a $30,000 maximum but requires less paperwork than a Keogh plan.

If you are not covered by a pension or retirement plan at work and aren't contributing to a Keogh plan, set up a tax-deductible IRA.

These four are terrific ways to save for retirement. With each —the salary reduction plan, the Keogh plan, the simplified employee pension plan, and the individual retirement account—you get to lower your current taxable income and compound your retirement fund tax free until you withdraw it.

The drawback, of course, is that you can't touch the money without penalty until you're 59½, unless you become disabled or die (in which case you certainly can't touch it, but your beneficiary can). You can't even pledge it as collateral for a loan. If you do, it's subject to penalties and taxes just as if you withdrew it.

Still, the 10% penalty for early withdrawal is likely to be outweighed by tax savings after just a few years' appreciation; and if you plan to have any money to supplement Social Security when you retire, at least some of it may as well be in the form of a tax-sheltered retirement account.

Proponents of these plans, myself included, used to argue that you could deduct your contributions now, when you're working and presumably in a high tax bracket, and then make withdrawals when you're retired and presumably in a low tax bracket. This isn't the certainty it once was, what with the new lower federal tax brackets—and the possibility of higher ones when you retire. But even if you don't get to shift income from a high tax bracket into a lower one, it will ordinarily pay to contribute to these plans. Why? Because you will have had working for you not just your share of the funds, but the share the government would otherwise have taken, too.

Over decades, the difference can be dramatic. Say you're 30 now and in the 33% tax bracket—and that you'll be there even after you retire. Contributing $2000 to your retirement each year (instead of just the $1333 you'd have had after paying tax on it) . . . and compounding that money at 9% (instead of just the 6% you'd have earned after tax) . . . will provide a retirement fund worth about $272,000 at age 60 (instead of just $106,000). True, that $272,000 would be taxed as you withdrew it. But if you withdrew it over 30 years (with the balance continuing to compound), your after-tax annual income would be $18,000. That compares with just $7000 a year you'd have going the nonsheltered route.

It's the same $2000 a year now. Which would you rather have to supplement Social Security over the last third of your life—$18,000 a year or $7000?

Of course, neither sum may buy much by then, which is why you should try to put away even more than $2000. But however little $18,000 may be worth in 30 years, it will be worth a lot more than $7000.

What's more, there is an enormous advantage to starting early. A single $5000 Keogh contribution at age 25, if you (or your child) can make one, grows at 9% to $250,000 by the time you have to begin withdrawing it at 70½. The same $5000 salted away at 60 grows only one-twentieth as large.

To get a rough idea how long you'd have to keep your money growing under the shelter of a retirement plan to come out ahead when you withdraw it—even if you're by then in a higher tax bracket or have to pay the penalty for early withdrawal—see the tables on pages 85 and 87.

The new tax law restricts the deduction you can take for contributing to a retirement plan. It cuts the $30,000 maximum on salary reduction plans (but not Keogh plans) to $7000. And IRA contributions are no longer deductible if *either* you or your spouse is covered by some other retirement plan—unless your adjusted gross income is under $35,000 (single) or $50,000 (joint). If it is, you're allowed $1 in IRA deductions for each $5 by which your income falls below those limits. That means you can take the full $2000 deduction, if either you or your spouse is covered by a pension plan or contributes to a Keogh plan, only if your adjusted gross income is no higher than $25,000 (single) or $40,000 (joint).

Should you still contribute to your IRA if it's not deductible? (Similarly, should you make voluntary nondeductible contributions to your company retirement plan, as many allow?)

Probably. It still compounds free of tax until you withdraw it. On the other hand, that's also true of life insurance products that allow more flexibility (you can borrow against them). And you could avoid federal tax altogether by investing in a no-load municipal bond fund.

Over long periods, a well-chosen common stock mutual fund compounding under the umbrella of an IRA should handily outperform an investment in either municipal bonds or life insurance (even life insurance that ties your cash value to its investments in common stocks, because the insurer may not select those common stocks terribly well and because the insurer charges a sales commission).

If you do make nondeductible contributions to an IRA, of whatever type, you will have to keep careful records. At withdrawal, the *non*deductible contributions you've made won't be taxed (that would be taxing them twice) or penalized for early withdrawal; but neither will you be able to withdraw them separately. In its zeal to make life complicated, the government says you'll have to treat each withdrawal as a proportionate blend of both nondeductible contributions and deductible-contributions-plus-appreciation.

You may contribute $2000 to an IRA each year (or 100% of your earned income, whichever is less).* There is no such thing as a joint IRA. Each spouse may contribute up to $2000 of his or her earnings to his or her IRA. If one spouse doesn't work and you file a joint tax return, you may set up a "spousal" IRA in his or her name, contributing up to $2000 to it—but not more than a total of $2250 between the two of you.

With the Keogh, the most you can ordinarily contribute is 20% of your self-employed income up to $30,000.** (You used to be able to put away the first $750 of your self-employment earnings without regard to the 20% test, under certain conditions, but no longer.) Check with your bank or accountant about the difference between a defined contribution plan (which is the most straight-

*Should you leave an employer and be given the retirement plan benefits you've earned, you will ordinarily be allowed 60 days to "roll them over" into an IRA rollover account, irrespective of any limit. In addition, you may still make your regular $2000 IRA contribution for that year.

**To confuse you, the IRS talks in terms of 25% of earnings, not 20%, but any normal human would describe it as 20%—and avoid the contorted calculations the IRS has contrived to match its contorted English.

forward) and a defined benefit plan (which may allow higher con- tributions but requires the blessing of an actuary and a lot more paperwork).

With an IRA, there's currently no special tax form to file each year. With a Keogh plan, there is form 5500EZ.

With either an IRA or a Keogh plan, you can spread your money across more than one investment. You could put half this year's contribution into a savings account and the other half into a mutual fund. Other than obvious questions of convenience—I keep all my IRA contributions in one mutual fund and all my Keogh money in one self-directed brokerage account—there's no limit to how many different IRA and Keogh accounts you can set up, so long as, in total, your contributions each year don't exceed your allowable limit.

At first, a bank may be simplest. But don't rule out the advan- tages of a no-load mutual fund.

If interest rates are high, consider locking in a guaranteed, compounded return with treasury-backed zero coupon bonds. (You'd do this through a self-directed retirement account at a bro- kerage house.)

You may transfer funds from one IRA trustee to another so long as you don't touch the money yourself. Most trustees have all the forms you'll need to effect the transfer. (If need be, you can take possession of the money yourself while it's between trustees, but not more than once a year and for not more than 60 days. Be very careful not to run afoul of this regulation.)

IRA and Keogh contributions for a given year may be made as late as April 15 of the following year. (With a Keogh, however, the plan itself must have been in place by December 31.) You may even be able to make your contribution later, if you've gotten an extension for filing your taxes. But why delay? If at all possi- ble, get into the habit of making this year's contribution the day after New Year's—not 15 months later. Your money will com- pound free of tax all the longer. Say you're 40 and just now begin to contribute $2000 a year to an IRA, investing it in a mutual fund that will grow at 12% a year. By making each contribution as soon as you're allowed to, instead of 15 months later, after 25 years you would come out more than $40,000 ahead. The first check I write each year is to the trustee of my Keogh plan.

(The second used to be to the trustee of my IRA, because you could have both. Now, you can still have both, but a Keogh plan is considered an employer-sponsored retirement plan in which you are the employer, so—in years when you contribute to it— IRA contributions may be rendered nondeductible, depending on your income level, as described above.)

With both the IRA and the Keogh plan you can't withdraw funds without penalty until you are 59½—but you're not forced to begin withdrawals until the end of the year following the year you turn 70½. In fact, you can keep making contributions up until (but not including) the year you reach that age. If you don't need it earlier, it makes great sense to keep your retirement money compounding tax free as long as possible. An awful lot of 65-year-olds live to be 80 or 90 or even 100, and you can't expect Willard Scott to support them all.

For further details on IRAs and other retirement plans, consult the specialist at any bank or brokerage firm or check the latest edition of *J. K. Lasser's Your Income Tax* ($8.95), widely available and invaluable. If you have employees, it is particularly important to understand the obligation you may have to include them in your plan. If you are nearing the age at which you choose or are required to begin withdrawing funds, be sure to check your options carefully.

SHOULD YOU CONTRIBUTE TO A RETIREMENT PLAN?

Retirement plans are great when they let you defer income from today's high tax bracket into tomorrow's lower one. They're even great if your tax bracket remains unchanged. But what of a situation where you suffer the 10% penalty for early withdrawal? Or where you defer income that would be lightly taxed today into a *higher* tax bracket tomorrow? This could happen if Congress one day jacked up the tax brackets or if you had built a small fortune that, by your later years, would throw off a large income—or if you simply decided to withdraw your entire $350,000 IRA nest egg in one lump sum.

The tables on pages 85 and 87 show how long a retirement-plan contribution has to sit until it's worth more at withdrawal than the same money invested *outside* such a plan. Obviously, if you're in the 40% bracket today (federal and state) but expect to be in the 15% tax bracket when you take the money out, break-even comes immediately. How can you lose?

On the other hand, if you're in the 15% bracket now but shoot up to the 50% bracket when you withdraw the funds, you'd be 250 before you came out ahead.

The tables are more precise than the real world, of course, and thus meant only as a guide. In the real world, the return you'll earn on your investment may jump all over the place—it won't be a steady 6% or 8% or 10% or 12% a year. In the real world, your tax bracket will vary from year to year—not sit at 15% for 10 years and then suddenly jump to 28%. And in the real world, you will have the option of withdrawing (and paying tax on) the money over a period of years. Perhaps you'll be in a high tax bracket at first, but a lower one as your retirement marches on.

Even if you're in the zero tax bracket today—you're a graduate student—chances are you'll be in a much higher bracket during most of the years your money would be compounding. So in looking at these tables don't think of "your tax bracket now" as zero, even if it is—think of it as what it's likely to be in a few years.

(But also, if you're in the zero or 15% tax bracket, consider making your $2000 IRA contribution *but not deducting it,* even if you're allowed to. Why deduct it now, when little or no tax would have been due on that income anyway, only to see it taxed at a high rate at withdrawal?)

Take the italicized "with penalty" numbers with a grain of salt, too. Yes, you'd have to pay a penalty if you withdrew the funds early. But if you did have to, might it not be because you'd lost your job or quit to write a novel? In such a situation, you might be in a lower tax bracket than planned. (Also, if you withdraw the funds early because you become disabled, the penalty is waived.)

In sum, these tables aren't meant to provide you with a single specific answer ("It will take exactly 6 years for my IRA contribution to break even if I withdraw it early"). They are meant to provide perspective on a wide range of possibilities.

POST-RETIREMENT

You should have a will. You know that, but you keep putting it off. Close this book and balance it on your head until you've gone to the phone and made an appointment with a lawyer to write your will. I'll wait.

Good. You'll find it's the cheapest legal fee you were ever charged, because for attorneys, wills are loss leaders. It's when you die that they reap it, as executors of the will.

An alternative is to establish a revocable living trust. You transfer all your assets to the trust, but by naming yourself the trustee, you can change its provisions whenever you like or dissolve it. You get—and are taxed on—the income from the trust and can withdraw principal. When you die, the assets in the trust are distributed as stipulated in the trust agreement. Your beneficiaries avoid many of the delays and fees involved with probate (the court-supervised process of administering your will). And the provisions of the trust, unlike a probated will, do not become a matter of public record and are harder to challenge.

HOW TO READ THIS TABLE: This table—and the one on page 87 for *non*-deductible IRA contributions—shows, under various assumptions, the number of years you'd have to leave this year's IRA contribution in an IRA before you'd have more at withdrawal, after taxes and penalties, than you would have had if you hadn't put the money into an IRA. Find your current tax bracket across the top and then look down to see how long break-even would take, assuming your money grew at 6%, 8%, 10%, or 12% a year. *The numbers in italics assume you'd have to pay the 10% penalty for early withdrawal.*

Say you're in the 33% federal-plus-local income tax bracket and think you can compound your money at 8% a year. If you were going to be in the 28% tax bracket when you withdrew the money, you'd immediately be ahead of the game by deferring today's income into tomorrow's lower tax bracket—it would take "zero" years to break even—*unless* you were hit with the 10% penalty for early withdrawal. In that case, it would take three years before you'd come out ahead by having put your money into an IRA. (See the number in italics that we've circled.) Anything short of that and you'd have been better off just paying tax on the income this year and investing the money without the benefit of tax shelter.

DOES A RETIREMENT PLAN MAKE SENSE FOR YOU?

Deductible Contributions

YOUR TAX BRACKET NOW:

	15%				28%				33%				40%				45%			
Assuming Your Money Will Compound At:																				
	6%	8%	10%	12%	6%	8%	10%	12%	6%	8%	10%	12%	6%	8%	10%	12%	6%	8%	10%	12%
You'd come out ahead after this many years:																				

YOUR TAX BRACKET AT WITHDRAWAL:

0% — In all cases, by shifting into the 0% tax bracket income that would otherwise be taxed, you come out ahead immediately. The number of years to break-even is "zero."

	6%	8%	10%	12%	6%	8%	10%	12%	6%	8%	10%	12%	6%	8%	10%	12%	6%	8%	10%	12%
15%	15	11	9	8	IMMEDIATELY															
28%	19	15	12	10	IMMEDIATELY															
	37	28	23	19	9	7	6	5	4	(3)	3	2								
33%	28	21	17	15	5	4	3	2	IMMEDIATELY											
	47	36	29	25	15	11	9	8	9	7	5	5	2	2	1	1				
40%	41	31	25	21	11	9	7	6	6	5	4	3	IMMEDIATELY							
	62	47	39	33	23	17	14	12	15	12	10	8	8	6	5	4	4	3	2	2
50%	62	47	39	33	23	17	14	12	15	12	10	8	8	6	5	4	4	3	2	2
	88	67	55	46	37	28	23	19	27	21	17	14	18	13	11	9	12	9	8	7

It costs more to draw up a revocable living trust than a standard will—perhaps $1000 or $2000 instead of $200 or $300—in part because your attorney has less to look forward to. There's also what may be the enormous headache of transferring your assets and then administering the trust. It's hard to imagine the average well-to-do forty- or fifty-year-old owning everything in the name of a trust. Life's too short for this nonsense. On the other hand, if you're a senior citizen, here's a way, in effect, to take care of some of the chore of settling your estate now, while you're alive, rather than leaving it to the executors of your will and the courts (although by then, what will you care? Personally, I'd rather deal with it after I'm dead).

HOW TO READ *THIS* TABLE: Just like the other one. The difference is, this one assumes your contribution is nondeductible—neither deducted from your taxable income when you make it nor taxed when you withdraw it.

NOTE: These tables are based on just this year's contribution. Whether to make another contribution next year is a separate decision to be made next year.

*Non*deductible Contributions

YOUR TAX BRACKET NOW:

	15%				28%				33%				40%				45%			

Assuming Your Money Will Compound At:

	6%	8%	10%	12%	6%	8%	10%	12%	6%	8%	10%	12%	6%	8%	10%	12%	6%	8%	10%	12%

You'd come out ahead after this many years:

YOUR TAX BRACKET AT WITHDRAWAL:

0% — IMMEDIATELY

15% — IMMEDIATELY (28% and above)

	6%	8%	10%	12%
15%	25	19	16	13

28% — IMMEDIATELY (33% and above)

	6%	8%	10%	12%	6%	8%	10%	12%	6%	8%	10%	12%
	31	24	20	17								
	53	40	33	28	17	13	11	10	9	7	6	5

33% — IMMEDIATELY (40% and above)

	6%	8%	10%	12%	6%	8%	10%	12%	6%	8%	10%	12%	6%	8%	10%	12%
	42	32	26	22	9	7	6	5								
	64	49	40	34	25	19	16	13	16	12	10	9	6	4	4	3

40% — IMMEDIATELY (45%)

	6%	8%	10%	12%	6%	8%	10%	12%	6%	8%	10%	12%	6%	8%	10%	12%	6%	8%	10%	12%
	57	44	35	30	20	16	13	11	12	9	8	7								
	80	61	50	42	36	28	23	19	26	20	17	14	15	12	10	8	8	6	5	5

50%

	6%	8%	10%	12%	6%	8%	10%	12%	6%	8%	10%	12%	6%	8%	10%	12%	6%	8%	10%	12%
	80	61	50	42	36	28	23	19	26	20	17	14	15	12	10	8	8	6	5	5
	107	82	66	56	53	41	33	28	42	32	26	22	30	23	19	16	22	17	14	12

PART II

Investing

"Wall Street," reads the sinister old gag, "is a street with a river
at one end and a graveyard at the other." This is striking but
incomplete. It omits the kindergarten in the middle.
—Fred Schwed

Chapter 6

MAKING MONEY THE OLD-FASHIONED WAY
Welcome to Wall Street

Discount broker Charles Schwab leads off *his* book of advice by describing an "eager-beaver stock salesman" he says he knew who took a prospect to look at the boats in the harbor. "As they surveyed the various luxury craft floating before them," Schwab writes, "the salesman pointed out all the yachts owned by successful brokers. 'But where are the customers' yachts?' the prospect innocently inquired."

It's odd Schwab would appropriate this famous bit of Wall Street lore as his own—the story was considered old even in 1940, when it was recounted in a wonderful book called *Where Are the Customers' Yachts?*—but it's a telling little legend nonetheless. An awful lot of money gets made in the investment world; but the exciting returns, by and large, are raked in by the croupiers.

I know a 23-year-old, first job out of college, who makes six figures trading foreign securities for a top-of-the-line New York firm. ("My job is to bullshit the customers," he says.)

91

I know an only slightly older fellow who makes seven figures trading bonds.

"*Whoa,*" I said when he first revealed the number—seven figures is a lot of money for a kid, even on Wall Street—"let me see the pay stub."

Maybe this isn't the sort of challenge one is supposed to pose in polite society ("My, my, Mrs. Partridge, what stunning jewels—are they real?"), but truth is my job objective, bluster my bête noire—and what connection have Wall Street trading desks ever had to polite society? Anyway, I wanted to see what a seven-figure pay stub looked like—if, in fact, this young man could produce it.

He could; he did. One million six hundred seventy-two thousand dollars. It was his bonus. (Otherwise, it looked pretty much like any other pay stub.) The problem was, he said, it wasn't enough. He'd been promised a percentage of profits on his trades—he is a very smart trader—and now they were trying to get off with a lousy $1,672,000.

It was the Richie Isaacs thing all over again. Richie, a classmate of mine, was trading GNMAs for Lehman Brothers and quit in a huff when his bonus check came through for just $2 million. He went to Donaldson Lufkin Jenrette, where he says he's much happier.

Of course, these aren't your average Wall Street traders. Your average Wall Street traders these days make, what, I don't know, maybe $200,000, $300,000 a year.

But for the good ones, you gotta expect to pay up. Here was this one kid at Hutton (or was it Shearson or Salomon?—my lips are sealed), again 23, making—well, it couldn't have been more than $70,000 or $80,000, one of his colleagues told me—but the entire GNMA desk at Merrill Lynch had up and left one day, en masse, for another firm, and now Merrill was, quick like a bunny, trying to regroup. (A GNMA desk is a bunch of guys connected to telephones and video screens trading millions of dollars of Government National Mortgage Association bonds and related securities.) So Merrill hired some senior fellow and charged him with putting together a new team. Which is how it came to pass that one morning, a year out of Princeton (or was it Yale?), the

23-year-old I'm thinking of came in to work and said he was leaving. He felt really bad, he said, but Merrill Lynch had made him an offer he couldn't refuse.

Now, you're thinking, How much of a bump would Merrill have had to offer a young guy like this to renege allegiance? Double what he'd been getting? Triple?

Merrill Lynch offered $600,000. But the kid didn't jump after all. You know why? His employer matched it.

"Hi, honey, I'm home!"
"How'd it go today?"
*"Not bad. I got a $530,000 raise."**

This chapter is about making money the old-fashioned way. If by the time you read it things on Wall Street have already collapsed, perhaps this will help to explain why. If they're still flying high, maybe it's time to take cover.

Not that the mid-to-late eighties bear much resemblance to the mid-to-late sixties, the last time we had some really good old-fashioned excess on Wall Street. Back then—*The Go-Go Years,* if you want to read John Brooks's fine account of them—champagne was flowing much as it is today. And then as now the Dow was not far from all-time record highs. But then you had daily merger-and-acquisition headlines, as financial wizards like Jimmy Ling used "funny money"—inflated stock—to build industrial enterprises of questionable long-term viability (LTV). Well, okay —today there are again daily merger-and-acquisition headlines. But with advisory fees to the investment bankers running routinely into the millions and very often the tens of millions—$100 million, in the case of Pantry Pride's 1986 acquisition of Revlon —you can be sure *these* deals are much more solidly grounded. This time, instead of shaky stock, they're using shaky bonds. Quite a different thing.

Then, you had celebrity money managers—the much publicized "gunslingers" like Fred Alger and Jerry Tsai; today, merely

---

*One trader who did jump to Merrill was Howard A. Rubin, lured from Salomon Brothers. In 1986 he was paid salary and bonus of $1 million. In April 1987, he was let go for losing $250 million.

the much publicized and occasionally incarcerated "arbitrageurs" (and, well, Fred Alger and Jerry Tsai back again, only bigger). Not at all the same.

Mutual fund sales were booming back in the sixties (remember Bernie Cornfeld?); today they're booming as never before, *but this time investors won't get hurt.* See the difference?

Seats on the New York Stock Exchange in 1968 went for prices exceeded only by the $625,000 record in 1929. Today, true, even that record's been broken (the $1 million mark was passed in April 1987, up from $95,000 ten years earlier). But after adjusting for inflation, $1 million isn't really that much anymore—and the seats are a lot more comfortable.*

Finally, today you've got a much saner new-issues market. Back then you had a company like National Student Marketing Corp. (*my* first job out of college) going public at $6 a share and rising in the first day of trading to $14 and then to $143. Today you've got Home Shopping Network going public at $18, rising to $42 that same day and, months later, hitting $252. But—and here's the critical difference—Home Shopping Network, unlike National Student Marketing (whose stock slid abruptly from $143 to $3.50), is no temporary marketing fad. Students graduate, but TV shoppers are glued to their sets for life. There's no way *that* stock could ever go down.

So the differences between that era and this are stark. No more have we a guns-and-butter policy in Vietnam sowing the seeds of inflation. Today our military and domestic spending are well within our means (give or take $200 billion).

But I digress. (And actually there really are enough differences to allow some hope, anyway, that we'll scrape through, as you'll see in the next chapter.) What I mean to be talking about here is compensation—specifically, the hint of unreality that has crept into pay at the apex. Has greed run amok? There was investment banker Dennis Levine earning $1 million a year, yet looking to

---

*Just kidding. There are no physical seats. Until the specialist system was introduced in 1872 or 1873 you really did get one—a carved cushionless wooden armchair in which to sit with your fellow members and make trades as the name of one stock after another was called out in turn. Now you don't even get that.

supplement his wage with some really serious money from insider trading.

"It's crazy, isn't it?" a young partner of what was once Lehman Brothers asked a group of us at an investment community dinner party. He was marveling at how much everyone, himself included, was making. Not that pay stubs were being passed around the room. But you had to figure average compensation for those in the circle was $500,000 to $1 million, if not higher. And this fellow, as he neared his 40th birthday, having built up a net worth of $5 million or so by going to the right schools and plugging away honorably and conscientiously for his firm, lo these dozen years, thought it was all a little crazy. "Isn't it?" he asked again. Apart from my own head, nodding like a piston, the rest of the heads in the circle seemed not to grasp exactly what he meant.

I sat next to a classmate at a similar dinner who had helped develop a financial planning program for households earning $250,000 a year and up, like his own. "Gee," I said, "that can't be a very big market. How many households have that kind of income?" Oh, I'd be surprised, he said, sipping the $50 wine that had been brought to our table. He didn't have the figures right with him, but it was several million—something like one household in 11.

One in 11 American households with an income of $250,000 or more!

In fact, of course, the number, though hard to ascertain exactly, is more like one household in 500. It's just that a preponderance of those happy households are clustered in this fellow's neighborhood.

And speaking of households, I asked this classmate and the others at the table, just to see if they would be as surprised as I had been when I ran across the figure, what proportion of American homeowners they thought had mortgage debt of $75,000 or more. I was relying on 1983 data, I confessed—home prices and, presumably, mortgage balances have risen since then—but this was the data I had, so this was the quiz. What did they think?

The consensus was around 30%.

What proportion of homeowners, I persisted, was $50,000 or more in mortgage debt?

The consensus grew to 50%.

Yet the answers, according to a government survey published by the Federal Reserve at the end of 1984, were 2% and 8%. Only 2% of American homeowners in 1983 owed $75,000 or more on their homes; only 8% owed $50,000 or more.

This is hard for investment bankers to imagine, because investment bankers live in Manhattan. In Manhattan, a three-bedroom apartment costs $800,000.

They're making so much money on Wall Street these days even the lawyers are "Leaving the Law for Wall Street," as the *New York Times* Sunday magazine titled an August 1986 cover story. In it, the senior partner of one top-paying New York law firm complained: "We are simply unable to pay the kind of money that a good man with two, three, four years of experience can get. The $200,000-to-$500,000 range just isn't possible."

Average American household income is in the $20,000-to-$30,000 range. Basically, it breaks down this way: Poor folks make four figures, most folks make five figures, rich folks make six figures, major celebrities and a select few plastic surgeons and business types make seven figures, Victor Posner and a very few others make eight.

Just what Victor Posner contributed to society to make him *worth* the $12.7 million salary and bonus he took from his financially troubled DWG holding company in 1985, theoretically with the shareholders' approval (DWG owns such companies as National Propane, Royal Crown Cola, and Arby's), is open to question — although he did once donate land to a Miami Bible college that he valued so highly on his tax return it led to his indictment on twelve counts of tax evasion.

But don't get me wrong. When Steve Jobs makes half a billion inventing the personal computer, that bothers me not a whit — all the less so, in fact, because making a bundle was not his primary goal. Invention and entrepreneurship are the internal combustion that drives the American dream. More power to them both. As for Johnny Carson and his NFL equivalents — more power to them, too.

Nor have I a beef with the first-year associates at Cravath

Swaine & Moore. ("When he landed a job with Cravath Swaine & Moore, one of the nation's most prestigious law firms," reported *The Wall Street Journal*, "the 25-year-old law student couldn't believe his luck. Then he got even luckier: the firm raised his starting salary by $12,000 to $65,000 a year—two months before he was expected to start work.") While it's undeniable we have too many lawyers, and hard not to wonder whether some are overpaid, I have no beef with the starting pay at Cravath. First off, $65,000 in New York is $45,000 anywhere else; second, associates earn that working 80 hours a week, which is simply two normal $22,500 40-hour jobs back to back. (Cry not, however, for Cravath's 56 partners, who averaged in 1986 a reported $970,000 apiece.)

I just feel uneasy when I hear that more than 20 employees of Merrill Lynch made over $1 million; or when I read that to elbow your way onto *Financial World*'s list of the 100 highest-paid Wall Streeters in 1985, you had to pull down a minimum of $3 million; or when I hear that a neighbor of mine, an arbitrageur, made $40 million that year and perhaps double that the next. Could junk-bond Jabberwock Mike Milken have been overcompensated at an estimated $100 million in 1986? What's theirs is theirs; I'm not trying to take it away from them—fair's fair. But could things in some sense be getting a little toppy? Could a bit of froth have bubbled into the market? Could some of the money going into their pockets be coming out of ours? If not, what planet *does* it come from?

I feel uneasy, too, when I read that top executive pay *outside* Wall Street keeps climbing faster than everyday wages—as if the contribution of the CEO grows steadily more important relative to that of the other 30,000 employees of the firm, or as if it's just damn hard to attract chief executive talent at $650,000 a year anymore, so you've got to sweeten the pot. (CEOs took home 18% more in 1986 than 1985, according to *Business Week*.) For it's not just on Wall Street that the deal makers, the guys with the leverage, reside.

Coopers & Lybrand compensation expert Edmund Schwesinger worries we may be creating a corporate "royalty" in this country with *such* luxurious perks, and *such* obsequious entourages, that morale down the line could suffer. "It's an inappropriate thing for a democratic society," he says, thinking not about the CEOs making hundreds of thousands a year but about some of those who make millions. "We shouldn't have a corporate royalty, or certainly not one fed by shareholders—especially when the shareholders are so largely pension funds."

In the last couple of years, he believes, things have gotten really out of hand. CEOs are rarely stars single-handedly responsible for the success of the enterprise; they're team captains. Yet instead of being paid that way, they're paid like Bill Cosby. Could it be that some of that money might more appropriately be paid to the shareholders?

There are ratchet effects at work here. Rather than base executive compensation on meaningful measures of performance (admittedly easier said than done), Schwesinger says there is a natural tendency to focus solely on what's "competitive." What's the competition paying *its* guys? Typically, an executive compensation study is commissioned and presented to the board. The board is then asked to approve pay at least equal to the industry average, to stay competitive. That pushes below-average companies up toward the average—and thus raises the average. (As you might expect, there's little downward pressure from above-average firms recommending to the board their pay be cut.) Ratchet.

The president and chairman don't recommend their own compensation, but if the board has just approved increases averaging 10.7% for the rest of top management, can they do much less for the CEO? Ratchet.

There's also the natural tendency for the lower-paying industries to compare themselves with higher-paying ones, with little enthusiasm for doing the opposite. Ratchet.

And there's this pressure on the board: If they let a valued key executive leave—like the CEO—they do a real disservice to the company (and saddle themselves with a major chore). It's more prudent to err by overpaying a little than to err by underpaying. Ratchet.

Fortunately, corporate lawyers generally have the good taste to put the really big numbers near the back of the proxy statement, not in that little table that shows shareholders what the directors and officers of their company earn.

It was clear to the shareholders of little National Bank & Trust in Norwich, New York, that its chairman earned $182,500 in 1985; but how many noticed the footnote on page 38 that disclosed his half-million-dollar retirement bonus? Some gold watch!

Nor is cash any longer the really meaningful factor in top executive pay. John Byrne was lured from GEICO to run Fireman's Fund Insurance for a salary of $283,333. But there was also the matter of his right to buy 2.5 million shares of Fireman's Fund stock at $26 a share after four years' stewardship. That right is already worth $25 million, if the stock holds its mid-1987 level for the next couple of years. Should it climb 10% a year to boot—not impossible—his four-year bonus would be $45 million.

So here I am, myself grossly overpaid, and I can't say I'm entirely sure what to make of all this excess—except, perhaps, that when things get so dizzy, they're poised to fall.

One thing not to make of it is a law or some special tax—the free market has a way of correcting excess all by itself. (You might, however, if you're a shareholder, vote against some of it, especially if you're the kind of shareholder who controls a million shares in a pension fund.)

And second is not to lose too much sleep envying it. I know that's easy to say, but I spent an evening with yet another investment banker classmate. This one has locked in a nice annual income for the next few years by setting up for his firm a profitable (well, okay, a *very* profitable) long-term hedge. (The idea with a hedge is that no matter which way things go, you make money.) He thought it up, he spends an hour or so a day overseeing it, to keep its ratios nicely balanced, and he gets his own little piece of it—$2 million a year. And do you know what? He's bored.

He makes 50 times as much money as you do (or maybe just 10 times as much if you've really turned out to be the hotshot your mom told me you'd be*) but gets to see only the same TV shows you do, sleeps in a bed very much like your own, eats and drinks only marginally tastier food and wine, and spends a good part of each waking day trying to figure out what to do with his life. He's not sure what he wants. That, at least, is no problem for you and me: we want what he has. Now that we've made a budget and dealt with some of the more mundane (but most important) issues of personal finance, let's see if we can't make a *little* headway, at least, toward getting you some of it.

---

*It's just that you *spend* it all, she says, which is beyond her, she says, because when *she* was a little girl, not even movie stars made that kind of money.

Chapter 7

A PRONG FOR ALL SEASONS
Formulating an Investment Strategy

> With the *MONEY Guide to the Stock Market* at your side,
> Wall Street can take you to Easy Street. And getting there has
> never been easier.
> —Ad in *People, Time,* and *Money*
> launched in the summer of 1986,
> after the Dow had climbed
> from 777 to 1900.

I can't remember this story exactly, but it comes from a *Ripley's Believe It or Not* I used to read over and over as a child. It may be familiar to you. Whatever the actual details, the essence is that they were holding an auction—in nineteenth-century England, I think—and the auctioneer held up a book purported to contain the secret of good health. The bidding became heated, and someone bought it for £1000, only to find, when he opened it, that all the pages were blank but the first. It read: "Keep your feet warm and your head cool." That was, after all, pretty much the long and the short of it.

Well, here's the long and short of it for investing: "Buy low,

The Only Graph in This Book

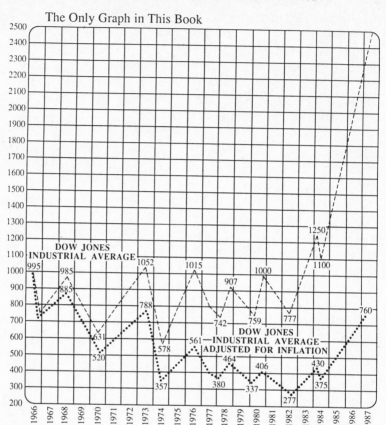

sell high—and, since it's tough to know without benefit of hindsight which is which, diversify."

BUY LOW, SELL HIGH

Most people do the reverse. When prices have dropped very low, it is by definition because few people are interested in buying. Yet that, of course, is the time to screw up your courage and part with the crowd.

What's low?

As I write, the stock market has tripled in the five years since its August 1982 trough, from 777 on the Dow to past 2500—and people are talking as if it may be the start of a great new bull market. Stocks are selling for nearly three times book value, higher even than in September 1929, yet there is much excitement that the Dow could be headed for 3600 (the number everyone seems to focus on, though lately there's been some talk of 5000) —and indeed it may be, and beyond.

But look how quickly the relative values have changed. For 30 years real estate prices outstripped inflation, getting more and more expensive relative to everything else. But only at the tail end of what had been a decades-long rise did real estate investing become truly popular. In the early eighties—exactly the wrong time to buy—we were flooded with get-rich-quick-in-real-estate books. Soon every UHF and cable TV channel seemed to be given over to late-night hour-long ads for $295 audiocassette real estate courses (A $1500 value! Not available in stores!).

Now, in 1987, several of the promoters have gone broke, the seminars aren't given much anymore, and interest in residential real estate as an investment has pretty well died. It's the stock market that's generating the interest now—and that may soon be generating books and tapes and seminars.

Is it possible, now that stocks are three times as expensive and residential real estate has remained flat, that real estate has become the better deal?

Or take farmland. In 1982, for the price of an acre of prime farmland you could buy 350 shares of Ford. (But did you?) Everybody wanted farmland because it was an inflation hedge. Today, for the price of the very same acre (down from $2500 to $1200), you can buy 12 shares of Ford.

Ford's great, and the negatives in farming are obvious—the stock market may have a lot farther to climb and farmland a lot farther to fall—but is it possible that the relative values have shifted a bit over the past half decade? In just those five years, Ford stock has become 30 times as expensive in relation to farmland. Is it perhaps no longer the better deal?

I'm not for a minute suggesting we all buy farmland (though you'll find a few paragraphs on this alternative, and dozens of others, in part III). I'm merely suggesting it's wise to think less about which stock your brother-in-law's dentist heard from his patient, *the chairman of the board,* would report great earnings, and think more about the larger picture. What markets, as you read this, seem cheapest relative to others? Oil stocks? Airline stocks? Real estate? Metals? Long-term bonds? Municipal bonds? Japanese stocks? (Talk about being poised for a crash!) Dutch stocks? Australian farmland?

Buy low, sell high.

Having said that, the fact remains that it's rarely possible to know with any real degree of confidence what is low or high. To know that you have to know what the future will bring—*and no one does.* As a result, the only sensible strategy for all but the most avid risk takers is to diversify.

DIVERSIFY

Spread your assets over four prongs: some liquid money first and then, if you can afford to, an inflation hedge, a deflation hedge, and, for lack of a better term, a prosperity hedge. Just how you weight these prongs depends on your own preferences, stage of life, and view of the future. But at least take a look to see how you're weighted now. If you're 95% in inflation hedges, ask yourself whether you're really *that* certain it's what the future holds.

1. Some Liquid Money

A bank or a money market fund is a great place for your first few thousand dollars. Relax. You're not a sucker—you're doing the right thing. Everyone needs some liquid funds—money he can get his hands on quickly, that's not frozen in an investment that's hard to convert to cash.

If you have just a few dollars—as may well be the case if you're young or burdened with family responsibilities—your challenge isn't deciding what to invest in, but resisting the temptation to "invest" at all. (Money in the bank *is* invested, but people tend to call that their savings, and other money their investments.) Cover the bases in part I of this book. Pay off your high-interest loans and obtain adequate insurance and buy your tuna by the case and salt away an emergency fund someplace safe, like a bank. Only then should you consider some of the jazzier (and frequently *worse*) alternatives in parts II and III.

There's no romance to a bank account (at least not to a little one). There's not that element of chance that makes investing so exciting for some people (and speculating so addictive). But there's this consolation: You won't lose your money.

Actually, even if you do have a lot of money, there are times when more than a little of it should be in cash. To hold cash is to sit on the sidelines. Not infrequently this is the wisest—but most difficult—thing to do. Cash burns a hole in an investor's pocket just as aggressively as it burns through a consumer's. Who wants to go to the track and not bet? An investor is at the track any time he picks up *The Wall Street Journal* or *Forbes* or listens to the nightly news (the French succeeded in launching a new satellite? Maybe it's time to short Lockheed or buy the France Fund or a time-share on the Riviera)—let alone when he's on the phone with his broker or a fellow investor. It's hard not to place a bet. But just because "cash" yields less than alternative investments is no reason to shun it. If you can't find investments that seem truly cheap—not fairly valued, *under*valued—wait. The day will come. Every so often, cash is king.

2. An Inflation Hedge

For most Americans that's their own home. If you're wealthy enough, someone else's home makes a nice inflation hedge, too. Not to mention gold and silver and diamonds and any number of other items that hold their value when paper money does not.

We face enormous budget deficits but are resistant—with good reason—to tax hikes. (The wrong kind of tax increase dampens incentive and could bring on the kind of recession that would make the deficit even worse.) The standard scenario for governments badly in deficit is simply to print more money. Inflation is the result and is nothing more (or less) than a relentless tax that needs no congressional approval.

Yet before you assume that inflation will come roaring back, and even more violently than in the last round—*as it may*—consider some other factors:

• We don't *want* more inflation. Just as you had a generation so scarred by the Depression that it was constantly on guard against another, now we've lived through a traumatic era of inflation that's attuned voters and legislators to its dangers.

• The budget deficit isn't as large as it seems when you add to it local government surpluses.

• There's nothing wrong with a deficit if it's incurred to make productive capital investments for the future, as some of ours is.

• A national debt, per se, is not a terrible thing. Healthy business enterprises have debts; wealthy individuals have debts. Each year's deficit adds that much more to the national debt. The key now is to have the national debt grow, if it has to grow, more slowly than the economy as a whole. The debt is $2 trillion (give or take). If the economy were to grow at 3.5% a year in real terms, and another 3.5% by way of inflation—7% in all—the $2 trillion national debt could also grow 7% a year—$140 billion—without getting any bigger relative to the economy as a whole.

This is no argument for $140 billion deficits, for if you aim for those, you'll get $175 billion deficits in good years and $400 billion deficits in a recession. But if we could gradually shrink the deficit, even without eliminating it, the national debt could actually shrink by the measure that's most important: its size relative to the economy as a whole. As you can see from the fourth-to-last column of the two-page table on pages 108–109, it has grown dramatically in the last few years, yet, historically, is not so frightening as it sometimes seems.

• We've become more productive. As technological improvements ripple through the economy—the increased efficiency on the horizon from this year's startling breakthroughs in superconductivity being perhaps the most dramatic example—*it makes things cheaper*. As we become more efficient, we can squeeze more goods out of the same resources—the cost per unit falls. Other things being equal, prices go down.

There's more that could be said about all this—the benefits of deregulation, the importance of free trade, the possibility that the dollar's inflation-producing slide (at 140 yen and 1.8 marks as I write this) may be nearly over—but I am no economist, and they don't know what's going to happen, either. Just don't assume our deficits make severe inflation inevitable.

3. A Deflation Hedge

Neither should you assume that all the debt we've piled up— Uncle Sam's but also Brazil's and your uncle Phil's and your employer's and perhaps your own ("When *I* was a little girl," your mom keeps telling me, "we didn't even have credit cards"*) —*won't* bring the financial world crashing down. That's the other quick solution to the debt crisis—have everyone go bankrupt. True, it could easily plunge the world into famine, warfare, and tragedy of truly epic proportions—so it's not a very *good* solution—but it's possible.

I suppose it wouldn't hurt to have gold or silver or diamonds in the event of such a disaster, but being far too much of an optimist to take any such scenario seriously, I own none of the above. (Well, a little silver, but that's another story.)

And there are other scenarios you can construct to throw the world into panic—author Paul Erdman has entertained millions constructing several—including the possibility of a 1929-style panic and crash in the Japanese market that could take all of about 11 minutes to spill over to U.S. and European markets. (Nippon Telephone selling at 250 times earnings? I've tried but can find no practical way to short it.) Or the possibility of a vicious circle of program trading and portfolio insurance (see pages 234 and 150), where one feeds upon the other, and around and around, until two 24-year-olds at Goldman Sachs and Salomon Brothers have bitten 500 points out of the Dow in a day. That could cause some loss of confidence, too. As could the California earthquake, when it finally comes.

Even so, none of this is likely to happen, or at least not get entirely out of hand, because too many people are in a position to control the damage and because our fundamental economic strength—our productive capacity and resources—is solid. All that's required to keep from coming unglued is a modicum of confidence and rationality. (Uh-oh.)

*When she was a little girl, they barely had plastic.

A TABLE THAT LOOKS BORING
BUT IS ACTUALLY MOST REVEALING

Year	Prime Rate	Triple-A Bonds	Municipal Bonds	Savings Accounts	Home Mortgages	Inflation
1920	6.58%	6.12%	4.98%	4 %	5.75%	2.3%
1925	4.98	4.88	4.09	4	5.90	3.8
1930	3.50	4.55	4.07	4¹/₂	5.95	−6.0
1935	1.50	3.60	2.40	2¹/₂	5.26	3.0
1940	1.50	2.84	2.50	2	5.40	.1
1945	1.50	2.62	1.67	1¹/₂	4.70	2.3
1946	1.50	2.53	1.64	1¹/₂	4.74	18.2
1947	1.52	2.61	2.01	1¹/₂	4.80	9.0
1948	1.85	2.82	2.40	1¹/₂	4.91	2.7
1949	2.00	2.66	2.21	1¹/₂	4.93	1.8
1950	2.07	2.62	1.98	2	4.95	5.8
1951	2.56	2.86	2.00	2	4.93	5.9
1952	3.00	2.96	2.19	2¹/₂	5.03	.9
1953	3.17	3.02	2,72	2¹/₂	5.09	.6
1954	3.05	2.90	2.37	2¹/₂	5.15	− .5
1955	3.16	3.06	2.53	2³/₄	5.18	4.0
1956	3.77	3.36	2.93	2³/₄	5.19	2.9
1957	4.20	3.89	3.60	3	5.42	3.0
1958	3.83	3.79	3.56	3¹/₄	5.58	1.8
1959	4.48	4.38	3.95	3¹/₄	5.71	1.5
1960	4.82	4.41	3.73	3¹/₂	5.85	1.5
1961	4.50	4.35	3.46	3¹/₂	5.87	.7
1962	4.50	4.33	3.18	4	5.90	1.2
1963	4.50	4.26	3.23	4	5.84	1.6
1964	4.50	4.40	3.22	4	5.78	1.2
1965	4.54	4.49	3.27	4	5.74	1.9
1966	5.62	5.13	3.82	4	6.14	3.4
1967	5.63	5.51	3.98	4	6.33	3.0
1968	6.28	6.18	4.51	4	6.83	4.7
1969	7.95	7.03	5.81	4	7.66	6.1
1970	7.91	8.04	6.50	4¹/₄	8.27	5.5
1971	5.70	7.39	5.70	4¹/₄	7.59	3.4
1972	5.25	7.21	5.27	4¹/₄	7.45	3.4
1973	8.02	7.44	5.18	5	7.95	8.8
1974	10.80	8.57	6.09	5¹/₄	8.92	12.2
1975	7.86	8.83	6.89	5¹/₄	8.75	7.0
1976	6.83	8.44	6.64	5¹/₄	8.90	4.8
1977	6.82	8.20	5.68	5¹/₄	8.68	6.5
1978	9.06	8.99	6.03	5¹/₄	9.72	9.3
1979	12.67	10.05	6.52	5¹/₂	10.94	13.0
1980	15.27	12.77	8.60	5¹/₂	13.50	11.9
1981	18.87	15.48	11.33	5¹/₂	16.31	8.6
1982	14.86	14.68	11.66	5¹/₂	15.30	3.9
1983	10.79	12.25	9.51	5¹/₂	13.11	3.7
1984	12.10	13.40	10.10	5¹/₂	14.00	4.3
1985	9.93	11.75	9.27	5¹/₂	12.13	3.6
1986	8.33	9.23	7.32	5¹/₂	9.90	1.9
6/87	8.25	9.75	7.96	5¹/₂	10.02	3.8

Average Price of Gold	Postage Stamp	Swiss Francs per U.S. Dollar	Year-end Dow Jones	GNP Billion $	Nat'l Debt as % of GNP	Fed Bdgt as % of GNP	Unem- ployment	Year
$20	2¢	5.9Fr	72	$92	26%	6%	5.2%	1920
$20	2¢	5.2Fr	156	$94	21	3	3.2	1925
$20	2¢	5.2Fr	164	$91	17	3	8.7	1930
$35	3¢	3.1Fr	144	$72	39	8	20.1	1935
$35	3¢	4.4Fr	131	$100	50	9	14.6	1940
$35	3¢	4.2Fr	192	$213	121	43	1.9	1945
$35	3¢	4.3Fr	177	$212	127	26	3.9	1946
$35	3¢	4.3Fr	181	$235	109	14	3.9	1947
$35	3¢	4.3Fr	177	$261	96	11	3.8	1948
$35	3¢	4.3Fr	200	$260	97	14	5.9	1949
$35	3¢	4.2Fr	235	$288	89	14	5.3	1950
$35	3¢	4.3Fr	269	$333	76	13	3.3	1951
$35	3¢	4.2Fr	291	$351	73	19	3.0	1952
$35	3¢	4.2Fr	280	$371	71	20	2.9	1953
$35	3¢	4.2Fr	404	$372	72	19	5.5	1954
$35	3¢	4.2Fr	488	$405	67	16	4.4	1955
$35	3¢	4.2Fr	499	$428	63	16	4.1	1956
$35	3¢	4.2Fr	435	$451	60	17	4.3	1957
$35	4¢	4.3Fr	583	$456	61	18	6.8	1958
$35	4¢	4.3Fr	679	$495	58	18	5.5	1959
$35	4¢	4.3Fr	615	$515	56	17	5.5	1960
$35	4¢	4.3Fr	731	$533	54	18	6.7	1961
$35	4¢	4.3Fr	652	$574	52	18	5.5	1962
$35	5¢	4.3Fr	762	$606	51	18	5.7	1963
$35	5¢	4.3Fr	874	$649	48	18	5.2	1964
$35	5¢	4.3Fr	969	$705	45	16	4.5	1965
$35	5¢	4.3Fr	785	$772	42	17	3.8	1966
$35	5¢	4.3Fr	905	$816	41	19	3.8	1967
$35	6¢	4.3Fr	943	$892	41	20	3.6	1968
$35	6¢	4.3Fr	800	$963	38	19	3.5	1969
$36	6¢	4.3Fr	838	$1015	37	19	4.9	1970
$41	8¢	3.9Fr	890	$1102	37	19	5.9	1971
$58	8¢	3.7Fr	1020	$1212	36	19	5.6	1972
$97	8¢	3.2Fr	850	$1359	34	18	4.9	1973
$161	10¢	2.5Fr	616	$1472	33	18	5.6	1974
$161	13¢	2.6Fr	852	$1598	34	20	8.5	1975
$125	13¢	2.4Fr	1004	$1782	35	20	7.7	1976
$148	13¢	2.0Fr	831	$1990	35	20	7.1	1977
$193	15¢	1.6Fr	805	$2249	34	20	6.1	1978
$307	15¢	1.5Fr	838	$2508	33	20	5.8	1979
$612	15¢	1.7Fr	964	$2732	33	21	7.1	1980
$459	20¢	1.7Fr	875	$3052	32	22	7.6	1981
$375	20¢	1.9Fr	1046	$3166	36	23	9.7	1982
$424	20¢	2.1Fr	1258	$3405	40	23	9.6	1983
$361	20¢	2.5Fr	1211	$3765	41	22	7.5	1984
$317	22¢	2.0Fr	1546	$3998	45	23	7.2	1985
$368	22¢	1.6Fr	1895	$4258	50	23	7.0	1986
$457	22¢	1.5Fr	2400	$4400	50	23	6.1	6/87

In any event, while everyone focuses on inflation, there is always the possibility of deflation. You know: like the Thirties, where everything got very cheap, but everyone was too broke to buy it. The best example of a deflation hedge is a 30-year non-callable U.S. Treasury bond (though through a quirk in the marketplace you'll often get a significantly better rate of interest buying the 29- or the 28-year bond). Imagine locking in 8% or 6% or 12% for 30 years—or whatever the yield as you read this—if the going rate drops to just 2% or 3%. You'll be the talk of the town.

Before you dismiss any such possibility, consider that from 1880 through 1965, in this country, there was no such thing as a home mortgage at over 6%. In that same 85-year span, treasury bonds rarely yielded more than 5%, municipal bonds rarely yielded more than 4%. Take a look at the table on page 108 to get a sense of how high or low today's interest rates really are.

(Another example of a deflation hedge? Cash. In times of deflation, money in the bank gets more and more valuable. So your liquid money—prong #1—doubles as a deflation hedge.)

4. A Prosperity Hedge

We just might muddle through. This has long been my own favored scenario, and it's actually got a fair amount pulling for it—including most of us. The combined talents and goodwill of a few hundred million people in the industrialized world should count for something. The danger in being too pessimistic is that it discounts the possibility that we'll be able to deal with problems as they arise. There is the tendency to believe that everyone in power is a total idiot and/or totally insensitive to anything but his own interests—but (despite much hard evidence) I believe this is only partially true.

So some form of prosperity is a definite possibility, in which case you will want to own a piece of it.

Your own business is great; failing that, shares in someone else's business—common stocks.

Over the long run, common stocks have always outperformed safer investments and, however cheap or dear they are today, over the long run should continue to do so. Not everyone can afford to wait, and it's obviously a good idea not to invest in stocks when they're about to drop through the floor (if only we could get a little warning), but in any 25-year period you choose, even the one starting in 1929, just before the crash, stocks always wind up outperforming bonds or bank accounts. The market pays you to take the risk.

The way to invest in common stocks is simple: Invest $100 a month or $500 a month or $5000 a month—whatever you can comfortably afford—in two or three carefully selected no-load (no sales commission) mutual funds. Be sure to see page 224 for details—and the sections on closed-end funds (page 195) and index funds (page 212) as well.

Just remember as you do this that the stock market is *not* the place for short-term money or money you can't afford to lose. Remember, too, that, over the long term, slow but steady wins the race. There's no need to switch in and out of funds trying to outguess the market (sure, it would be great; but it's awfully hard to do). The main thing is to develop the discipline to save money in the first place and then put it to work at what, in the long run, is likely to be a superior rate of return.

How are your assets deployed over these four prongs? Is there a way to make limited funds stretch to cover more than one? Cash covers both liquidity and deflation. Convertible bonds (page 201) straddle two or three prongs. They provide a nice fixed income in the event of deflation (unless the issuer goes broke), and the value of the bond will rise if the common stock into which it's convertible rises—as in periods of moderate inflation or prosperity it might. U.S. savings bonds (page 248) are relatively liquid (in an emergency), provide a guaranteed rate of interest (in the event of deflation) and even provide for the possibility of higher interest (in the event of inflation).

Once you start thinking this way, you realize that your liabilities, and not just your assets, can be made part of your strategy, too. You might, for example, try to arrange to carry no appreciable debt yourself, lest we have deflation (debt's no fun in a deflation because you have to repay it with ever more valuable dollars)—but *invest* some of your money, at least, in common stocks of companies, or in partnerships, that do have a lot of fixed-rate debt, lest we have inflation. (A company with lots of fixed-rate debt may fare well with inflation, as its assets appreciate but debt stays unchanged.)

But enough of the broad strokes. The prudent thing to do now would be to skip chapters 8–12, because they're about investing in the stock market and limited partnerships, while you'd be better served investing in no-load mutual funds and perusing the investment alternatives on display in part III. But please don't skip these chapters, because this is no time to be prudent. This is just a book. *Real life* is the time to be prudent.

Chapter 8

SPREADS
Minimizing Your Transaction Costs

A price for everything and everything has its price. A wise Oriental said that thousands of years ago—"plice," he said, actually, which some Cockney correspondent mistook for "place," which got twisted, as these things do, into an old saw he never intended to invent (a *place* for everything...)—but that's the way life works, isn't it? Just when you've invented what you think will become a tired old truism, somebody comes along and totally misunderstands you, and you become famous for something you never did. Like the late James Cagney, who swore he never did say "you dirty rat" in any of his pictures.

Well, there you are.

I call this to your attention to point out that the old saw he did intend to coin—a price for everything and everything has its price—was wrong.

Everything has two prices.

There is the price you can buy it for and the price you can sell it for. In the difference between these two—the spread—resides the entire world of commerce. Retailing, wholesaling, garage saling—the works.

In much of the business world this difference is called the

113

mark-up. On Wall Street it is the spread. In Paris, I'd guess, *la différence,* whence the cheer of the French brokerage community, *Vive la différence!*

This chapter is about spreads, with particular reference to the higher-priced spreads. Spreads are less visible and surely less bitched about than commissions, but often far the more important cost.

BONDS

Take bonds. Many firms will charge as little as $30 or $40 to buy or sell 10 bonds. To buy or sell an equivalent amount of stock— $10,000 worth—the commission could run to $200 or more.

What you never see on your confirmation slip, and what many brokers are reluctant to disclose even if you ask, is the spread. Ask your broker for a price on such and such number of bonds, and he will respond with a question of his own: Are you buying or selling? If you say you'd like both prices, the bid *and* the ask, you're likely to be told that his trading desk won't give quotes that way.

Even if it did, and you saw what it was really costing you to trade the bonds, how likely would you be to open an account at another brokerage firm just to shave a few bucks off the spread— if you could find another broker who would shave the spread— and how much could we be talking about here, anyway?

I called a broker from whom I had purchased for my Keogh plan $250,000 of zero coupon bonds maturing May 15, 2007. Zero coupon bonds pay no interest (*zero coupon*) and so don't cost much to buy. Although they may be issued by corporations or municipalities, most of them are the actively traded offspring of long-term treasury bonds (never mind how they off-sprung*), and

*Okay, here's how. The U.S. Treasury issues $1 billion of bonds that promise 8%, say, for 30 years. That's 60 semiannual $40 interest payments on every $1000 bond, plus a 61st payment—your original $1000 back—when the bond is redeemed. Some big firm like Goldman Sachs buys the entire billion and "strips them" into 61 separate pieces of merchandise, as a chop shop strips a stolen car. You want to buy just the 48th semiannual interest payment? You got it. Twenty-four years from now, when the treasury pays it, it will be used by

these particular ones cost me $21,450 in 1985, geared to compound at 11.8% to their glorious quarter-million-dollar maturity 22 years hence. (Something you buy for $21,450 that grows to $250,000 in 22 years is growing—trust me—at 11.8%, compounded.)

But now that interest rates had fallen and zeros needed only to promise to compound at 9% or so to attract buyers, I could sell mine not for the $21,450 I had paid, but for around $37,500. At that price, a buyer holding on for 21 years until the glorious maturity would have seen *his* money compound at a little more than 9%, while I, meanwhile, would have turned a $16,000 profit on $21,500 in a year and a half. Not enough to make up for some of my other brainstorms, perhaps, but something.

Of course, there would be commissions. My broker offered to do the trade "for an eighth," meaning $312.50,** to cover the cost of the three minutes he and his trading desk would spend handling this transaction. But what's $312.50 when you're talking a $16,000 profit? (Never mind that it would have been the same $312.50 if we had been talking a $16,000 loss.) And, really, I'm not being fair. They've got $50-a-square-foot rent and mega-mega computers and million-dollar bonuses and a national TV ad campaign to pay for. So $312.50 (and a similar commission when I bought the bonds) is not so bad.

But what about the spread?

"What spread?" my broker grins over the phone.

Understand: my broker and I are very good friends. It has given

---

Goldman Sachs to pay off your bond. Until then, nothing. That particular piece of merchandise is called a 24-year zero coupon bond. The treasury may have thought of it as "just another $40 million semiannual interest payment we'll have to make on September 1, 2011—don't forget," but the clever folks at Goldman or Salomon or Merrill, in return for a nice spread, turned it into a $40 million zero coupon bond issue that they sold to brokers like yours or mine to sell—with another nice spread—to you and me.

**Bonds are sold in $1000 increments but quoted in cents on the dollar. A bond trading at par (face value) is quoted at 100, not 1000. So adding "an eighth" makes it 100.125—$1001.25 per bond. Of course, *my* bonds would not be up to par for another 21 years. They were quoted around 15—$150 a bond—so adding an eighth meant $151.25. Multiply that extra $1.25 by 250 bonds and you get $312.50.

me enormous pleasure over the years to see his net worth mount.

"The *spread*," I persist.

"Oh, the spread!" he says. "Hold on."

My broker has never, ever dealt any way but fairly with me, but he has put me on hold. And even then he has the ability to make me feel like his only client. Sometimes he puts me on hold to exchange a few more words with someone else he has on hold, but sometimes, as now, he puts me on hold knowing I'm impatient and am likely to let him off the hook.

He comes back half a minute later. "You there?"

"Yeah," I disappoint him.

"It's a great life if you don't weaken," he says, apropos of nothing in particular, which is exactly what he hopes we will now discuss.

It's not that he means to conceal the spread his firm maintains in trading these bonds or avoid the hassle involved in finding it out. What he hopes to avoid, I think, is the inevitable bitching and moaning he knows he'll have to sit through and the same old discussion where I say the spread's outrageous and he says, "Hey —if you think it's an easy business, go ahead—set up shop yourself."

"What's the blinking spread?" I remind him gently.

"Oh, blink you," he says. "Hold on." This time I know he means for me to stay on the line, silently, while he calls his bond trader to find out the spread.

The spread on these zero coupon bonds turns out to be 45 basis points. A basis point, as you may know, is one-hundredth of 1%. A bond that yields 9.02% is trading one basis point higher than a bond that yields only 9.01%. In this case, the brokerage firm would sell the bonds at a price that would yield the buyer 9.00% but buy them at a lower price that would yield 9.45%. I know this can get confusing, but the dialogue's a snap:

"Forty-five basis points!" I wail, reaching for my calculator. (My broker makes a point of not having one nearby.) "That's some spread! What does that work out to in dollars?"

"I don't know," he says, handling our conversation on autopilot. He can talk to me and be hypnotized by his computer screen at the same time.

"Well!" I announce triumphantly, having caught the brokerage industry in its act yet again. "That's a thirty-four-hundred-dollar spread!" Meaning, they would buy the bonds for $3400 less than they would sell them for.

"It is?" mumbles my broker. "Well, I don't know—it's not a round lot. The spread's narrower with a round lot."

(With stocks, 100 shares constitute a round lot. Buy fewer and there's a small nuisance charge to pay. With zero coupon bonds, although you can buy them in virtually any quantity, the really big players—pension funds and such—deal in multiples of $5 million.)

"What's so puny about a quarter-million-dollar face value?" I demand.

"You want to get into this business?" he asks, still on autopilot. "No one's stopping you."

"I mean," I continue, "it's not as if these were some obscure municipal bonds that trade once every four months." (If they were, the broker might have to hold them in inventory for a while in hope of finding a buyer—albeit collecting interest on them all the while.) "I mean, these things trade like crazy." If the obscure municipal bond issue were the equivalent of a flight from Allentown, Pennsylvania, to Omaha, Nebraska—not the sort of route much subject to discounting—my zeros were New York to Chicago.

"You're going to Chicago?" my broker chuckles.

"Oh, forget it," I give up.

"Have a nice tr—"

The spread in this case was so wide—it worked out to $37,500 bid, $40,900 asked—that, combined with my guess that interest rates might continue to decline (and, thus, bond prices continue to rise), I decided to sit tight. Sitting tight, in a world where each transaction clips you for commission, spread, and taxes, is often a swift maneuver.

GOLD

The wider the spread, obviously, the tougher it is to make money.

If you're buying gold, you would as I write this pay $431 for a one-ounce bar or sell it for $421. That was the spread—$421 bid, $431 asked—at Ruffco, a courteous and trustworthy outfit that specializes in precious metals for the little guy. Check around and you may find spreads a little wider or a little narrower, but you get the idea. For its trouble and the cost of maintaining its toll-free line (800-722-7833), Ruffco takes $10 an ounce—about 2.5%. That's its spread. There is also a $20-per-order handling fee, whether you buy a single ounce or 10.

Add in about $7 in postage when you trot down to the post office to accept your gold bar, which is mailed registered insured postage collect, and you get the total price for buying the ounce: $458. Total price for selling it, less postage and a 1% handling charge: about $410.

"How's gold?" you shout up to the mythical trader in the sky.

"How much you interested in?" he booms back from across the heavens.

"One big one," you yell over the din.

"Ten to fifty-eight," he roars ($410 bid, $458 asked), figuring you're hip to the jargon.

Whereupon you must decide, if you're thinking of buying a single ounce of gold, whether it would be smarter to buy 10 ounces instead and reap economies of scale (it costs only $3 more to mail and insure 10 ounces than one)... or to buy without accepting physical delivery of the metal (call 800-223-1080 outside New York to buy Citicorp gold certificates on your Visa or MasterCard with a spread generally under 50 cents an ounce but a 3% commission and an annual storage charge)... or (my personal favorite) not to buy at all.

If gold hits $3000 one day, the spread and commissions won't have made any difference. In the meantime, though, gold would have to rise more than 10% just for you to break even buying a single ounce through the mail. That's a hefty handicap in a world where earning 10% on your money safely, after tax, can take two years.

Spreads—and transaction costs like commissions, postage, and handling—make life rough for the small investor.

They even make life rough for the big investor. The reason the average money manager does a little worse than average investing the millions or billions entrusted to him or her—and he does—is that the averages against which he's measured, like the Dow or the Standard & Poor's 500, have an edge: they're just averages. They do no buying or selling, pay no brokerage commissions, suffer no spreads. They're even safe from that tiny but annoying penny-per-$300 levy you may never even have noticed the Securities & Exchange Commission chips off all sales of New York and American stock exchange stocks. A penny per $300 here and a penny per $300 there—sell $3900 worth of stock and you're hit for 13 cents—but over the course of the year it mounts up: $40 million. (Not that the treasury can't use the extra money.)

PENNY STOCKS, MEGA SPREADS

Here is the headline of the March 26, 1986, $150-a-year *Penny Stock Ventures* newsletter: WHAT YOUR IRA NEEDS IS A GOOD PENNY STOCK. This is exactly what your IRA *doesn't* need, of course, because penny stocks—typically thought of as those selling for under $3—are for the most part highly speculative. If you buy them at all, you're better off buying them outside your IRA. That way, if you lose your money, you'll at least be able to get Uncle Sam to shoulder some of the loss by subtracting up to $3000 of it a year from your taxable income (no such break is available for losses suffered under the umbrella of an IRA).

But forget that. What about penny stocks themselves?

On the back page of *Penny Stock Ventures,* published by the Money Growth Institute (37 Van Reipen Avenue, Jersey City, New Jersey 07306), is a list of all its featured recommendations since July 1982. The first one, for example, Gen'l Dev. (General Devices of Norristown, Pennsylvania), is shown as having been $2 bid when it was recommended in 1982 and $3 bid when it was recommended for sale some unspecified time later, for a gain of 50%.

The thing about the 50% gain in Gen'l Dev., as I'm sure *Penny Stock Ventures* would agree, is that it's not really a 50% gain.

Say you had gone to buy 500 shares when it was recommended at 2. Two was the "bid." The spread was probably something like "two to a quarter," meaning $2 a share if you were selling, but

$2.25 if you were buying—and you were buying.

But chances are you would have paid at least an eighth of a dollar more per share—$2.375—because when a little stock is recommended in a newsletter and the phone starts to ring at the market maker's trading desk, the market maker does what any good market maker should: he senses an increase in demand, and unless he's also getting a lot of calls from people wanting to sell, he bumps up the price. Supply and demand. You know.

Often, by the time you get your crummy 500 shares, the stock has risen substantially. But let's say it was up just an eighth. You've now paid $2.375 a share for the stock (not $2)—plus a commission. The exact size of the commission will depend on your broker, but let's say he had a heart and charged you just $32.50. That brings your price per share to $2.44.

Sometime later the bid climbs to $3, and the stock is recommended for sale. Again the trader's phones light up, but this time he's notched the stock down an eighth by the time you reach him, and you get, after commission, $2.81 a share. Net gain before taxes: 15%.

So the spread and commissions cut a 50% rise in the stock—for it had assuredly become 50% more expensive to buy—to a 15% real gain before taxes.

Today, Gen'l Dev. is quoted "one and three-eighths, seven teenies" (a teenie is a sixteenth of a dollar)—meaning $1.375 if you want to sell it, $1.4375 if you want to buy it—while the stodgy Dow Jones average, in the same time period, has nearly tripled and paid four and a half years' worth of dividends besides. But no one ever said penny stocks were forever. You get in, take your profit, and get out.

Penny Stock Ventures recommended National Superstar, Inc., at a quote of three-eighths of a dollar to five-eighths. That's $625 plus commission if you want to buy 1000 shares, $375 minus commission if you want to sell them. If you did buy 1000 shares, you'd be instantly down 47% or so even if the stock held firm, which, given the nature of its business—selling financial-seminar tapes on late-night cable TV—something told me over the long run it might not.

Had you bought the eight stocks recommended as a "Penny Stock IRA Portfolio" by the folks at Money Growth Institute, you would a year later have lost most of your money in two of them and half your money in three. You would have broken even in one, made 30% in one, and doubled your money in the last (ironically, at $4 when it was recommended, the least pennylike of the lot). During the same period, the Dow rose 500 points.

I own some penny stocks, most of which, sadly, were not penny stocks when I bought them. One, Offshore Logistics, was recommended by a successful investment banker in Houston at $27 a share. The spread then was an eighth or a quarter—12.5 cents or 25 cents a share—which, as a percentage of the whole, was insignificant.

By 1985 you could have bought it for around $1.25 a share— or sold it for 75 cents. The spread had widened to half a point— 50 cents a share—which works out to 40% (before commissions).

Mystical Question #1. Is it insane to buy a stock that instantly loses 40% in value were you to turn around and sell it? *Absolutely—unless it goes back to $27 someday (and Sirhan Sirhan becomes mayor of New York, New York).*

Mystical Question #2. How come the spread in issues like these is so wide? *Because the market makers are pigs.*

Okay, that's a little harsh—cowardice plays a part in it, too. The wider the spread, the less risk the market maker takes.

WHO SETS THE SPREAD?

On the stock exchanges, prices are set more or less by supply and demand with a little help from a fellow called the specialist. The specialist chips an eighth of a dollar off most trades he's involved with, but on a $20 or $40 stock, who cares? That's his cut for taking the risk of maintaining an orderly market when buyers and sellers don't show up at his post at the same time. Not that a specialist ever went broke taking that risk, so far as I know—specialists *mint* money—but why quibble over an eighth?

For "listed" securities, then, stocks and bonds traded on the

New York and American stock exchanges, spreads are not much of an issue. One guy is offering to buy shares at 47⅛, another is offering to sell them at 47⅜, so the spread is described as "an eighth/three-eighths." Big deal.

But there are another 15,000-plus stocks and tens of thousands of bond issues traded "OTC"—over the counter (well, OTP, really—over the phone). There the spreads can range from a quarter of a dollar on a $65 stock like Apple Computer—less than half a percent—to a nickel spread on a stock like Magnum Resources, quoted two cents to seven cents. That's two cents if you want to sell shares, seven if you want to buy them—a 250% spread.

Several things determine the spread in a security, but the overriding one is volume. If lots of shares are being sold each day, week in and week out, the spread will be narrow because lots of market makers—firms you know, like Merrill Lynch, and firms you may not know, like Troster Singer, and firms you surely don't know, like Mayer & Schweitzer—will be competing for the business.

If there are only three or four market makers in a stock, they may not beat one another over the head to narrow the spread. They may even, tacitly or not so tacitly, agree that "two to three-quarters [$2 bid, $2.75 asked] looks about right." Who's to know? We're talking major backwaters in thousands of these stocks. Unlike the most actively traded over-the-counter issues, whose best bid and asked prices are instantly available on every brokerage computer screen in the capitalist world (though even many of them sport gaping spreads), there are 11,000 scarcely noticed public issues listed only in the pink sheets each day.

The pink sheets, in this age of instant electronic communication, are indeed pink, as they have been since the thirties. (The yellow sheets are for corporate bonds and the blue sheets for municipal bonds.) If a brokerage firm wants to be listed as a market maker in the stock of Natural Beauty Landscaping, as eight firms not long ago did, it just lets the National Quotation Bureau of Jersey City know by two o'clock the previous afternoon and pays the bureau 31 cents to list its name and toll-free number. (I'm oversimplifying, but this is more or less how it works.) For the National Quotation Bureau, that's 31 cents a line times several market makers in each of 15,000 issues every trading day; and then $42 a month plus delivery to each of the brokerage offices around the country that subscribe—and every one of them does.

When you call your broker and ask to buy 1000 Natural Beauty, the order he writes up gets routed to his firm's trading desk, where a very junior trader looks in the pink sheets to see who has any for sale. Then, if he's not too busy, he'll call three or four of them in search of the lowest price, as he should, or, if he is a little busy, he'll just close his eyes and call whichever one his finger lands on. Hey, it's not his money—why should he beat his brains out trying to save *you* $50?

Some market makers include bid and asked prices in the pink sheets, others prefer not to tip their hands. Of the five who recently listed prices for Natural Beauty Landscaping (three others chose not to), two were asking 12 cents a share, two were asking 14 cents, and one wanted 15 cents. That's if you were buying. If you were a seller, one was offering 7 cents a share, three were offering 8 cents, and one was offering a dime.

There's usually less variation, but in this case, presumably, your broker's trader would, at the very least, call one of the outfits that was asking just 12 cents (Fitzgerald DeArman & Roberts of Kansas City or Cutler Hunsaker of Salt Lake City) and perhaps check, as well, with the three who had not included prices with their listings.

The firms asking just 12 cents for Natural Beauty may have been doing so because they had a little more Natural Beauty on hand than they wanted. The firm offering to pay a dime for shares (Olsen Payne, also of Salt Lake City) was probably in just the opposite spot. It may previously have sold all the Natural Beauty shares it had, and more, and so now wanted to cover its short position and perhaps even get a few shares back on the shelf.

It all sounds capitalist and freewheeling in the extreme until you notice how often the spreads are (a) wide and (b) virtually in lock step between the various firms, the disparate quotes on Natural Beauty notwithstanding. I'm not suggesting that the spreads are explicitly rigged, although inevitably some of that goes on;

but price fixing need not always be explicit. In many thousands of inactively traded stocks, it's probably not unfair to say, market makers show little interest in taking much risk or rocking the boat.

For example, rather than compete by narrowing their spreads and offering the best prices, which would benefit you, some market makers will entertain the traders at your broker's firm with the hope that, when you place an order, the trader who gets it will first call the guy who took him to *Cats*—and maybe not bother to call anybody else. Hockey tickets, limos, champagne . . . one young trader at a now defunct discount brokerage house was given such carte blanche, he was allegedly able to attract the interest of Morgan Fairchild. (A spokesperson for Ms. Fairchild cannot recall her ever having dated a discount broker.)

What kind of way is this to do business? Far better, some brokerage firms have decided, to take the payoff themselves—not in champagne, but in cash payments of as much as a nickel a share for every share funneled through a particular market maker. Market makers call this "paying for order flow" and are happy to do it—it was their idea to do it—because if the orders flow through them, so do the profits.

Fidelity Brokerage was offered a penny and a half a share to trade with one large OTC market maker, "and that," says a Fidelity executive, "was just for openers—but we said no, we didn't want to pursue it." For Fidelity, it would have meant an extra $4 million or so annually ($12 million at a nickel a share)—pure profit—just for directing its OTC trades to a particular market maker.

Other brokerage firms have been unable to resist.

The rationalization is that the spreads are the same everywhere, so why not do business with the firm that offers the biggest kickback? But if the market makers can afford to give back a nickel a share on each spread—even the spreads that are only an eighth of a dollar, as many of them are—maybe the spreads are a nickel a share too wide.

broker*—or by getting your full-service broker, if you do enough business with him or her, to knock 50% or more off the posted rate. It may not *seem* like much on any given trade, once or twice a month (and it won't be if your trades are small—even the discounters typically charge a $35 minimum), but it can quickly mount into the thousands.

(Another way to cut the cost of commissions and spreads is simply to jump in and out less often. Buy and hold.)

If by shaving your transaction costs you can cut 1% from the cost of each trade—a $50 commission on a $7000 trade, say, instead of a $120 commission—you will have cut 2% from each round trip. If your performance would otherwise have averaged 10% a year, now it will average 12% (if your average holding period is a year; far more if you trade more frequently). One way, your $10,000 grows over 30 years to $175,000; the other, to $300,000. So don't let your broker soothe you into thinking it doesn't matter.

When it comes to stocks and bonds, you're free to complain about the spread. Whining is a good idea, too: sometimes the spread is negotiable. Don't let your broker off accepting the first quote he's given—try to get him to get his trader to shop around. And, most important, *don't invest in the first place* in a stock or bond—or anything else—that involves a wide spread unless you truly understand the handicap this places on your chances and have reason to think it's a handicap worth accepting—as it sometimes is.

With the best of the thinly traded stocks that sport big spreads, it's really as if you're buying into a private company. The spread between what you could get if you had to sell, and what you'd have to pay if you insisted on buying out one of your partners, can be very wide indeed. Yet despite this illiquidity, this enor-

---

*The two largest are Charles Schwab & Co. (800-648-5300) in San Francisco and Fidelity Brokerage (800-225-2097) in Boston, both of which offer myriad 24-hour services and low rates. There are other good discounters as well, but unless you trade in very large size (in which case you can find even lower prices—check the ads in *Barron's* and *The Wall Street Journal*), either of these should serve you very well.

mous spread, some private companies do indeed thrive and, eventually, make their shareholders very rich.

With the best of these thinly traded stocks, two things will happen. First, their prices will rise dramatically over the years as they grow; second, the spread will become progressively narrower as, having grown, their shares become more actively traded.

But your average guy doesn't invest in stocks like National Superstar for the long term, he invests because he can buy 10,000 shares (*gosh,* that has a nice ring to it) for a mere $6250 (or sell them for $3750), and if the stock just hits 10 in a year or two—is 10 a big number? No, it is not—he's turned his $6250 into $100,000.

(National Superstar is today quoted "a nickel, a dime," meaning he'd so far have turned his $6250 into $500—before commissions.)

Chapter 9

SYSTEMS

A Dozen Ways to Beat the Market
(A Couple of Which May Actually Work)

I sit, guilt dripping down my spine, implementing my system. Free drink in hand, playing roulette, I am steadfastly betting on red. If I win, I double my money. If I lose, I double my bet.

I am doing this, I'm compelled to admit, with $1 chips. This was a long time ago.

I bet $1 on red, and if I win, I bet $1 again. If I lose, I bet $2. If I lose again, $4. Then $8. Then $16. Any time I win, which should be just shy of half the time, I immediately go back to betting a single dollar.

The result is that every time I win, whether it be on the first try or the second or the fifth, I win $1. (Losing $1, $2, $4, and $8 and then winning $16 works out to a net gain of $1.) Not much to you, perhaps—and by now I just leave singles on the table or use 'em for scratch paper or toothpicks—but a buck's a buck (I actually smooth out their little creases and lay them tenderly in my wallet), and with this system, they just mount up hour after hour, night after night. Endless dollars.

To speed things along, you could make your basic bet $5 or

$10 or $100 instead of $1, but then you'd be more likely to run into the Snag.

The Snag is that ever so rarely you'll get such a long string of losers—black will come up so many times in a row—that you just don't have enough cash to keep the system going, or else you bump up against the betting limit on the table (which is one of the reasons they have limits).

The odds are very much in your favor. (Well, they're not, of course, but let's enjoy this for a minute.) The chances of black coming up nine times in a row, by which time, having begun betting $1, you'd be out a total of $511, are around 1 in 500. Nevva happen! And if it *did* happen, you'd just place your next bet in the progression, $512—which I'll admit is a lot, but it's not all *that* much—and you'd win it all back plus $1.

Unless it came up black again, in which case you'd be out a total of $1023, which is probably more than you went into the casino planning to lose, but come on: the chances of losing ten bets in a row, when you're betting on red, are about 1 in 1000, and no one's that unlucky.

So there I was, minting money, Harrah's Lake Tahoe Casino oblivious to the siphon I'd stuck in its vault. Lose, win, win, win, lose, win, lose, lose, lose, win, win, lose, lose, lose, win, lose, lose, win, win—fine. My dollars mounted and mounted. Then I lost once, lost twice, and again and again—this wasn't supposed to happen too many more times—and again, and again, and now, facing my seventh bet in the progression, I was up to serious money. I still don't exactly toss $64 to the wind, but back then, down $63 and facing yet a further $64 hit, I had entered the Dostoyevsky stage of America's second favorite late-night pastime.*

The drama was heightened by the fact that beyond this $64 I could not go. The table limit was $500, but they don't let you bet your shoes and socks, and that last $64 was all I had left to bet.

---

*"As I was going out of the station, I looked—and there in my waistcoat pocket was one surviving gulden. 'Ah, so I shall be able to have dinner,' I thought. But when I had walked about a hundred paces I changed my mind and went back . . ."—*The Gambler.*

I took a deep breath—when you *have* to win, you don't—and put down 64 big ones on red. And it came up red. I had added yet another $1 to my horde. But I decided it wasn't worth it.

And of course the odds *are* against you, because, by a stroke of genius that long ago made the Roulette family one of the very wealthiest in France, there are *37* little clicky-slot things on a roulette wheel, not 36. The thirty-seventh, technically known as 0 or snake-eyes or *merde,* is neither red nor black. It is the house edge. (In America, unless you use a discount casino, there are *two* sets of zeros and twice the edge for the house.)

Even so, you will generally win with this system at roulette (it's just that when you lose, you will lose a fortune). It is, in fact, the oldest system in the book. And if you can do it at roulette, why not with stock options? The odds are less precise, but the idea's the same. Bet $500 on some soon-to-expire Amerada Hess options and then, if you lose it, bet $1000 the next time, $2000 —you can imagine the possibilities. For when an option does pay off, it can pay off big. (See page 228 for an introduction to options.)

Your broker, bankruptcy lawyer, and bartender will all love you, because the house take on each options bet—the commission—is around 10%; you are almost sure to lose in the long run; and win or lose you'll be buying a lot of drinks.

In the long run, this system doesn't work.* But have you ever wondered whether there are any that really do? Have you never had your emotions thrown into confusion by a friend's confiding, "He's got this system, see . . . ?" You wish to appear worldly, so part of you is saying, "Sure, sure." But you are, in truth, yearning to be let in on the secret and, while doubting it could possibly amount to anything, hoping that it might.

In the financial world, systems abound. They range from the

---

*Among kids, this system is called "double or nothing" and works a little differently. The idea there, if you've lost a few dollars shooting baskets, is to keep doubling the bet not so much because you think you'll eventually win (though it's likely you eventually will), but rather to get your losses up so high that what had started out as a small but serious bet becomes, obviously, just an abstract, hypothetical thing. You owe your 14-year-old friend $200 million. Swell. Let's go cruise the mall.

truly dumb (sell stocks when the average numbers of sun spots per month exceeds 50) to the fairly dumb (buy whatever is making new highs) to the not so dumb at all (stay out of the market in the first half of each presidential term, when most of the tough medicine is likely to be administered; come back in for the second half). The not-so-dumb ones might better be tagged with the more dignified label "strategies." Gamblers have systems; investors have strategies. Not that it necessarily does them much good.

The beauty of systems is that they eliminate the need to think, reducing what would otherwise be an extraordinarily complex array of factors to something as simple as "If hemlines are going up (a sign of increased liberality), so will the market." Easy women, easy money—like that. It's a roundabout sort of indicator but more fun to watch than the money supply.

PRESIDENTIAL CYCLES

Holding a representative basket of New York Stock Exchange stocks in the second half of each presidential term from January 1, 1960, through the end of 1980, and treasury bills in the other years, reports *Market Logic* (3471 North Federal Highway, Fort Lauderdale, FL 33306), would have netted you better than 11 times your money. Compare this with holding stocks in the *first* two years and T-bills in the latter years. That back-assed strategy, says *Market Logic,* would have *lost* almost half your funds.

Long-time market observer Yale Hirsch, publisher of the annual *Stock Trader's Almanac,* has tracked this phenomenon back to 1832 and reports a net market gain of 515% for owning stocks in the latter two years of each administration versus barely more than a break-even for the first two years. (His figures ignore dividends and compounding.)

But will the pattern hold? It only sort of did for Reagan's first term (1982 and '83 were the good years, not 1983 and '84), and would have had you sat out the first two years of his second term, 1985 and 1986. If you had, you would have missed a 56% rise in the Dow, from 1212 to 1895.

THANK GOD IT'S FRIDAY

If you could keep your commissions low enough, you'd certainly want to buy stocks or options two or three days before Thanksgiving, because in 31 of the 34 Fridays *after* Thanksgiving, from 1952 through 1986, the market has risen. (Two of the three exceptions, however, were 1985 and 1986.) In fact, Fridays generally tend to be a lot better than Mondays, and *Market Logic* reports that *the last trading day of each month and the first four of the following month* form a highly favorable five-day span. Not to mention the two days preceding market holidays.

If this sounds like hocus-pocus—the reasons for it are subtle at best—consider this. Had you bought the Standard & Poor's 500 index at the beginning of each favorable five- and two-day period, and sold at the end, between December 30, 1927, and December 30, 1975, *Market Logic* calculates $10,000 would have grown to $1,440,716 (not counting dividends or commissions or taxes). Remaining fully invested throughout those years instead of jumping in and out, the same $10,000 would have grown to just $51,441. And jumping in and out backward—buying when you should sell and selling when you should buy—would have shrunk your $10,000 to $357. In other tests after 1975 and involving real money, the phenomenon has been confirmed.

Unfortunately, if your broker charges 2% every time you buy or sell a stock, the only millions generated by such a system will be his. Still, if you're thinking of selling a stock, you might wait until the fourth or fifth trading day of the next month in hope of making an extra few dollars on the trade. And if you play the index-options game—where you can indeed bet on the S&P 500, the S&P 100, or several other baskets of stocks, with relatively low commissions—these timing hints should obviously be considered.*

You might even add two more *Market Logic* refinements:

1. Take advantage of Friday's strength. If the five- and two-day periods mentioned above begin on Mondays, jump the

---

*You'll still lose your money, but it will take longer.

gun a day to include the previous Friday (buy at the opening). If they end on a Thursday, stretch them out a day to include Friday (sell at the close).

2. Adjust your trading for the knowledge that "if the market is up today [particularly if it closes strong in the final few minutes], the odds are it will also be up tomorrow; and if the market is down today, the chances are better than even it will be down tomorrow."

Then adjust for this *Stock Trader's Almanac* refinement: The market does much better from November 1 through April 30 (climbing at a 13% average annualized rate in those six-month periods since 1950) than from May 1 through October 30 (up just 1.7%).

If past patterns hold, you could theoretically type up a page of rules for your broker, work out an extra-low commission rate in recognition of all the trading you'll be doing, throw a few thousand dollars into the till, and leave for a 20-year trip to Alpha Centauri. When you got back, you'd not only be younger (isn't that the way it works? Did you see *Back to the Future*?), you'd be rich.

A SIMPLE SYSTEM FOR OPTIONS

A genius I'll call Biff—obviously not his name; in all of recorded time there has never been, nor ever shall there be, a genius named Biff—developed a simple system for beating the options game. It had nothing to do with doubling his bet after every loss. Quite the contrary, it had to do with *winning* most of the bets. "It's easy," he told me as he ran an initial $400 stake up to $18,000 in a matter of months. He tried to describe it to me, but it never fully penetrated my veil of skepticism, which is why—forgive me!—I can't pass it on to you. What I do know is that *with the exact same system* in the months that followed, he proceeded to lose the full $18,000 and then some.

The worst thing that can befall someone in a game of chance—particularly one like the options game that purports to involve an element of skill—is early success. It hooks you.

It is for this very reason that the slot machines at the Las Vegas airport are geared to pay out 140 cents on the dollar. It is a savvy investment on the part of the casino owners. They let you win a few bucks while awaiting your Vuittons, which gets you primed to do some real gambling when you get to the hotel. And when you straggle back out to the airport a couple of thousand dollars later, tossing your last few into the slots in disgust while you wait for United to call your flight, they let you win cabfare home. That reawakens the spark for your next trip. (None of this is true—so far as I know. It does sound plausible, though, doesn't it?)

A MORE COMPLICATED ONE

I related the prior story, sans the Las Vegas fantasy, to the Investment Club at Harvard Business School. Afterward, a student topped it. It seems he had run $5000 into $150,000—we are beginning to talk some serious money here—*in five days,* using a system that linked Dow theory (which tells you where the market's headed by comparing the Dow Jones industrial, transportation, and utility averages with their past highs) to the important observation that Teledyne stock, then in the 90s, was breaking through its 200-day moving average. Thus inspired, he bought $5000 worth of far-out-of-the-money Teledyne November calls, which is a fancy way of saying he bet $5000 the stock would soar. *Mirabile dictu,* it did.

I began to take notes—forget journalism, these were notes for *me*—when he smiled and acknowledged that using the exact same analytical tools over the subsequent year and a half, he, too, had managed to give back all his winnings.

HOLD THAT HEMLINE!

Since the first Super Bowl in 1967, the Standard & Poor's industrial average had gone up *without fail* in years a premerger NFL team had won and gone down *without fail* in years when an AFL team had won. Knowing, this, the market shuddered and dived after the Los Angeles Raiders, a premerger AFL team, won in January 1984. That was the first year broad attention had really been focused on the indicator, which had by then racked up a perfect 17-year record, and, as often happens with these things, that was the year it faltered. The market should have gone down in 1984 because the Raiders won, and in truth, for a lot of investors it did. The Dow Jones industrial average was down. But the Standard & Poor's industrial average was up a hair, from 184.24 to 184.36.

Does this invalidate an otherwise solid principle of finance? Certainly 1985 and 1986 were good years, just as they should have been after San Francisco and Chicago (premerger NFL teams) whomped Miami and the Patriots; and 1987 was gangbusters after the Giants beat Denver.

Maybe the guys who rig professional football are the same guys who rig the market! Maybe the Trilateral Commission has something to do with it. Have you noticed how truly powerful men cannot communicate an economic thought without using a football analogy? There's definitely something going on here.

Professor Steven Goldberg of the City University of New York, an ex-Marine and something of a Renaissance man (his articles include "Bob Dylan and the Poetry of Salvation," "Is Astrology Science?" and "Does Capital Punishment Deter?"), has written what may be the definitive dissertation on the NFL/AFL phenomenon—and it has nothing to do with the Trilateral Commission (though I'm still suspicious).

"Whenever you are surprised," writes Professor Goldberg, "it is because you are comparing the thing that surprises you to some background expectation in your mind. You would be surprised to hear that it snowed 300 times in Hawaii last year because your understanding and expectation are that it hardly ever snows in Hawaii. You would, of course, be justified in your surprise. Surprise, however, is not always justified."

We *think* the Super Bowl's ability to call the market 17 times in a row (through 1983) is like flipping heads 17 times in a row. The odds against this are 130,000 to 1. But coin tosses, unlike Super Bowls, are 50–50, random affairs.

From 1967 through 1983, Goldberg argues, because of inflation and economic growth, the market actually had a strong bias to rise. Combine that bias with the NFL teams' tendency to win

—if only because in 5 of the 17 games *both* contestants were premerger NFL teams—and the odds come down to 36,000 to 1.

Oh, hey! So no big deal.

Goldberg can get the odds down even lower, to 13,000 to 1, if you'll buy his notion that, just as the market was more likely to rise than fall in any given year, a premerger NFL team was more likely to win than lose. That would have been because the NFL teams were better than the AFL teams, but I don't want to start any fights over anything as idiotic as football (I mean it! You guys are nuts!), so let's let that lie.

"I can tell," Goldberg writes, "you're still not impressed. After all, 13,000 to 1 doesn't happen every day, does it?" To which he answers, *"Yes.* And this is infinitely the most important point. Surprise is justified only if an *unexpected* event takes place. This would be the case if someone had, *in 1966,* predicted a correlation between future Super Bowl results and the S&P." But no one did. It was only looking back that the coincidence was noted.

"On the other hand," explains Goldberg, "had someone predicted, in 1966, that some variable, *he did not know which,* would offer a sequence perfectly matched" to the annual direction of the S&P, "we should not be in the slightest surprised in 1983 to find that he turned out to be correct."

If it hadn't been the Super Bowl, it would have been temperature readings in Grosse Pointe or any of 13,000 other variables you could look at. Except that the Super Bowl correlation got noticed because so many guys who follow football follow the market. Other chance correlations, he says, are out there—you're just not likely to notice them.

Case closed. Except, boy, it's still a heck of a coincidence to be just a coincidence. . . . Do you think Howard Cosell could be involved in this thing someplace?

CHARTS

Most investment systems are technical in nature. I don't mean technical in the sense of complicated, though many are that, too; I mean technical as distinguished from fundamental. A fundamentalist looks at stocks in terms of the underlying assets they represent. What kinds of profits and dividends can they generate? How will economic developments affect them? A technician looks at charts of price movements and trading volume.

For a good dose of this, you might try to scare up a copy of *How the Average Investor Can Use Technical Analysis for Stock Profits* by James Dines (Dines Chart Corporation, 1972). Dines, long associated with his enthusiasm for gold, was described in Adam Smith's *The Money Game* as being "slightly to the right of Nahum the Elkohite. He is so pessimistic he must make up adverbs—'unmeechingly'—to describe his pessimism."

But Dines—whose pessimism has waned a bit—is also one of the smartest technicians around. His book is 599 pages long, but that shouldn't stop the average investor. In it, he will learn of pennant bottoms, megaphone bottoms, wedge bottoms, false breakouts, head-and-shoulders formations (for those embarrassing white flecks on your charts), saucer tops, tombstone tops, Prussian helmet tops, the Seasonal Rule for Years Ending in "8" (not once in this century has the Dow ended lower than it started in a year ending in 8, which would seem to be tied in to the presidential cycle already described), the Dines Buoyancy Index, the Dines 30 Tick Rule, the Dines 90–109 Rule, and more.

Here's the way I read charts: If a stock is real low, I take it as a good sign. If it's real high, I steer clear.

I am vaguely aware of some of the more sophisticated charting techniques and of the relationship, held by chartists to be crucial, between price movements and trading volume. There are even logical underpinnings for some of this. But to put more than a little weight on a stock's chart in deciding whether to buy it is . . . well, listen to a writer named Thomas Gibson, as quoted in *The Money Game:*

"There is an incredibly large number of traders who pin their faith to the so-called chart system of speculation, which recommends the study of past movements and prices, and bases operations thereon. So popular is this plan that concerns which make a business of preparing and issuing such charts do a thriving business."

This quote, Adam Smith tells us, comes from a book called

The Pitfalls of Speculation, published by Moody's in 1906. It continues:

"There are various offshoots and modifications of the system, but the basic plan is founded wholly on repetition, regardless of actual conditions. [Meaning that past patterns will repeat themselves, regardless of the fact that out in the real world a leak may have occurred in a fertilizer plant owned by the company whose stock chart you are analyzing, killing and injuring 200,000 people.] The idea is untrustworthy, absolutely fatuous, and highly dangerous."

This, Adam Smith notes, was published before Moody's went into the chart business.

FOLLOWING THE INSIDERS

A lot of study backs up the commonsense notion that, over time, insiders are likely to do better buying and selling their own stocks than you or me—even when they do it legally. They're by no means infallible, either at judging the prospects of their own companies or in judging the market's reaction to those prospects. But they have an edge.

Several services will help you follow and assess insider moves, all of which must promptly be reported to the Securities and Exchange Commission. One is *The Insiders* ($100 a year—800-327-6720), a sister publication of *Market Logic*. But how much can one afford to spend on newsletters? And what if you're only out to buy a handful of good stocks and hold them for the long term? What do you do with five or six newsletters arriving each week offering several hundred recommendations a year? Tending your investments could quickly become a full-time occupation, with no guarantee you'll do any better than, or even as well as, you'd do in a no-load mutual fund or a bank.

THE CYCLE JOCKEYS

An otherwise respectable Harvard Business School graduate several years into a successful career on Wall Street came to me in the late seventies with a book relating phases of the moon to cycles in human emotions. Those cycles, he argued—the market being driven as much by emotion as anything—could be used to predict movements in the stock market. The book, by Dr. Arnold Lieber, was called *The Lunar Effect: Biological Tides and Human Emotions* (Anchor Press, 1978). Everybody knows the moon's effect on water—high tide, low tide—and everybody knows human beings are 80% water, so there you are! There are certain days every few months, my friend said, when the heavenly alignment virtually guaranteed a major stock market move.

Being a charitable fellow, I decided not to tell anyone of his theories or reveal his name (Mason "Speed" Sexton, Harvard MBA '72). I figured I would wait a few years and then track him down, promising anonymity, to find out just how badly his astrological fling had gone and what business he was in now.

Well!

Far from his having given it up or desiring anonymity, I found him and his then partner Michael S. Jenkins, a seasoned mutual fund manager, sitting at the then offices of Rooney, Pace in New York, in 1985, managing money and publishing a biweekly newsletter called *Harmonic Research*. The moon thing was part of it (well, people *do* become more aggressive during periods of full moon, if only because they have more light to fight by; weather and agriculture *are* affected by lunar forces), but *Harmonic Research* was attempting to encompass all kinds of cycles, not just lunar ones, ranging from the long waves, like the 50-year Kondratieff Wave, to the rather more complicated Elliott Wave, to waves that have no names but slosh off the charts at you if you just know how to look.

Sexton and Jenkins see the markets (be they in stocks, gold, or whatever) as psychological lakes. Into those lakes from time to time have been dumped all manner of pebbles, boulders, rocks, and sand, each rippling out endlessly, forever and ever. (They could explain this better than I can, but they're tied up on the phone.) Often, the lake is a jumble of these waves, with, say, a couple of big up cycles more or less canceling out a bunch of down cycles. But from time to time there's more of a confluence

—*all* the important waves are running in harmony, *all* headed up or down in their cycle—and then, oh, boy, big stuff. (You may recall the *Not The New York Times* parody that reported the Queensboro Bridge collapsing from the harmonic vibrations of 10,000 New York City marathoners all jogging in cadence.)

The essence of the newsletter each issue is a calendar for the ten trading days ahead, telling what the market will do on each of those days. For the day I was in their office, they had predicted a trend change between noon and one, with the Dow showing a loss for the day. I arrived at one, their prediction, published a week earlier, firmly under my arm, and found them in a state of excitement. "It's turning! It's turning!" they were saying as the Dow, which had been up as much as eight points that day, began to fall. "This could turn out to be one of our most courageous calls," Speed was saying to Mike, in between efforts to explain to me how their system worked. By 1:13 the Dow was up only five.

By 1:20 it was up only three, and Mike began placing shorts, betting the market would go lower.

Speed was telling me about "killer waves." Mike was telling me about "master reverse mirror-image symmetry." If you look at a chart of the stock market, or a single stock, you'll see it—the left side of the mountain looking like the reverse of the right side, the whole thing looking like jagged edges cut out of a folded piece of paper that's then unfolded. You think all this happens by chance? By 1:40 the Dow had bounced a hair, but by 2:07 it was up only 2.80 on the day.

Mike points to the market first hitting 1000 in 1966, takes a tape he's marked off, and stretches it out 1000 days. It falls on another market top. You think that's coincidence? We try it at a market low, 570 on the Dow in 1974, and stretch the tape ahead 570 days to the next major high. You think *that's* coincidence? There is a definite relationship between price and time in these cycles. Amplitudes and periodicity. You and I don't understand it, but then you and I haven't spent years working with the charts and the computers learning to interpret these things. The Dow, at 2:13, is up less than a point. It could go negative.

Say I, "Gee. Once you program in all the cycles, like big and little undulating strands of spaghetti, your computer could print out the ups and downs of the market for the next ten years! Does this mean you could actually write all your newsletters at the beginning of the year and then go fishing?"

I am being cute, but Speed says, "Yeah. Probably." (The Dow, at 2:28, is now down three.) Only, as Mike points out, wavelengths are not always constant and vary with the height of the Dow (or whatever else you're scoping out). What's more, while the interacting cycles are awfully good at calling turning points in the market, sometimes—maddeningly—the major move turns out to be the opposite of what's predicted. Instead of zooming on the appointed day, it may plunge. (Of course, even the knowledge that the market will move sharply on a particular day can be played to great advantage by buying options straddles—a put and a call simultaneously—or by limiting your losses with "stop-loss" orders, in case the call happens to be backward.) The Dow, at 2:42, is now down less than a point—but *Harmonic Research* has called for a strong close this day, so I shouldn't be too surprised, Speed says, now that it has indeed dropped about eight points since one o'clock, to see it close up for the day.

Mike shows me more of the cycles on the charts, more of the symmetry, more of the 30-degree, 45-degree, 60-degree, and 90-degree angles that have special meanings, and the half, third, and quarter cycle points. There's a natural rhythm to it, he says (and this is a man whose mutual fund, when he managed one, was up 45% in 1979), a cadence, a harmony. Mike has been working on translating the chart into—yes—a symphony. It's not done yet, but one day you could sit back and listen to *The Dow Jones Industrial Symphony*—the 1982nd or the 1988th (I'd like to hear the 1929th), with the oboe, tuba, and flute, perhaps, representing the separate price and volume movements of Merck, GM, and Sears.

The Dow closes the day down 4.30.

I had promised Speed that I would keep an open mind, and while it was naturally impossible for me to keep it open very far, I was more impressed than I had expected to be. Not by that day's call, which by itself meant nothing, but by the overall effort.

There are lots of "cycle jockeys," Speed and Mike admit, but probably few, if any, who've developed the art as far as they have.

This isn't to say the Dow will necessarily peak at 3600 in November 1988, as they were predicting in 1985; or that they'll be able to compound their money, or yours, at 10% a month as they hope (which turns $10,000 into $10 billion in 12 years); or even that they won't ultimately wind up losing a bundle. But their predictions, I thought, would be fun to track.

I decided to tally their performance for the next three months.

Every two weeks their newsletter arrived with a capsule of what to expect of each of the next ten trading days, like a two-week weather forecast. For each day an arrow pointed up or down, indicating the direction of the Dow, with occasional comments such as "Strong opening, weak close" or "Big decline possible!"

I awarded two points for each day they were right, one point if they were sort of right, subtracted one if they were sort of wrong and subtracted two if they were all wet. Days they starred as being particularly noteworthy I tripled in importance.

Right all 60 trading days, they'd score 120 or more; wrong all 60, *minus* 120. If they were no more right than wrong—which is exactly what you'd expect—they'd score zero.

Admittedly a crude gauge, but not without foundation. Final score: minus three.

Lest my awards be too subjective, I also tried a more mechanical approach. On days they said the market would go up, I gave them as many points as it did go up—or subtracted the number it went down. And vice versa. On days they said it would be flat, I credited them for each point fewer than five the Dow moved and subtracted for each point over five.

Here they had a maximum-possible score—if the market had always gone in the direction they predicted—of around 330 points (or minus 330 if it always foiled their predictions). Again you'd expect a score around zero, the good calls canceling the bad. But you'd hope these guys could do better, because they're nice guys, smart guys, hardworking guys, and it would be great to think they've found the key to the market. They scored minus 55.

This doesn't mean their long-term forecasts won't be astoundingly good—time will tell. But it does make one doubt whether with cycle analysis they, let alone us amateurs, can beat the market.

Subsequent to my dramatic afternoon, things became a little less harmonic over at Harmonic Research, and Speed was left to publish the newsletter on his own, which last I checked he was doing from offices at 650 Fifth Avenue in New York with a heavy schedule of advertising in *Barron's*.

WHEN JUPITER IS IN URANUS

The Second Annual Harmonic Research Seminar was held December 6–7, 1986, at New York's Waldorf Astoria Hotel and cost $600 a head, plus lodging and meals. I didn't get to go myself (and had somehow missed the first annual seminar), but I did get one of Speed's brochures promoting the event. The five speakers included Arch Crawford ("Astrocycles in the Stock Market"), Marc Chaiken, first vice-president of Drexel Burnham Lambert ("The Use of Gann Turning-Points and Price Harmonics with Momentum Bands and Internal Volume/Breadth Indicators"), and Shearson Lehman's John Tirone ("An Overview of Trading Oscillators Focusing on Stochastics and Relative Strength Indexes").

The most interesting speaker, judging from their biographical paragraphs, was Norman Winski ("The Utilization of Price and Time Vectors to Optimize Trading Strategies"). If you were hesitating over the $600 seminar fee, his brief bio might have pushed you over the edge:

Norman Winski has been trading professionally for more than eleven years. Beginning in 1970, while pursuing degrees in economics and finance, he became interested in financial astrology and found that he was able to use it successfully investing in the stock market. In 1975, he became a member and market maker on the floor of the Chicago Board Options Exchange. During an eighteen-month period, 1976–1977, he successfully parlayed $500 into nearly $1,000,000 [it would have been hard to do this unsuccessfully]. Mr. Winski's library contains over 3000 volumes on cycles, harmonics and astrology, including the collection of the late Evangeline Adams, J. P. Morgan's renowned personal astrologer.

Think of it. Five hundred dollars into nearly a million in a year and a half. That's not 2000% appreciation, that's 2000-*fold* appreciation. Skeptical though I am about these things, it's hard to argue with results. (You know the old put-down definition of an academic—someone who worries that what works in practice won't work in theory.) But 2000-fold! At that rate, in a second 18-month period beginning in 1977 his million would grow to $2 billion, then $4 trillion—and still six years to go before the Second Annual Harmonic Research Seminar he was about to address.

Okay, so as a trader right there on the floor of the exchange, he's going to have advantages you and I, as amateurs, can't duplicate. But heck—for $2 billion, I'd go to work on the floor of the exchange for a couple of years, too.

Anyway, as I say, I couldn't attend the seminar, but neither could I resist calling Mr. Winski to find out how he'd done since. And it turned out that, first, Norman Winski is a fine fellow, and that, second, the reason his trading credentials were limited in Speed's brochure to those fabulous months in 1976–1977—hey, there isn't room to put *everything* in a little brochure—was that, in September of 1977, he went broke. Not from high living; Mr. Winski is not a high liver. His positions just went against him. You Winski some, you—oh, forget it.

"What did I know back then?" he asks, seeming to marvel at the folly of it all—"I was twenty-six." He's learned a lot since and added a lot of analytical tools to his repertoire, including one proprietary astrological indicator that's been working beautifully for him of late.

So is his net worth back in seven figures? I wondered. "Well, it was until this year," he says. "I've had a down year. Wait a minute—no, I mean six figures. Never mind."

And yes, he still believes you can beat the market with technical and astrological analysis. One is certainly inclined to root for him. He sounds like a very nice guy.

• • •

It may be that readers with no money for the stock market, or with the eminent good sense to invest only through no-load mutual funds, have already heard more than enough about market-beating systems and should skip the next chapter. Otherwise, fellow market nuts, take a minute to freshen your drinks. There's more.

Chapter 10

SYSTEMS II
The Sequel

"Don't tell anybody about this," a big-city radio talk show host tells me, but he's found one of the keys to the market. The talk show stuff he just does as a sideline. Full-time he is a stockbroker "with the best record in the country." I ask him just what that means and whether he is very, very rich. He says he *would* be very, very rich if only his partners didn't keep stealing from him. But he's got a photographic memory, studies 40 pages of computer printouts every morning, and is better than anybody at psyching out the market.

I'd voice my skepticism, except that we are about to go on the air, and, frankly, I'd like to know about this key to the market he's found. So I ask him what it is, and he says it's simple. In the first minutes of trading he can always tell—well, nine times out of ten—what the market will do that day. A short-term orientation, to be sure, but one that could be leveraged to considerable advantage all the same. How can he tell? It's a secret he wouldn't want to have get around—why give away something so valuable for nothing?—but "Just check out the opening on AMR." He doesn't know why (does it matter?), but if American Airlines (symbol: AMR) opens up, the market will have an up day. If it opens down, the market will have a down day. Think you can remember that?

Naturally, since this guy has the best record of any broker in the country and would be very, very rich if only his partners weren't stealing from him, I got set to multiply my own consider-able fortune by going long or short stock market futures each morning as soon as I saw how AMR opened, then closing out my position with a fat little profit each afternoon.

But first I figured I'd try a dry run. And do you know what? Over 20 consecutive trading days it worked not nine times out of ten, as advertised, but only a little better than half the time, as you'd expect. (You'd expect better than 50% accuracy because AMR is most likely to open up if the market as a whole opens up; and if the market as a whole opens up, it's already got a head start on *finishing* up.) On the first day of my test, AMR opened up an eighth and the market finished up three points. Score one for the talk show host. But the second day AMR opened *down* a quarter and the market finished up 15. The real big day, when the market jumped 21 points, AMR had opened unchanged. On its biggest losing day of the 20, AMR had opened up a quarter. Damn!

It's tough to find systems that work, but, at least in hindsight, it's possible to find systems that have. (Once you subscribe to a single financial newsletter, your mailbox will be stuffed with offers for them.) At best, they worked in the past for a *reason,* as opposed to a random correlation, like the Super Bowl. Whether they'll continue to work is another story entirely.

THE STOP-LOSS STRATEGY

One tenet of Wall Street runs like this. You've probably heard it. *Cut your losses and let your profits run.*

So a system many investors use is to place "tight stops" on all their positions. When their brokers call to confirm that they've just bought a stock at $50.75 a share, for example, they may say: "Good. Now put in a stop at forty-nine."

A stop-loss order ensures that even if you're off in Africa and

not paying attention, you will be "stopped out" of your stock—
your shares will be sold—if it ever touches 49. The less room
you give your stock to fall, the tighter your stop. What's more, if
and as your stock starts to rise, you can continually "raise your
stop" right along with it, like a ratchet wrench, to lock in your
gains.

I'll grant two parts wisdom in this. The first and most obvious
is that if you arbitrarily set a 10% limit, say, on the loss you'll
accept, you'll never lose more than 10%. The second is that it's a
big world out there, and you can't know all its secrets. If your
stock is falling, there may be a reason. Rather than wait around to
find out what it is (by then the stock could be down 40%), it
might be better to scram.

Even so, there are problems with this strategy.

First, it's not entirely true that by setting a 10% stop you'll
never lose more than 10% because (a) you have to pay commissions, which can easily bump your 10% loss up to 14% or more;
and (b) if the stock should encounter truly major bad news, closing at 50¾ one night and opening at 33½, you may not have a
chance to limit your loss to 10% (which is to say 14%). You will
be off shooting emus, or their photographs, and your broker will
be dutifully selling you out on the opening at 33½. So you're not
entirely protected.

Second, what often happens is that you do indeed get stopped
out at 49, or whatever price you specified, only to see the stock
bounce back to 50¾ and beyond. This is called getting whipsawed. The floor of the New York Stock Exchange is ankle deep
in whipsawdust.

So if you do use stop-loss orders, you might be best served
using them selectively. They're fine if you're jumping on board a
rising stock simply because everyone else is buying it and you
hope it may have a ways yet to climb (the musical-chairs method
of stock selection) but less obviously useful if you're buying a
stock you feel represents great value. If it was a good buy at 50 ¾,
it may be an even better buy at 49 or 46.

PORTFOLIO INSURANCE

Taking stop losses a step further is so-called portfolio insurance. This has caught on big among institutional money managers and is basically pretty dumb.

Instead of placing a stop-loss order on one stock, you place it on your portfolio as a whole, either by selling more and more of your stocks as the market falls or, more conveniently, by selling market index futures or buying market index puts. (You'll find some of this in part III, but the specifics aren't important.) Then, when prices have climbed back a little and it's safe again, you buy back those stocks (or close out your futures position). You've lost money by doing this (and paid commissions and, possibly, taxes), but you've insured that you won't lose too much—unless you keep getting whipsawed as the market bounces up and down (it does that), in which case you'll lose everything.

There's no free lunch. Portfolio insurance makes the stock market less risky—at a price. An alternative would be simply to invest someplace less risky in the first place.

Certainly there are situations in which it might make sense to hedge your stock market bets. But the cost of *continually* making the market less risky in the short run with a system of portfolio insurance will of necessity hurt your performance over the long run.

THE MERRILL LYNCH SYSTEM

If most investors think the market's going up, it goes down. The more enthusiastic they are, the more dangerous the situation. This is because, being sure the market's going up, they've presumably bought heavily to capitalize on that gain (surely they don't buy when they think it's going down). But if everyone's already bought, there's no one left to buy more, so the rise never materializes. By contrast, when everyone knows the stock market's a terrible place for money, and so have theirs elsewhere, there are few remaining sellers and tons of cash available someday to move back into stocks and drive prices up.

All you have to do to beat the market, therefore, is to figure out

what everybody else thinks, and when a great preponderance of
them are leaning one way, lean the other. What's often hard, however, is to gauge what "everybody" thinks.

According to Stephen Leeb, editor of the *Investment Strategist,*
"One of the most reliable measures of market sentiment is the
thinking of Merrill Lynch. Merrill is always a long-term bull
[they're in business to sell stocks], but intermediate term it is now
bearish—as it was in the first quarter of 1978, the summer of
1982 and in the fall of 1985. All these periods turned out to be
historic market bottoms." Leeb wrote this in September 1986,
with the Dow at 1781. Over the next several months it rallied to
2400.

When Merrill Lynch talks, listen—and do the opposite. (Well,
in fairness it should be said that even this sensible system is likely
to work only about half the time.)

TELEPHONE SWITCH SYSTEMS

Many mutual fund families let you switch from fund to fund by
phone, often at no charge. A couple of newsletters specialize in
telling you when to switch from common stock funds into money
market funds and back (*Telephone Switch Newsletter,* 800-772-
7272; *Switch Fund Advisory,* 301-840-0301).

It's an appealing notion. Instead of entrusting your investments
solely to a mutual fund manager (who's not about to sell all the
stocks in his fund even if he thinks the market's headed lower),
you pay an extra $150 or so each year for a newsletter that will
keep you out of the down markets. Over the long run, if it can
really call the major turns in the market, you'll do awfully well.
With no brokerage commissions to pay or spreads to endure, it's a
much cheaper way to go in and out of the market than buying and
selling stocks.

"Most switching services purport to produce fantastic results,"
writes Gerald W. Perritt in the *American Association of Individual
Investors Journal.* "However, most of the claims made by these
services turn out to be highly misleading. All ignore the impact of
taxation"—not a problem, if you own your shares under the um-

brella of a retirement plan—"[and] some services compute their purported returns without deducting their fees"—a handicap if you've got just $4000 or $5000, not really significant if you're investing $40,000 or $50,000. "A few," he writes, "even go so far as to report 'hypothetical' historical results." (On Wall Street, hypothetical fortunes are a dime a dozen.)

One advantage of these newsletters is that for a modest annual fee you get someone else to make the decisions for you—and someone to blame if he doesn't make them right. Another advantage is that they focus on the intermediate to long term. They don't have you jumping in and out; they try to catch the broad, long-term swings.

If you do subscribe, subscribe to just one and make up your mind not to second-guess it—you're paying, in effect, not to have to think about this. Otherwise, save your subscription fee. You can get plenty of expert opinion on the direction of the market, every bit as unreliable as what you'd get from these newsletters, just by reading *Barron's*.

THE EX-DIVIDEND SYSTEM

Stocks pay dividends—if they pay dividends—four times a year. The "record dates" for those dividends are known well in advance. Those are the dates used to determine, for dividend-paying purposes, who is a shareholder. If you own the stock that day, you are eligible for the dividend even if you sell it before they actually get around to mailing out the checks. You'll find record dates in the dividends column of *The Wall Street Journal*.

Say General Motors is selling at 80, and, by buying on margin, you can afford to buy 1000 shares. (Dream a little.) You do that Monday, five business days before the record date. Tuesday, you sell it back at 80. (To own a stock on the record date, you must actually have purchased it five business days earlier, because it takes five days for a transaction to settle. You can sell it the very next day, because the sale, too, takes five days. It's like the world's most out-of-sync movie: the lips move five days before you hear the words.)

You paid $80,000 for the stock and got $80,000, so that's a wash. You also paid—if you've got the right broker—a rock-bottom $250 in commissions. And you paid interest for a day on the $40,000 your broker loaned you (half the purchase price). That's another $14 or so.

But you got the dividend, which in GM's case might be $1.25 a share, or $1250.

After your expenses you made almost $1000—in one day—on $40,000 of your own money (plus $40,000 you borrowed), which is 2.5%. *In one day!*

And tomorrow you can take your $40,000—correction, your $41,000—and use it to buy some other stock that, like a mare in labor, is about to bear a dividend.

Do this every day and, compounded, you'll soon own the world. The annualized rate of return comes to around 14,000% (before taxes).

Here are the problems.

The first is that it's even more crucial than usual, in a scheme like this, to keep your commissions low. To do that, you've got to be playing with big chips. If you tried to do this with just 50 shares of GM—which is still $4000—the dividend you'd get, $62.50, would be less than the commissions you'd pay to do the trades.

But as it's little or no more difficult for a broker to trade 1000 shares of GM than to trade 50, and as with this system you'd generate monumental commissions, it wouldn't be too hard to find a broker who agreed to take a straight eighth of a point per share. That's 12.5 cents for each share you buy, 12.5 cents for each share you sell, $250 in all for buying and selling 1000 shares of stock.

The second problem is a lot stickier. Who says, having bought GM for 80, you'll be able to sell it back at that price the next day? What if you can only get 77?

In point of fact, four days before a stock's record date, it "goes ex-dividend." That means three things. First, somebody makes sure a little x appears next to it in the stock pages of your newspaper. Second, anyone ignoring that x and buying the shares anyway is buying them ex—without—the dividend (because when the trade finally settles, five days later, the record date will have passed). Third, the value of the dividend will automatically be subtracted from the quoted price of the stock the next morning— at least until it opens for trading.

If you're lucky, investors will be little troubled by the lack of this dividend and immediately bid the stock back up to the $80 you paid for it (in which case, the newspaper will report it as having gone up 1¼ that day).

But if you're not, the stock will open just where, rationally, it should—at 78¾ (80 less the dividend)—and minutes later crash to 63 on news that Subaru has invented a V-8 engine that—yes, that's right—actually runs on V-8 juice (and gets 300 miles to the gallon). In Detroit they'll be screaming bloody Mary, and in the meantime, in your quest for a lousy $1250 dividend, you'll have lost $17,000.

Lots of work, lots of commissions; a highly uncertain reward. The one man I know of who tried this on a large scale, persuading private investors to provide him with a pool of money to manage in 1985—a good year for the market—lost a significant sum.

RELATIVE STRENGTH

Have you ever noticed how, when the market is going down, some issues seem to avoid most of the loss? They're stronger than their brothers and sisters, and many believe this relative strength will translate, when the market starts back up, into superior gains.

Dan Sullivan, who says he's more than quadrupled his own portfolio since 1969 (though to do so in 16 years is merely to compound one's money at 9%), has made a science of calculating stocks' relative strength and a business out of selling his advice to others (*The Chartist,* Box 3160, Long Beach, CA 90803). He says he really doesn't care what the companies he invests in do; he cares only how their stocks move relative to others and which way the market is headed. Into the computer go stock data, and out come relative strength ratings based on a formula he's developed.

MARKET TIMING

With real estate, everyone knows it's location, location, location. With investing, writes Dick A. Stoken, the three crucial elements are timing, timing, and timing. It is vastly easier to make money in stocks or precious metals or real estate when the general trend of stocks or metals or real estate is up. Just which stocks you choose, or which metal, or which rental property, is secondary.

That much is sure. Whether, in addition, you should buy stocks "when either short- or long-term interest rates have fallen to a fifteen-month low" and hold them until both long and short rates have risen to seven-year highs, I cannot say. But if you like this kind of thing, Stoken's book, *Strategic Investment Timing* (Macmillan), is excellent. Certainly, with the perspective it provides on political and economic cycles, and its rules for interpreting four commonly available indicators (interest rates, the political cycle, the producers price index, and the Dow), when you lose money in the market, your losses will be based on much more sophisticated misjudgments.

Had you followed Stoken's rules from 1921 through 1983, you could have parlayed $1000 not into the mere $19,000 you'd have had standing pat with the Dow Jones industrials, but—by sidestepping declines in the market and then coming back in—$2,714,466. Tailoring your investments not just to the Dow but to rotating groups of stocks that perform best in various phases of an up market, you'd have done yet another four times as well. None of this takes into consideration dividends or taxes, but what it really doesn't take into consideration is that, sadly, Stoken's book appeared in 1984, not 1921. As he would surely acknowledge, it's far easier to formulate rules that fit the past than the future. That said, you're a lot less likely to buy at the top or sell at the bottom after reading it.

THE LOW P/E SYSTEM

Every stock can be described in terms of its price/earnings (P/E) ratio—what the stock sells for divided by the profits it reports. If IBM is selling for $150 a share and reports $10 in earnings, its

P/E is 15—its stock sells for 15 times last year's earnings. If other things were equal (and, of course, they're not—one stock's earnings may triple while another's might turn to losses), you'd want to buy stocks with the lowest P/E's.

Technology may be the future—how could it not be?—but you might do a heck of a lot better buying old shoe machinery companies at 9 times earnings than Digitalis at 50 times. For a 300-odd-page elaboration of this notion, see David Dreman's much-praised *The New Contrarian Investment Strategy* (Random House).

THE NO P/E SYSTEM

The case for buying real losers (for many of which P/E's cannot be calculated because they have losses instead of earnings) is made in William Grace's *The Phoenix Approach* (Bantam), subtitled "The Contrarian Investor's Guide to Profiting from Out-of-Favor, Distressed, and Bankrupt Companies."

THE LOW P/S SYSTEM

More constant than earnings are sales. And while sales alone do not a rich company make, a company with lots of sales relative to the price of its stock need only see a small increase in its profit margin to show a dramatic increase in earnings. A highly profitable company highly valued by Wall Street, by contrast, selling perhaps at 30 times earnings and 3 times sales, need suffer only a minor profit margin squeeze to see its earnings—and stock price—collapse. Money manager Ken Fisher likes established companies selling for 40% or less of their sales-per-share—and shuns those selling for more than 80%. (For small growth stocks, he's willing to accept much higher price-to-sales ratios.)

THE SMALL STOCK SYSTEM

It's easier to grow when you're small. It's also easier to be overlooked. Does that give small companies an edge? One study compared the performance of the Standard & Poor's 500 average, which is made up of big companies, with the results you'd have achieved buying only the smallest stocks on the New York Stock Exchange—namely, those in the bottom 20% in terms of market value (so-called small cap—small capitalization—stocks). From 1926 through 1985, the study found, you would have compounded your money at 9.8% a year with the S&P 500, including dividends—but at 12.6% with the small stocks.* Your $1000 would have grown to $273,000 in the S&P, but to more than four times as much with the small stocks.

THE GENERIC STOCKS SYSTEM

Avner Arbel's *How to Beat the Market with High-Performance Generic Stocks* (William Morrow) makes a strong statistical case for buying neglected stocks. His notions overlap the good cases others make for buying low P/E stocks and doghouse stocks and "small cap" stocks. But Arbel says a company doesn't have to be small to be neglected—almost a third of the big blue chips in the Standard & Poor's 500, he says, are not regularly covered by Wall Street analysts—and that, in fact, some small companies are *not* neglected and tend to be poorer buys than those that are.

Arbel advises that we look up a potential purchase in the *Standard & Poor's Stock Guide* (any broker has this on his desk, if you don't) and check the column that tells how many different financial institutions own it. As a rule, he says, a stock held by fewer than 10 institutions can be considered neglected. If you further screen your choices to weed out the financially infirm, you're likely to be left with a portfolio of what Arbel calls "generic stocks"—stocks whose prices are not inflated by a brand-name premium.

"Amazingly," he writes of the results of one study, "the return of the most neglected stocks was more than 60% higher than for

Stocks, Bonds, Bills, and Inflation, 1986 Yearbook (R. G. Ibbotson Associates of Chicago) as summarized in *A Lifetime Strategy for Investing in Common Stocks,* a pamphlet by James B. Cloonan published by the American Association of Individual Investors (612 N. Michigan Avenue, Chicago, IL 60611).

the most followed stocks even after adjustment for total risk!"

One clear advantage: a stock owned by a lot of institutions can one day be *sold* by a lot of institutions, crushing it, while a neglected stock may someday catch their eye, causing it to soar.

CATCH A RISING STAR

But there's more than one way to beat the market. Two highly successful mutual funds, Twentieth Century Select and Twentieth Century Growth, have long outstripped the competition by seeking companies on a roll. If reported sales and earnings from continuing operations begin to accelerate—never mind why, and never mind that others may have anticipated this before the reports were issued—these funds buy, and never mind the price. What's more, far from hoping a stock is neglected, these funds will only buy if trading volume is in an uptrend. Says *Forbes* of Twentieth Century's James Stowers, "He wants proof that other investors are interested, and he wants to see the price moving up." "If you're the only one who knows about it," *Forbes* quotes Stowers, "nothing's going to happen." Or, as *Forbes* quotes John Maynard Keynes (no mean investor himself): When betting on the outcome of a beauty contest, don't bet on the girl you think is prettiest, bet on the girl others think is prettiest.

Of course, if you like this system, you're probably best off letting Twentieth Century execute it for you.

THE WINDOW-DRESSING ADVANTAGE

At the end of each quarter (the end of March, June, September, and December), large institutional money managers are prone to a certain amount of "window dressing." In anticipation of reporting their holdings at quarter's end, they'll kick out the embarrassments (driving their already low prices even lower) and purchase a few names anyone will recognize as having done well that quarter (driving their already high prices even higher). This is ridiculous, to be sure, but because the managers don't have to include the prices at which they bought or sold, it can help to make them look good. It can also help to make you money.

"When making an investment decision," writes Francis X. Curzio (*The F.X.C. Report,* 62–19 Cooper Avenue, Queens, NY 11385), "fundamental analysis is primary. But window dressing by the institutions may result in a greater gain or smaller loss for the individual investor." Avon in 1984 looked good at 27, down from 37. "Two weeks before the end of the quarter it was 19." Coleco attracted a lot of interest at 30, down from 65. "Yet if investors waited for the institutional managers' end-of-quarter cover-up, they could have bought it at 15."

THE *VALUE LINE* SYSTEM

Value Line (711 Third Avenue, New York 10017; 800-223-0818) divides the 1700 stocks it follows into five groups—100 in group 1, 300 in group 2, 900 in group 3, 300 in group 4, and 100 in group 5. If you were a stock, you would very much want to be in group 1. It's like getting into Harvard. Group 5 is reform school.

Investing in nothing but group 1 stocks in 1965, when this ranking system began, and replacing them when they fell into group 2 with the new group 1 stocks, would have multiplied your fortune over the ensuing 20 years 90-fold (ignoring taxes, commissions, and dividends). You had a million. Now you have $90 million. Had you instead invested only in group 5 stocks over the same years, you would have cut that million down to pocket change.

And remember: this record wasn't built hypothetically, with hindsight. This is a real-life, real-time record built over two decades. The only unsure thing is whether it will continue to work. To quote the immortal if cloying Emilio Estevez (you know—Martin Sheen's kid), "That was then, this is now."

The Value Line rankings consider many factors but are weighted heavily toward earnings momentum, which is usually not established until long after a stock has touched bottom. So if you like to find truly neglected stocks and buy at the bottom (easier said than done), Value Line's rankings are not for you. If you prefer to find healthy, profitable companies whose stocks have already risen a lot but may have a lot further to go, they may be.

There are three ways to take advantage of *Value Line:*

1. Subscribe for $425 and get its huge 2000-page loose-leaf reference, with a dense page on each stock, plus weekly updates throughout the year. Spread your investable funds over as many group 1 issues as you can (because not all do well; *on average* they do well), and sell when they are demoted to group 2. This is not practical for the small investor—$425 a year takes a big bite out of a $10,000 portfolio, and $10,000 cannot be spread over many stocks—but perhaps you can get your library to subscribe to *Value Line* and to lend you an extra $30,000 to invest (it is a lending library, isn't it?).
2. Forget subscribing. Invest in the Value Line Fund and let Value Line do all this for you. The fund's record in recent years has been notably uninspired. But it's a no-load with low expenses that might regain its touch.
3. Send $55 for the introductory subscription each household is permitted once every two years and get the 2000-page reference, plus 10 weeks of updates. But if you do the sensible thing—invest in the stock market through no-load mutual funds—why would you need this nifty reference book at all?

THE JANUARY SYSTEM

If the S&P 500 is up in early January, chances are the year as a whole will be a winner, too—and vice versa. The significance of this is that, by seeing how the S&P has done, you can presumably figure out how to bet on Super Bowl Sunday.

January's other special feature is as a trampoline—traditionally, it's a time for stocks to bounce back from tax selling. That might change now that the favored treatment of capital gains has been suspended, but I think not. People are still likely to be selling losers at the end of the year to offset their gains. Buying those losers in December when you think they've bottomed and holding them for a few weeks until they've bounced back—sometimes as early as the first week in January—is a risky (well, these are losers, after all) but often successful strategy.

Or you could simply try to take advantage of the difference between institutional behavior and individual behavior. Most institutions, like pension funds, are exempt from tax and so don't do year-end tax selling. Many individuals, by contrast, do—kicking out losers, but also, sometimes (to balance gains and losses or to get a charitable deduction), kicking out winners, too. This would suggest that the kind of stocks the institutions favor —the big capitalization stocks—will go down less at the end of the year and rise less after the start of the new year than the kind of stocks individuals lean toward—the smaller stocks. One way to try to profit from this, suggested by Professors Donald Keim and Jay Ritter, is to buy futures on the Value Line index at the end of the year, because it includes a lot of the smaller stocks individuals might lean toward, and short a corresponding position in the S&P index, because it's weighted more toward what the institutions own. The idea is that the Value Line index will bounce back from tax selling more than the S&P index, and that by going long and short the two at the same time, you reduce the risk inherent in the futures market.

Reported *Fortune* in 1986: "Even small investors willing to take a flier can afford to play. A discount commodities broker will demand a minimum deposit of $1100 and about $50 in commissions. In mid-December [1985] a Value Line contract expiring in March was quoted at 216.05, vs. 212.75 for a March contract on the S&P 500 index, or a spread of 3.30. If the Value Line index rises more, it generates a profit of $25 for each additional .05 in the spread. In some years the spread has widened most in the first two weeks of January. But in January 1985, Ritter reports, the spread widened the most in the latter half of the month. Both Ritter and Keim say they have managed to roughly double their money each January."

Of course, it's just when these plays start to make it into *Fortune* that you've got to watch out. Had you put on this spread at the end of December 1986, following the instructions above, you might have been horrified in January 1987 to have seen the S&P

500 index soar 13%, as institutions went on a buying binge; while the Value Line index, which you were hoping would rise faster, rose only 10.6%. You would have lost about $4000 on each $1100 you bet.*

Even the most logical market systems are risky, because the markets are markets of human beings. It's never been easy to predict their behavior.

*Ah, but you need only hold this position for the first few days of January, says Professor Keim, during which, even in 1987, the Value Line outperformed the S&P 500. The trick in 1987 would have been to get out in time, or at least to instruct your broker to limit your loss to some acceptable amount.

Chapter 11

REAL DEALS
Severely Limited Partnerships

In eight years as a Merrill Lynch broker, I never sold a limited
partnership that made money.
—Mary E. Calhoun,
as quoted in *Money*, December 1986

Much is written about the little liquid investments we can make in
stocks and bonds and options. And much is written about the *big*
investments some people make—Larry Tisch buying CBS, Carl
Icahn buying TWA, Rupert Murdoch buying everything else. But
what about the little deals? The $1 million deals split 35 ways.
The ones that may still be out of your league—you've budgeted
that $30,000 for your daughter's wedding—but that you can be
sure your pediatrician has a piece of.

In this chapter, I want to tell you about some of these deals and
how they turned out. Humor me. This chapter cost me a lot of
money. In the next chapter, *you* get to decide which deal to go
into.

OIL AND GAS

Until the Tax Reform Act of 1986, most limited partnerships were almost entirely tax-motivated, but the guy presenting them to you, whom you'd known since you were sophomores in college, would say, Hey, *forget about the tax advantages!* He's putting his *grandmother* into this deal (and he probably was). She's got zero use for tax shelter, he would say, but this deal's so good that even without the tax advantage blah blah blah, blah blah blah, yuppety-yup-yup-yup.

My first such deal had amazing credentials. There were, to begin with, my college buddy's grandmother and my college buddy's Harvard Business School degree. There was the general partner who had been at the top of his Yale Law School class. (When you or I invest from the comfort of our La-Z-Boy recliners, we are *limited* partners. The fellow to whom we send our checks, or the corporate entity erected to protect him, is the *general* partner.) And there were the sensible shoes this deal wore. Seven wells would be drilled, not one—low-risk development wells, not wildcats—to assure that the law of averages would be firmly on our side. We would not go into debt to drill these wells —that can be risky. Only if the wells lived up to expectations would we borrow enough, with the first seven as collateral, to drill a second set of seven. That would give us twice the tax deduction and, down the road, twice the royalties. We had to sign personally for the loans, but where was the risk? The cash would be borrowed only *after* the bank had been satisfied as to the value of the first set of wells. If the price of oil, then $12, held firm or rose, we'd be flush.* *This* deal didn't assume oil was on its way to $75. As I say, this deal wore sensible shoes.

The prospectus talked about potential conflicts of interest and 100 other reasons not to invest, but that's what prospectuses do. For the best deals and the worst deals, prospectuses all read maddeningly alike. What really matters are the people. A college buddy, a brilliant Yale grad, a grandmother. How could it miss?

What was truly extraordinary (I was young) was that one of the

*Or perhaps he said "flushed."

seven wells had already been drilled, even though not all the money had yet been raised (I never did quite understand this), and *wow!*—it looked as if it could carry the whole program by itself. That's why my buddy was putting his grandmother into the deal.

Finally, even though the minimum unit was $50,000—it said so right in the prospectus—he *thought* he could get the general partner to make an accommodation and sell me just a half unit. And he did.

The wells were drilled; they looked promising just long enough to secure the bank loan; seven more wells were drilled; and then all fourteen wells dripped and dribbled like the last few drops from a well-squeezed lemon. (In theory, the loan to drill the second seven wells would not be drawn down unless the flow from the first seven warranted it. But the bank was hardly going to quibble over geology when it had 35 financially robust signatures guaranteeing principal and interest at 2.5% over prime. It was not loans like *this* that brought down the Penn Square Bank and Continental Illinois. Don't blame *me* for the near collapse of the Western world.)

The important point to make is that while some oil deals hit nicely (I've never been in any), most bomb (I'm in six). This story isn't unusual—it's the norm. As it turns out, they've *always* just drilled one of the wells even though the cash has not all been raised, and—confidentially—it's *always* a zinger! What's more, these deals are made up *mostly* of grandmothers who need no tax shelter—or so it sounds—and they're *always* able to make a special exception and let you have just half a unit.

And the funny thing is, your college buddy really did mean to do well by you and took the commission he made selling you and the rest of the frat house and invested in a half unit himself. The general partner, too, was eager for you to succeed, not least because he retained a 25% interest in the wells. If they bombed, he only made a fee for drilling them and a fee for maintaining them and a fee for trying to rescue them and a fee for putting the deal together in the first place.

My college buddy went on to bigger and better things and was soon making more money than the president of the United States. The general partner, last I looked, had moved to even plusher offices. He doesn't write to us directly; he has a much-abused vice-president of investor relations send us the bad news each year. He's had five of them since we started.

PAPER CASTLES

Before the new tax law, real estate developments were erected entirely on tax opinions. Many promised three-to-one write-offs (invest $60,000, write off $180,000, save $90,000 in taxes). Yet —whatever additional wrath the IRS may ultimately wreak on some of these deals—Congress in 1986 clipped the wings of even the legitimate ones in midstream. Where before you could deduct partnership losses against your regular income, now you can only deduct them from passive income. Which sent everyone scrambling for PIGs (passive income generators) to pair off against their PALs (passive activity losses). The test of passive income or loss is essentially that you take no active role in drilling the wells or managing the real estate or leasing the airplanes.

You now have three kinds of income to keep straight:

1. Ordinary income, against which you can deduct things like local income taxes, home mortgage interest, and charitable contributions, if you itemize. You can also deduct up to $3000 a year in capital losses. (You can deduct these things against any kind of income.)
2. Portfolio income (dividends, interest, and capital gains), against which you can deduct investment interest (such as margin interest) and capital losses.
3. Passive income, against which you can deduct passive losses. (Passive losses in excess of passive income remain 65% deductible for 1987, 40% in 1988, 20% in 1989, and 10% in 1990, with the nondeducted portion added to the basis of your investment and thus eventually figured into your gain or loss.)

A special exemption allows taxpayers with less than $100,000 a year in adjusted gross income to deduct up to $25,000 in losses from rental properties that they actively manage. For each dollar above $100,000 in adjusted gross income, 50 cents of the $25,000 deduction is disallowed, so that none of it may be deducted by anyone who reports $150,000 or more in adjusted gross income.

The tax advantages of limited partnerships have thus greatly diminished. But the volume of limited partnerships thrown onto the market may not slacken at all. Gone are the three-to-one write-offs; long live the passive income generators and deals that generate cash that won't be taxed for years.

Your broker will eagerly show you deals like this if he thinks you've got the kind of money to participate, usually $50,000 or $100,000 payable in multiyear installments. But there are also little deals your accountant or lawyer or a local real estate developer might be putting together for just a few investors.

I was a tiny partner in one such New York City co-op conversion, where by doing some paperwork and paying some attorneys' fees (and being patient), we turned what was once a shabby $350,000 brownstone with five rental apartments into exactly the same shabby brownstone with five *cooperative* apartments that could then sell for $120,000 apiece—$600,000. This was not a $250,000 profit on a $350,000 investment, it was a $250,000 profit on a $100,000 investment, because the rest of the purchase price was borrowed against the value of the building.

But it's more satisfying to see your dollars go actually to build something. This can be risky. We took a run-down eight-story building, gutted it, put in a new elevator and eight new apartments, sold them—which was not easy in 1982—and after two and a half years barely broke even. Such was the leverage in that deal (the bank having put up most of the money) that had we just hung on for another year before selling—which, by gritting our teeth a little harder we could surely have done—we would have gotten 30% or 40% more for each apartment and, instead of breaking even, tripled our cash. The three keys to success in real estate are location, location, location. But timing, timing, and timing don't hurt, either.

Witness a deal to build 200 rental units in Longview, Texas. To the substantial credit of the general partner, the project was built on time, on budget; the units were fully rented on time, on budget; and the first checks the partners received were for more than had been projected. Then Longview's largest employer, a steel mill, laid off 3000 people. There have been no checks since. At least we did build 200 attractive housing units. (Well, a bunch of hardworking guys I've never met built the units; but we paid them.)

RESEARCH AND DEVELOPMENT DEALS

Before the new tax law, research and development deals were another fine way to feel good losing money. Almost all these deals failed, but you got to write off your investment in the year you made it, much as if it were a charitable contribution; and any money that did come back was likely to come back as a lightly taxed capital gain. More than that, you had the feeling that, even if you only vaguely understood it, you had attempted something worthwhile: the development of a more efficient electric engine, the construction of a revolutionary ultralight graphite fuselage, the design of an improved solar collector, the development of a machine that eats tires and excretes energy, the development of electric-power-line fault meters—and so on.

The fault-meter company actually went public in 1986 and paid back handsomely after what had been a six-year wait, and I retain distant hopes for the tire eater, but otherwise my own success has been confined to one venture—and even that was limited. A group of us who had only the vaguest idea what monoclonal antibodies were put up $1.8 million so that a handful of people who knew awfully well what they were (and who had several months earlier invested $500,000 of their own) could develop a new kind of diagnostic kit. The kit would assist hospital pathologists in making rapid analysis of suspect tissues. If things worked out, we were guaranteed three times our money back, or (at our option) double our money and 10% of the company. The latter option was particularly intriguing, because although only a few high-risk deals like these succeed, those that do can succeed on a grand scale.

This one was succeeding on only a fairly grand scale—and running out of cash just as some powerful competitors were stirring—when, happily, after a mere 18 months, Johnson & Johnson agreed to buy it for $18 million. This may or may not have been the most acute strategic move Johnson & Johnson ever made, but it was a blessing for us.

Interestingly, for all its girth, the sheaf of papers underlying our $1.8 million investment did not specifically deal with such an eventuality. It was not entirely clear how the $18 million should be split up.

Obviously, the folks who'd invested $500,000 and their extraordinary talents deserved most of the bonanza. They were the entrepreneurs; their brains were the prime assets. All we had done was risk $1.8 million to pay their salaries and expenses, which hardly seems like much of a contribution after a deal has turned to gold. (Try raising it beforehand, however.)

So the general partner decided it would be fair to split the $18 million this way: We would get back our $1.8 million plus a $900,000 profit; he and his colleagues would get back their $500,000 plus a $14.8 million profit. A 50% return on our money; a 2900% return on theirs.

After much howling by the limited partners, and much pointing to what would appear to have been his contractual obligation to give us at least three times our money in the event of success, the general partner upped our return from one and a half times our investment to double—$2 back for every one risked—but no more.

Double your money in less than two years, with tax advantages to boot, was more than an adequate return, he felt. Many of the limiteds (certainly those of us who joined to sue him) felt that, while marvelous in the abstract, such a return was unfair. If most such deals fail, then, when you finally have one that hits big, the return has to be awfully high to justify the risk. All we wanted him to do was live up to the terms of the prospectus.

We retained a lawyer who did an energetic job of rounding up $3000 from each of us but then seemed to lose interest. There was the temptation to sue *him,* or at least to put sugar in his gas tank, but the whole effort just sort of petered out.

HAVE I GOT A DEAL FOR YOU?

You may be wondering, Where does he *find* such great deals? Where do *I* find such great deals?

As I've tried to suggest, it's not entirely clear you should be looking. Especially now that the losses won't offset your Christmas bonus. But chances are, if you can afford them, they'll be looking for you. Your broker will be suggesting them, your accountant will be suggesting them, friends who can't afford a half unit themselves and want to split one will be suggesting them, and, once you go into a deal where your name shows up down at the courthouse as one of the limited partners, even strangers will be calling to suggest them to you.

Did you go to college? Did you have buddies in college? Are their grandmothers still living? You should be all set.

Even so, I've got three more for you.

Chapter 12

MORE REAL DEALS
Choose One

Here's $25,000; I'm giving you a choice. You may invest it in a musical comedy about four dead nuns, in Iowa farmland described as consisting of "poorly and very poorly drained soils," or in a real estate partnership consisting of three apartment complexes and two brand-name roadside inns.

Take your time. Twenty-five thousand dollars is a lot of money. Which do you go for—the dead nuns, the poor soil, or the motels?

Ah. I knew you'd say that.

Well, the answer is no. You can't just take the cash. I know you. It would be gone before you could say 380SL (and even then you'd need financing). I want you to invest this money. And no, you can't just spread it over all three choices. Great fortunes were not built by hedging bets. They were built by the Bold Stroke— that special insight that allows one to distinguish the nuns from the mud from the motels.

Being a bit of a wuss myself, and possessed of no such special insight, I put a little something into each. But I'm giving you the $25,000, so I get to set the rules. Choose, please: dead nuns, poor soil, or the partnership.

I guess you need a little more information.

The play about the nuns is called *Nunsense*. The music is terrific, the lyrics are tasteless and sophomoric but ultimately pronun, and the plot—well, briefly, this is the story of the Little Sisters of Hoboken, 19 of whom were out playing Bingo when Sister Julia, child of God, served tainted vichyssoise to the rest. The 19 return to find their 52 sisters facedown in the soup (let me say again: the show is, at heart, pro-nun), whereupon they bury 48 of them (all of this off-stage, to keep the actual cast down to five sisters plus the band), and the remaining four—well, there was much sentiment for burying them, too, but funds were scarce and Mother Superior decided to put them in the freezer and buy a Betamax for the convent instead.

As the play opens, the New Jersey Board of Health has threatened to shut down the convent if the sisters don't get those four blue nuns out of the freezer and into the ground by morning. So the sisters have, in desperation, thrown together a little talent show to raise the needed funds.

The farmland is in western Iowa. It's flat—no problem with its washing downhill onto someone else's farm—but its soil is not like that rich brown earth on sale in sacks at Sears. It's more like the surface of a clay tennis court. Of course, as any tennis buff knows, vegetation can grow through clay if not properly discouraged. *En*couraged, it can grow as high as an elephant's eye.

This particular land can produce 100 bushels of corn per acre (not 100 bushels of ears, I was amazed to learn; 100 bushels of just the little yellow kernels themselves) unless, because of its very poor drainage, showers have turned it into a lake during what would otherwise be the relatively brief opportunities for planting and harvesting, or drought has turned it into a desert during the growing months in between.

The real estate partnership includes five separate, existing, attractive operating properties in Virginia Beach, Sacramento, Fort Lauderdale, Indianapolis, and Tomball, Texas. Unlike the nuns and the farm—tiny, private offerings—this is a multimillion-dollar partnership put together by a large real estate syndicator.

(A real estate syndicator arranges to buy property jointly with a bunch of dentists and airline pilots. The syndicator, or general partner, puts together the deal; the dentists and airline pilots [limited partners] put up the money. After certain fees to the general partner, whatever profit or loss the property generates gets passed through to the limited partners. If it appreciates, the partnership may either sell it, with the investors taxed on the gain, or take out a bigger mortgage, with the investors sharing, tax free, the extra millions borrowed against it.)

In this deal, the syndicator guarantees distributions to the limited partners of at least 6% in the early years of the deal (shielded from tax by depreciation), even if the revenues from the three apartment complexes and two motels lag projections. Projections call for much higher returns thereafter.

So now are you ready to choose? Yes, you are. You have long since figured out that this must be a trick question, so the solution is simply to pick the worst-possible investment. A lot of us— perhaps feeling that life itself is something of a trick question— seem to choose our investments very much the same way. (Surely you know someone who's proclaimed that from now on he'll beat the market simply by deciding whether a stock should be bought or sold and then, because he's invariably wrong, doing the opposite.)

But in order competently to beat this trick question—if it is a trick question, and I didn't say that it is, just that you'd concluded it must be—you need to decide which of the three *is* the worst investment, and for that you need more information.

Did I mention, for example, that the "large real estate syndicator" guaranteeing 6% minimum distributions (and whose name I'm sure you noticed I did not reveal, to make you smell a rat) is actually a well-regarded, highly profitable New York Stock Exchange–listed firm (Southmark Corp.)? The guaranteed distribution checks have been arriving quarterly, like clockwork.

Did I mention that the bricklike Iowa soil comes with a water well and a gigantic pivot sprinkler, unlike anything you have ever seen on your lawn or any other? (It looks like the world's tallest crane, keeled over on its side, with a well at its base and big rubber wheels at intervals for support as it imperceptibly describes a damp circle around the parched farm, except for the corners, on which you could bake bread.) This enormous piece of machinery (if it works) helps to assure that, drought or no, in most years we'll get our 90 or 100 or perhaps even 120 bushels per acre.

Did I mention that this land sells for just $500 an acre, compared with the $1200 to $1500 it fetched just a few years ago, when inflation raged and farmland was hot?

You should also know that the United States is swimming in corn; that this land is not suitable for raising aspartame, aloe, or artichoke hearts; that corn prices fell under $1 last year for the first time since 1953 (so at 100 bushels in a good year, you're talking $100 an acre in revenue, less perhaps $75 an acre in seed and fertilizer, for a gross profit—*before* the cost of labor or of equipment or of the land itself—of $25 an acre); and that your tax dollars effectively kick in another $1 or more per bushel in government subsidies, bringing the true revenue per bushel up closer to $2.50 (and the gross profit per $500 acre to more like $175 in a good year), except that there's no telling how long Uncle Sam can continue these mind-boggling subsidies.

Oh, yes. Will Rogers said, "Buy land; they're not making any more of it." And we've all seen *Gone With the Wind.*

As for the nuns, did I mention that, as investors in the original off-Broadway play, we would be entitled to a small piece of all ancillary rights, such as movie rights, sitcom rights *(The Flying Nun's* been done, but never a sitcom about dead nuns), rights to the record album, and royalties on out-of-town productions? Did I mention that virtually all New York theatricals, whether on Broadway or off, lose their backers' money? I've been in several —a Mike Nichols–directed award winner, a show by the author of *A Chorus Line,* a musical about the first woman ever to run for president—and to date I have gotten back, in total, $146. Even the big hits that run a year or more often don't return their backers' money, let alone a profit.

Now are you ready to choose?

I grant there's a lot more you need to know, but that's always true. And even if you knew it—if you read the 200-page real estate prospectus, with descriptions of, and computerized projections for, the three apartment complexes and two motels; if you went out to Iowa and kicked the tires of the pivot irrigator and boned up on U.S. farm policy; if you read the *Nunsense* script and saw the sisters sing and dance—there would still be more you needed to know. Are the people you're relying on honest? Have they been realistic in their projections? Will we have inflation or deflation? Will the demand for corn sweeteners surge? Do Catholics have a sense of humor? (Is the pope Catholic?) And, as always, if this deal is so good, how come they're offering it to us?

So this is it. Seriously. Write your choice here, *in ink* _____, and then read on to find out how, as of this writing, these deals are working out.

I bought the farm in 1986 because it was about as bad a time to own farmland as anyone could remember. This doesn't mean that by the time you read this things won't have gotten worse. If the price of farmland drops further, I plan to buy more. (This is the quicksand theory of soil management.) But when loads of people want to sell and almost nobody wants to buy, that's sometimes sign of a bottom. After all, food is always likely to be worth *something;* and without farmland, it's hard to grow.

I was struck by the fact that for the same money, one could either buy a single condo parking space in Boston's aforementioned Brimmer Street Garage or a 160-acre farm. And if things failed to work out (one should never underestimate Boston's parking problem), I could always echo the haunting preamble to *Out of Africa.* "I . . . had a farm . . . in Iowa," I could say, softly.

Because, in truth, my farm may not make it. When the massive government farm subsidies wither, as it seems inevitable and reasonable that they will, only the more economical farms will survive. The marginal land will go out of production. Prime farmland in the Midwest runs more to $1200 an acre these days (down from $2750) than to the $500 I paid. Whether it will remain economical to farm ground like mine remains to be seen. In the meantime, it's rented to an excellent farmer who owns land of his own nearby, and it throws off 10% a year in rent after expenses (principally, property tax and a management fee).

Those of you who chose to sink your 25 G's into the farmland: smart move! (I hope, I hope, I hope.)

(If you *have* just inherited half a million and want to risk a sixth of it on 80 acres of prime ground in the nation's heartland or 160 not-so-prime acres near me, two of the hundreds of farm managers who might be eager to help are Murray Wise of the Westchester Group in Champaign, Illinois, and Richard Thoreson of Security National Bank in Sioux City, Iowa. I'm assured you won't be driving anyone off his land—the bankers have already done that. Nor will you be expected to plow the fields yourself; farm managers will arrange for tenants and handle most of the details for 5%, if the farm is rented out for cash, or for 10% if, as is more likely, it's leased under a crop-share arrangement. In the latter case, you share the expenses of planting the crop and reap 50% of the proceeds, if there are any.)

I went into the real estate deal because it was geographically diverse, because its attractive projections were based on existing, operating properties, and because I wasn't keen on paying 59% of my income in federal, state, and city taxes. (This was in late 1984, before Congress killed, retroactively, some of the tax advantage of investing in real estate.)

Even so, I have always had a problem with real estate syndications. Most of them eat up about 15% of your investment in sales commissions and other costs, leaving only 85% or so actually to be invested in real estate. Lots of investors accept this haircut who would never consider paying $205,000 for a house they know is really worth only $174,000. Yet that's the difference 15% makes.

Not only that, real estate syndicators, in their hurry to get something to syndicate, haven't always the same incentive as you or I. Where we might hold out for something really irresistible, the syndicator may very reasonably pay fair market value— which is to say full market value—or perhaps even a little more. After all, it's not his money. And how many dentists and airline pilots know whether a shopping center is worth $4.9 million or merely $4.3 million, anyway? What's more, if inflation comes roaring back and this shopping center is sold for $20 million, who cares? So *what* if the investors put up $5.75 million to buy for

$4.9 million (what's left after 15% in fees) a property that a really tough, patient negotiator might have snagged for $4.3 million?

The syndicator would certainly like to see you do well—he likes to do a good job, just as you do, and the better you do, the better he'll do, both in future business from satisfied investors and because he shares in the ultimate profits on the property. But most of that incentive is years off. The incentive now is to put tens or hundreds of millions of dollars' worth of deals through the pipeline, getting an immediate cut thereof. That's what stocks the refrigerator and fuels the private jet.

Anyway, for those of you who placed your $25,000 on the three apartment complexes and two motels, I have bad news. It turns out that things have not been going so well. The memos you've gotten from the general partner are cheerful, to be sure,* and your quarterly checks come just as promised; but the 1985 financial statement, issued in the summer of 1986, tells a worrisome story. Revenues from all five properties have been lower than projected. They're not just generating tax losses (what with the depreciation), they're generating real losses. Huge ones.

So what else is new, right? But there's a distinction here. It's one thing if you go into a chancy gold mining deal and, guess what, it doesn't pan out; or if you buy into an office building in Houston and then, months later, the price of oil collapses.

You pays your money, you takes your chances. Nobody likes a sore loser.

But in this case, you bought into five operating properties in late 1984. Isn't it odd that all five, in five different parts of the country, should turn in results sharply below projection for 1985? Was there a recession in 1985? I missed it. Were there unexpected economic shocks or a sudden steep decline in motel occupancy? No, 1985 bumbled along much as 1984 had.

Yet here were the property-by-property projections for 1985 used to sell the deal in late 1984, and now here were the actual

*My first inkling there was something wrong came early, when I received an empty embossed three-ring binder into which it was suggested I might want to put those forthcoming memos. Call me hard-nosed, call me cynical, but I've become leery of general partners who send embossed three-ring binders. It may be just a little too much attention to marketing, perhaps not quite enough to business.

1985 results. Rent had come in 8% under projection from the Fort Lauderdale apartments, 21% under projection from the Virginia Beach apartments and 26% under projection from the Tomball, Texas, apartments. (Did *your* rent go down 20% in 1985?) Gross revenues from the Sacramento and Indianapolis motels had come in 26% and 27% under projection, respectively, while their "cost of sales" had unfortunately come in 43% *higher* than projected.

Bad results or no, the mortgages still had to be paid, along with some other expenses, leaving a nearly $2 million cash shortfall on an overall investment by the partners of just under $8 million.

That's not much of a shortfall for a small nation, but it's a lot for three small apartment complexes and two motels. Is it conceivable the projections were based more on what it would take to make the deal look good than on the professional judgment available to a New York Stock Exchange company? (Is *that* the way the world works?) Yes, the general partner is making cash distributions of 6% per annum anyway—those checks just roll in—but they take the form of loans to the partnership and, in any event, cease after three years.

Now, you say, calm down. They got off to a rocky start. Given two or three years, those 26% shortfalls in revenue will gradually disappear and everything will be fine.

But it's not enough that the properties eventually start bringing in what they were projected to bring in for 1985, because for the deal to succeed, net income had to rise every year from the 1985 level.

The general partner projected that for 1986 "net income before other expenses" (primarily, $3,468,510 in mortgage interest) would outstrip the 1985 target by 15%. And perhaps it did; I'm no longer privy to the numbers. To have done so, however—to have gotten back on track (even without recouping the 1985 shortfall)—would have required a jump in net income of 160%. And then, to stay on track, another 12% gain in 1987, 10% gains in 1988 and 1989 and—well, there's not a lot of time in these projections to stop and catch your breath, let alone suffer a downturn.

Anyhow, having studied the projected and actual numbers, which neither I nor most investors, I think, generally do (what's the point? Once you're in one of these deals, you're in for a decade or more), and having noted that all five geographically diverse properties were performing under projection, I called the general partner to comment on the coincidence.

"You dumb sons of bitches robbed us blind!" I said—nicely.

"What's the problem?" asked the investor relations department. (Again, I am paraphrasing liberally.) "The program's going to work out great! It's just that the economy was terrible in 1985."

"It was?" I said.

"Well, and we're not sure the sellers of the motels were entirely candid in their representations to us."

Ah. Now we were getting somewhere.

I muttered something about "due diligence" and a couple of other legal phrases I don't really understand but that I thought might conceivably apply ("class action" may have been one of them), and within minutes—in the scale of time at which things like this move—the general partnership had agreed to buy back my interest for enough, after taking into consideration the tax benefits I had received less the taxes I'd now have to pay, to come out whole. "We think it would be unwise for any investor to sell out," read the gracious letter. "Nevertheless, if you are dissatisfied and wish to sell at this time . . ."

Whether any other limited partners took the time to compare the annual statement with first-year projections, and whether, if so, any of them squawked, I cannot say. But if you chose this particular deal for your $25,000, it might have paid you to do so.

And now for the nuns. I know that's what you chose, hard as I tried to deflect you. You're not stupid; I'm not stupid. If you had just three choices—farmland, real estate, or a musical comedy about dead nuns—your money was on the nuns.

I went into it myself for several reasons. First—with all due respect—I thought it was hysterical. Second, it was capitalized at a mere $150,000—versus perhaps $500,000 these days to put on your average off-Broadway number and $4 million to mount a full-fledged Broadway musical. Third, unlike most shows, where for each 1% of the capital investors put up they are entitled to just half a percent of the profits (with the general partner in line for the other half), in this case we were offered a full point for each point invested. Presto: the odds, though very long, just doubled.

Fourth, this was a show I actually got to see before investing. With most, you're asked to attend a backers' audition in the producer's living room to hear a description of the plot and 8 of the show's 14 songs. In this case, a shoestring production of the actual show, with the actual cast, was playing on a high school stage in my neighborhood. And fifth, they needed the money.

The devil made me do it.

And though not a penny's profit has yet to flood my coffers ("You're so rich, the banks are charging you storage," my broker likes to tell me, as accurate in this appraisal as in most others), things are looking good on the nun front. The sisters in *Life,* the sisters on Phil Donahue, separate productions in Boston, Philadelphia, San Francisco, Toronto, Sweden, and Australia, a fat amateur-and-stock rights sale, a cast album, Peggy Cass in a Michigan production, Kaye Ballard and Jaye P. Morgan in Miami —it looks as if you grabbed that $25,000 by the dollar sign and slammed it down on the right choice.

Nice job.

If you haven't the money to invest in deals like these for real, this chapter and the last may suggest you're not missing much.

If you do have this kind of money to invest, here's a checklist to consider first:

1. What's the spread? How much of your money actually goes to buy the property or drill the wells and how much goes to drawing up that huge prospectus?
2. Are you buying this deal—or is it being sold to you? As highly as I regard your broker, you may be better off deciding on your own the kind of deal you're interested in and then seeking out the right one. For help, subscribe to *Brennan Reports* (Box 882, Valley Forge, PA 19482; 215-783-0647) or even to *The Stanger Register* (1129 Broad Street, Shrewsbury, NJ 07701; 800-631-2291), though it is written for the salesman or financial planner as opposed to the investor. Because they're expensive, request a back issue as a sample, first.

3. *All* deals include a page of attractive projections. Yet many deals don't work out. Given that the projections are more likely to be optimistic than pessimistic, you must at the very least play an aggressive devil's advocate with the numbers. How much are they predicated on inflation? With many deals—like the real estate deal described above—inflation is crucial to success.

4. Is there an overcall provision? If there's any possibility of your being called upon to pony up additional funds, you should assume you will be called upon to do so.

5. If there's not, how is this deal likely to support itself if it falls short of money?

6. Are there tax benefits? If so, how would the deal look without them? The more aggressive the tax benefits, the more likely you are never actually to receive them.

7. What are the potential conflicts of interest? Typically, they're listed right in the prospectus; but typically, too, one feels awkward imagining that the general partner would succumb to them. After all, he was forthright enough to warn you of them in the first place*—you just know he's not actually going to take advantage of you. And he probably isn't planning to, either. But things have a way of happening.

8. Do you truly understand this deal? If not, are you sure you want to invest $25,000 or $50,000 or $100,000 in it? If it seems as if you'd never really be able to understand it, or as if there's no time to study it (the deal's hot, says your broker, but if you get the papers to him by messenger, he thinks he can reserve you a spot)—pass it by. Other opportunities are sure to follow.

9. Does the deal seem to respond to some genuine economic need? Or is it a thoroughbred-horse-breeding deal?

10. How guaranteed are the "guaranteed cash distributions," if any? Will the general partner really be able to make good on those guarantees? And, if so, will the cash be coming from the general partner to the limited partners with no

*The SEC makes him.

strings attached—or merely as a loan to the partnership, to be repaid later? Are these guaranteed returns on your money or merely returns *of* your money? (Give me $1000 and I'll gladly guarantee to return 25%—$250 a year—for three or even four years.)

11. Is the return you expect high enough to justify the loss of liquidity? Should you invest in one of these real estate deals or oil deals—or might the same money be better invested in a publicly traded REIT (real estate investment trust) or MLP (master limited partnership) that you can sell whenever you want?

12. Before you lock away big money for a decade or more (well, it's *fun* to be able to say yes to your broker and play big-time financier), consider your alternatives.

PART III

A-Iternativ-Z

The people who have gotten rich quickly are also the ones who
get poor quickly.
—John Templeton

A-LTERNATIV-Z
Decisions, Decisions

There are dozens of places to bury your treasure. Herewith your alternatives, from A to Z.* As new ones come along and old ones are repackaged, ask yourself how they compare with those below. How do they compare in terms of risk? Potential return? The spread involved in buying and selling them? Liquidity? Tax advantages? The hassle factor? If they compare very favorably, remember to ask yourself one other thing: Why, if they're so good, are they being offered to you?

If the array of alternatives seems vast, please note that you needn't torture yourself trying to find the best alternative. Except with hindsight, there *is* no best alternative. Any of a dozen—and, more likely, a mix of a few—may do very nicely. Your goal is merely to find investment vehicles appropriate to you. Most of the alternatives that follow are offered more to improve your cocktail party acumen than as investment vehicles you should seriously consider.

*In Hawaii, where there are only 12 letters in the alphabet, A, E, I , O, U, H, K , L, M, N, P, and W, the investment process is simplified substantially.

ADRs. When you see Sony and a few other big foreign companies trading on the New York Stock Exchange, it's not actually Sony stock they're trading, but Sony ADRs—American depository receipts. Buying these saves having to exchange currency or fly to Kyoto to open a brokerage account.

ANNUITIES are the opposite of life insurance contracts. Instead of paying a lot of little premiums and then eventually having your beneficiary collect a large lump sum, with a "single premium deferred annuity" you pay the insurer a large lump sum now in return for its promise of smaller sums each month as long as you live—which it hopes will not be long. You say you smoke four packs a day and dismantle bombs for a living? Welcome!

Annuity contracts are like large nondeductible IRAs. Your money compounds free of tax until you withdraw it.

Annuities may be written to promise monthly payments for a set number of years or for as long as you live or even for as long as you or your spouse lives, whichever is longer. Payments may begin right away or only after a certain age.

Annuities are illiquid. As with IRAs, there's a 10% penalty for withdrawing funds before age 59½ (except in cases of death or disability), and the insurance company may also impose a charge if you choose to cash it in during the first few years.

You can buy a fixed annuity, which will typically guarantee a 4% return on your money but pay more if the insurer's conservative investment portfolio permits. Or you can buy a variable annuity, directing that your funds be invested in one of a handful of mutual funds the insurer manages, with the payout determined by how well those funds do.

An alternative, if you're looking for tax shelter: municipal bonds and municipal bond funds, where the income is not just tax-deferred, but entirely tax free.

An alternative to the variable annuity, meanwhile, may simply be to buy and hold common stocks. Without the shelter of the annuity your dividends will be taxed, it's true; but appreciation will be taxed only when you take profits, which need not be often (particularly if you get into the habit of making your charitable contributions with appreciated securities—see: Charity).

The trade-off with an annuity is between its tax-deferral advantage, on the one hand, and its illiquidity and sales charges, on the other.

If you're seriously considering the purchase of a single premium deferred annuity, be sure to see also: Single Premium Life.

ANTIQUES. Duck decoys and weather vanes fetch six figures. An American Chippendale wing chair sold for $2.75 million in 1986—a record for furniture. Can you imagine how dumb whoever sold it will feel when it fetches $500 million at auction a few years from now?

ART. Buy what you like. Display it out of reach of children and pets. Don't count on its appreciating, or on your being able to sell it readily even if it does. Personally, I collect original *New Yorker* cartoons. If you see one you like, call the magazine (212-840-3800) and ask whether it's available. Prices start at around $300.

BANK ACCOUNTS are fine places for your first few thousand dollars. Stick to those with federal deposit insurance. If you belong to a credit union, you can often earn a little more on your money or borrow for less. In choosing a bank, don't agonize over service charges or a quarter of a point in interest. Even if you can determine which bank offers the best overall deal, that could change in a month. Then what do you do? Move your account?

Concentrate, instead, on convenience and on dealing with a bank where it's possible to develop a personal relationship with one of the officers. Don't expect miracles—banks are banks— but nothing cuts through red tape like a little personal rapport.

See: Credit Unions.

BASEBALL CARDS, says a friend with $20,000 invested in 10,000 of them, have reached the tulip-bulb phase. All his cards, which would now cost about $50,000 to replace, are pre-1961 vintage. He's been collecting them ever since he was a kid. Unfortunately, his mom threw out most of *those* cards when he was off at camp one summer, which is where the $20,000 comes in (moms loom larger in all this than one would at first imagine).

It's no longer just a matter of little kids trading baseball cards back and forth or even of some of the old ones in good condition commanding big money. (My friend has a 1951 mint Mantle he says would go for anywhere from $600 to $1500.) It's gotten to the point where genuine adults are buying cases full of newly printed cards, as many as 12,000 to the case, and putting them into storage or trading them—unopened—as if they were cases of wine. Imagine the value someday of a case of cards that—though unopened—is assumed to contain approximately a dozen 1987 mint Dwight Goodens.

Although Topps is the big name in baseball cards—any kid knows that—two other companies, Fleer and Donruss, are of interest to collectors as well. No one wanted their cards when they were readily available several years ago, but then, allegedly—the companies deny it—they hit on printing up just a fraction of the number that had been ordered. That made them hard to get, and that made everybody want them, and that boosted sales.

Little of this has to do with baseball anymore and none of it, as far as I can tell, with chewing gum or tooth decay. But for the real story and up-to-the-minute market information, you'll want to subscribe to that *Barron's* of baseball cards, *Sports Collectors Digest* (700 East State St., Iola, WI 54990—$14.50 for 26 weekly issues). Cases of 12,000 current cards start at $140, but 1985 and 1986 cases—good years for baseball cards—already fetch $750 or more.

BOND FUNDS are mutual funds that invest in bonds. The question is: bonds of what maturity? And what quality? Taxable bonds or tax free? And what are they going to charge by way of a sales fee and annual management and administrative fees to invest your money? One percent may not sound like much (if that's what it is—and it can be even more), but if bonds are yielding 8% and this outfit is taking 1%, leaving you with 7%, that may be just 1% of your overall investment each year—but it's 12.5% of the annual income. Bond fund managers will tell you they can more than make up for that handicap by their expertise in selecting and trading the bonds. Pastry chefs will tell you that cannoli aren't fattening. At the very least, stick to no-load bond funds that charge a very low annual fee for expenses and administration.

See also: Unit Trusts.

BONDS are $1000 IOUs issued by corporations or governments and traded thereafter on the New York Stock Exchange (in the case of many corporate bonds) or over the counter. Bond interest is paid semiannually. If a bond has an 8% "coupon," that means it promises $80 a year interest—$40 every six months—until it matures. *Quel excitement.* A bond's "current yield" is its coupon —$80, in this example—divided by its market price. If you could buy the bond for just $800 in the open market (because the general level of interest rates had risen and no one was willing to pay $1000 for it), its current yield would be 10%—$80 a year on $800. Its "yield to maturity" would be higher, because it would reflect not just the current yield but expected appreciation, as it eventually rose from the $800 you paid to its full $1000 redemption value ("par").

"Yield to call" can be even more important than yield to maturity for a bond that pays high interest, because when interest rates fall, bond issuers like to do the same thing homeowners do: refinance. It may be fine to pay $1200 for a $1000 bond that yields $150 a year (say). That works out to a current yield of 12.5% ($150 a year on a $1200 investment). But if the bond can be called after just two more years—at its $1000 par value or perhaps a tad more—you wouldn't want to go near it. After adjusting for the $200 you'd lose when it was redeemed, its yield to call would work out to only 4.4% a year.

It's vital, in buying a bond, especially a bond that sells above par, to understand its call provisions—including some of the sneakier ones that may be buried down deep. Rather than worry about this, you may simply wish to stick to bonds that, because they were issued with low coupons when interest rates were low, currently sell substantially under par. If somebody wants to redeem for $1000 the bond you paid $720 for—well, worse things have happened.

An alternative to becoming a bond expert yourself is to stick with bond mutual funds. But even then you have to decide what type of bonds to buy. Corporate bonds are taxable; treasury bonds are subject to federal tax but not local income tax; municipal bonds are generally free of federal tax and their own local income tax but are more complicated than they used to be.

You also have to decide what sorts of maturities to go after—bonds maturing a few months from now, a few years from now, or in the year 2017—and how much risk to take. The two are related, because the longer the maturity, the more time there is for something to go wrong.

When you buy a bond, you subject yourself to two risks. The first, called *credit risk,* is that the bond issuer will go broke. You may get some or even all your money back eventually, but it's not going to be fun. The second risk, called *market risk,* is that the general level of interest rates will rise after you buy your bond, causing its value in the marketplace to fall. If newly issued bonds similar to yours pay $100 a year in interest—10%—who in his right mind would pay you $1000 for yours, which pays only $80? (On the other hand, the general level of interest rates could fall, causing your bond's value to rise.) You can't do much about the general level of interest rates (other than sticking with short-term bonds that will be redeemed soon for $1000 no matter what interest rates do), but you can protect yourself against credit risk by buying only high-quality bonds. Rather than rely on Moody's and Standard & Poor's ratings of corporate bonds, if it's safety you're after, I would stick to government bonds (or highly rated municipal bonds).

Safe bonds don't pay as much interest as riskier ones, and the overwhelming majority of risky bonds scrape through (or have so far, anyway), so if you can afford to diversify over a couple of dozen different issues, you may wish to go for more risk and a higher yield. The only problem is that it's a nuisance, and the spread involved buying and selling just a few thousand dollars' worth of any given bond can be very wide. More reason to do your bond investing through bond mutual funds.

Finally, note that bonds are quoted in cents on the dollar. A bond trading for $800 would be listed in the paper at "80." A bond quoted at "129⅜" would cost $1293.75.

If any of this is new to you, again, stick to bond funds. (Or as Humphrey Bogart said to the young Bulgarian girl trying to get exit visas for her and her newlywed husband to leave Casablanca: "You want my advice? Go back to Bulgaria.")

See also: Bond Funds; Convertible Bonds; Junk Bonds; Municipal Bonds; Original-Issue-Discount Bonds; Zero Coupon Bonds; Zero Coupon Convertible Bonds; and U.S. Savings Bonds (to which absolutely none of the foregoing applies).

BROADWAY SHOWS. People who invest in Broadway shows are called "angels." There is a reason for this.

CABLE TV DEALS. Once upon a time, these limited partnerships offered great tax advantages. Now you might be better off just buying stock in a cable TV company. Naturally, it all depends on the deal and the stock.

CALLS. See: Options.

CASH. Cash is variously meant to mean *cash,* as in dollar bills, tens, and twenties, or "cash equivalents"—things like money market funds or treasury bills that you could immediately turn into cash, but that have the added attraction of paying some interest until you do. To hold cash (of whichever variety) is to sit on the sidelines. As argued on page 105, this is frequently the wisest —but most difficult—thing to do.

CATS. A brand of zero coupon bond. See: STRIPS; Zero Coupon Bonds.

CERTIFICATES OF DEPOSIT. Remember the old savings account passbooks? With CD's you get higher interest but no passbook. They're no good if you're trying to put away $6 a week, but fine if your savings can be invested in larger increments. The more you invest and the longer you're willing to tie it up, the higher the rate of interest.

But should you tie up your money for six months or five years just to get a little higher rate of interest? The answer is "yes!" if having the money tied up helps you to keep from spending it.* Otherwise, how about treasury bonds instead, subject to no local income taxes and readily sold without penalty (except for a small commission and spread)? How about a conservative no-load bond fund? How about tax-free municipals?

(If you have an account at discount broker Charles Schwab & Co., you can call toll free and be quoted competitive CD rates from banks all over the country. Then, if you want to invest, Schwab can shoot the money straight from your account into the CD at no charge. Just don't entrust more than $100,000 to any one bank.)

CHARITY. Definitely one alternative for your money—but give wisely. Your donation is an investment of society's scarce capital. Do you want it to go toward keeping a drought-stricken family alive or toward resurfacing a prep school's tennis courts? Save the Children or Save the Whales? These choices sound much easier than they are. Perhaps the main thing is that your dollars, wherever you direct them, not be wasted.

Just as it's rarely wise to invest in something brought to your attention by bulk mail, so is it risky to give money to a charity based on a slick or plaintive solicitation. One of the more remarkable examples was a group that granted the wishes of dying children. According to *The New York Times,* the group raised $237,000 in 1984. Of that, $10,000 went to grant wishes; the rest was spent on "professional fund-raising organizations, salaries, car rentals, jewelry, rent, unsecured personal loans, a VCR, and a videotape entitled *Sex Games.*"

Write the National Charities Information Bureau for its free *Wise Giving Guide* (19 Union Square West, New York, NY 10003). Or call the Council of Better Business Bureaus (703-276-0100) for reports on specific charities or for a free copy of *Give but Give Wisely,* which rates charities across 22 parameters.

---

*The answer may also be yes if you're over 59½ and this is IRA money. The law is that no penalty can be imposed on early termination of a CD in such circumstances. Check with your bank to be sure this is still the law. If it is, you might as well get the highest rate.

One key factor, naturally, is the proportion of your dollar eaten up in fund raising and overhead. But with an organization like Mothers Against Drunk Driving, where the fund-raising expense is a whopping 38% of total revenue (versus 2% for the American Red Cross), keep in mind that the act of fund raising itself— sending out all those heart-rending letters—gets the word out and builds a constituency, which is the point of the organization in the first place.

A charity I've long recommended, though it's hell on our bal- ance of trade, is the Foster Parents Plan (155 Plan Way, Warwick, RI 02887). If you can spare $22 a month, it will have a real impact on an entire family in the Third World.

For large contributions, consider giving appreciated property or securities—that $3000 worth of Gap Stores stock you bought for $500 years ago. By giving it to the charity directly instead of selling it first, you avoid ever having to pay tax on the long-term capital gain. Be careful never to do this with property in which you have a *short*-term gain (you'll be allowed a deduction only for its cost, not its current value). And note that under the new tax law, your untaxed capital gain ($2500 in this example) becomes a preference item that may, along with others, subject you to the alternative minimum tax.*

Rather than wait weeks or months to receive the actual stock certificate from your broker and then mail it to the Fund for a Bigger Little League, give your broker written instructions to transfer the stock immediately from your account to the account

---

*Under the new law, the alternative minimum tax is a flat 21% of your "alternative minimum taxable income." If that works out to more than your regular income tax, you pay it instead. Only a few hundred thousand high- income taxpayers are likely to have to, but you could be one of them if you have a complicated tax return filled with deductions that are okay in figuring your regular tax, but *not* okay in figuring your AMT income. These include the appreciated portion of a charitable contribution; state and local income and prop- erty taxes; the interest and tax-shelter deductions still allowed in part in figuring your regular tax (65% for 1987, 40% for 1988, and so on); the extra home mortgage interest that comes from taking out a larger mortgage on your home— and more.

If even without being able to take these deductions your taxable income adds up to less than $112,500 ($150,000 joint), you should be okay, because you get

of the Fund (which is easy for him to set up). He should then call the Fund for you, advise them of the gift, and solicit instructions for disposition of the stock. Do they want to hold it? Do they want to sell it? In case they're not sure, have your broker give them this hint: They want to sell it.

Discount brokers probably won't go through all this for you, but a good full-service broker will.

And this final note. One of the times you may have the most money to give and miss it the least is when you're dead. Warren Buffett, whose fortune is already estimated at $1.6 billion and which will be $152 billion if it keeps growing for the next 25 years as it has for the last 25, has already told his kids they'll get almost none of it. It's his feeling, shared by many others, that to do otherwise is to deprive children of the chance to make it on their own, in their own way. So what you may wish to do is leave the bulk of your empire to trusts that benefit your spouse while he or she is alive and that then revert to the charities of your choice.

You can actually get a head start on all of this, and a meaningful tax benefit if you're of reasonably advanced years, by setting up a "charitable lead trust." You get the income from that trust while you're alive; the charity gets the principal at your demise; the IRS allows you a current tax deduction for the *present value* of that future gift. If you're only 35, the present value will be negligible (the promise of $50,000 40 years from now isn't worth much in today's dollars). But if you're 65 or 70, the deduction could be for as much as half the ultimate value of the gift. The IRS has actuarial tables and a "discount rate" that govern such transactions; big charities will have someone on staff who can answer a lot of your questions before you actually get to the point of calling your attorney or tax adviser.

---

to knock off $30,000 ($40,000 joint) before subjecting what's left to the 21% tax. But that automatic exemption shrinks by 25 cents for each dollar by which your AMT income exceeds $112,500 ($150,000 joint), disappearing altogether once it reaches $232,500 ($310,000 joint). Even then, you won't have a problem unless you have so many deductions that, far from paying 28% of your income in federal tax, as envisioned by the new law for 1988 and beyond, you'd be paying less than 21%. Beneath that, the AMT kicks in. And why shouldn't it? The only truly obnoxious thing about the tax is its complexity, not its amount.

CLOSED-END FUNDS are mutual funds that sell a set number of shares to the public—15 million shares at $10 each, say—and then close the doors to further investment. Once sold to the public, the shares trade in the open market, just as if 15 million shares of General Motors had been sold, except that instead of shares in a car company, these are shares in a pot of other stocks and bonds. Technically, you'd expect each such share to sell for its proportionate share of the pot, rising and falling as the value of the pot increases and shrinks. But in the real world, these shares will sometimes rise to a premium over their "net asset value"—if the public thinks the managers of the fund are so good that it's worth paying a little extra to get in on it—or, more often, fall to a discount. The discount may run to 10% or 20% or even 30%, which is like selling dollar bills for 90 or 80 or 70 cents, except that with a dollar bill you can always get 100 pennies or 10 dimes. With shares in a closed-end fund, you can only get what someone is willing to pay you for them. *Invest only in closed-end funds selling at a significant discount.* For one thing, you get a dollar's worth of assets working for you for only 80 or 90 cents. That alone is a big plus. For another, the discount might someday narrow, particularly if someone takes it into his head to buy control of the fund and convert it to an *open*-end fund. (With an open-end fund, you can redeem your shares for 100% of their true proportionate value.) The obvious problem with buying closed-ends at a *premium* (on the initial public offering, say, when an underwriting fee may be added to the cost of the shares) is that once the excitement causing the premium subsides, the premium is likely to turn into a discount. Even if it doesn't, you've paid more than a dollar to get 100 cents working for you.

There's actually a sound reason for closed-ends to trade at a discount. They're burdened by a handicap—namely, the 1% or more in management and administrative fees that are subtracted each year. If the stocks in the fund grew by 10% a year including dividends, the net asset value of the fund itself would grow at only 9%, after expenses.

Funds may also trade at a well-deserved discount if their managers have demonstrated a consistent talent for making poor investments.

And they may trade at a discount if, through making *good* investments, they've piled up large unrealized capital gains in stocks they've not yet sold. When those gains are finally taken, whoever's holding shares in the fund will have to pay tax—even if she just bought the shares yesterday and realized no gain herself. (Such funds are thus best suited for a tax-sheltered portfolio.)

You can find the prices of many closed-end funds, also called "publicly traded funds," in the paper as you would any stock. *The Wall Street Journal* publishes a separate list each Monday showing the premium to or discount from net asset value at which each is trading.

Closed-ends offer two conceptual advantages over open-end funds. First, as mentioned, when trading at a substantial discount, a closed-end is like a *less-than-no-load* fund. You get $1 worth of assets working for you for 80 cents. That's never true of an open-end fund. Second, closed-end fund managers need not worry that, in a down market, they will be flooded with redemptions, forcing them to dump holdings at what may be exactly the wrong time. So they may be able to do a better job managing the fund. True, they don't have the same incentive as open-end funds. (With an open-end fund, good performance draws new investors, swelling the management fee; poor performance leads to redemptions and lower fees.) But they still have an incentive, because increasing the value of the fund also increases the management fee. And there is the ego factor—particularly now that "personality" closed-ends have appeared on the market along with the faceless institutional funds.

Four such closed-ends issued to the public in 1986 were the Zweig Fund, Gabelli Equity Trust, Growth Stock Outlook Trust, and Schafer Value Trust, managed by Martin Zweig, Mario Gabelli, Charles Allmon, and David Schafer, well-known figures in the investment world. It would have been foolish to buy shares in these new funds when they were first offered to the public, because the offering price included about a 7% premium to pay the costs of selling the issue to the public. But soon the funds were trading on the New York Stock Exchange sans any sales fee and, in fact, at 10% *discounts* to their net asset values. For 90 cents you could thus have purchased $1 worth of these funds' assets and had that $1 managed by one of these pros, to boot. There was always the very real risk these discounts would widen further (or that the pros would pick lousy stocks or that the market would collapse altogether—or all three). But for a portion of the money you can afford to risk in the stock market, these closed-end funds, *when trading at significant discounts* to their net asset values, make sense.

To find out which of the many publicly traded funds may offer the most intriguing values at any given time, write Thomas J. Herzfeld & Co. and ask for a complimentary copy of its monthly $200-a-year closed-end fund newsletter (7800 Red Road, S. Miami, FL 33143). One he was recommending in the spring of 1987 was Worldwide Equities Ltd., then trading on the Toronto exchange at about a 20% discount to fully diluted net asset value. Interestingly, this fund is managed by the same John Templeton organization famous for its huge open-end funds that people clamor to pay an 8.5% load to buy into. (Not surprisingly, the Templeton telephone sales staff either doesn't know about, or won't discuss, this closed-end no-load fund. "Oh! You must mean our Templeton World Fund," they say. But at least as of this writing, the Templeton group really was its manager.)

Really savvy investors—this is *not* for most people—might consider shorting shares in closed-end funds that sell at a premium when first offered, assuming that that premium will disappear and turn negative fairly soon after the sales effort ends. To hedge the bet, lest the market as a whole zoom, you'd buy a like amount of stock in another closed-end fund (with similar kinds of holdings) selling at a discount.

Typically, the discounts in closed-ends widen in bear markets and narrow when everyone is smiling.

See also: Country Funds; Dual-Purpose Funds.

CMOs are collateralized mortgage obligations. This is the generic term for any securities backed by mortgages. The best known are Ginnie Maes (see page 209).

COINS. If you're buying American Eagles or Canadian Maple Leafs for their gold content or bags of silver dimes or quarters for their silver content, try to pay as little as possible above the actual value of the metal.

See also: Rare Coins; Gold; Silver.

COLLECTIBLES. The real trick is to find the next "collectible"—something that could appeal to people with money that has not yet benefited from an organized collectors' market. But the best advice is to collect what you enjoy collecting. Life is not a business.

See also: Baseball Cards; Comic Books; Rare Coins; Scripophily.

COMIC BOOKS should be wrapped in three-mil Mylar, stored in acid-free archival boxes, and kept in a cool, fairly dry (not superdry) dark place, says Cambridge, Mass., investment strategist Donald W. Mitchell, who keeps the 100,000 or so he's bought recently at 50 degrees. Some of his comics are old single copies; many are new, bought in bulk. He bought 3000 copies of the first in a new series of Superman comics last year (you get a 40% to 60% discount off the cover price when you buy in bulk) and figures they will be worth a pretty penny for his kids one distant day.

The primary purchasers of comic books, not counting the collectors, are 18- to 27-year-old American males and the Japanese. Comics are much bigger in Japan than in the United States—a best-seller there, like the "Lone Wolf and Cub" samurai series the Japanese have recently begun exporting here, will sell six million copies an issue. In the United States, best-sellers rarely hit one million.

As you probably know, comic books fall into five primary grading categories: mint, near mint, fine, good, and poor. What I never realized is that even most brand-new straight-off-the-presses books qualify only as near mint because of printing imperfections.

Mitchell bought a single copy of one of the very earliest Superman series in fine condition for $400 last year and figures it's worth $1000 today. "The number of collectors is growing rapidly, and with it, the prices," says Mitchell, who holds two Harvard degrees and in real life consults to multibillion-dollar corporations.

To profit from America's love affair with semiliteracy yourself, you will want to subscribe to the weekly *Comics Buyer's Guide* ($12.95 for six months, 700 East State Street, Iola, WI 54990) and write away for the annual *Official Overstreet Comic Book Price Guide* ($11.95, 780 Hunt Cliff Drive, NW, Cleveland, TN 37311).

Figure you should be able to buy a well-bargained-for comic from a dealer at a little under the *Overstreet* price—and then sell it back the next day, if you had to, for perhaps half. Private transactions avoid the dealer spread but may entail advertising and other costs.

COMMODITIES. "Robert Hocker told a federal court in Wyoming that he didn't even know what a commodity was when a broker for First Commodity Corp. of Boston phoned in 1983. But after listening to the broker's tales of huge profits to be made in silver," reports *The Wall Street Journal,* "the unemployed oil-field worker sent the firm more than $55,000. First Commodity took 39% of his money in fees the first day, then lost most of the rest in volatile futures markets. Mr. Hocker eventually got back $1387.64, about 2.5% of his original investment."

If you speculate in commodities—which have come to include not just agricultural products but metals, foreign currencies, interest rate futures, and stock market index futures—*you will lose your money.* In fact, it is even possible to lose more than you bet. I could tell you a lot more about commodities, *but this is all you need to know.*

COMMODITY FUNDS. With a commodity fund you pay dearly for the privilege of having someone else lose your money for you. The good news is that ordinarily you can't lose more than you bet.

Commodity funds are far more risky than stock or bond funds. Sadly, you are not rewarded for taking that extra risk. In any given year, of course, a few of the commodity funds will do spectacularly well. But their prior performance says very little about how they will do in the future. A study by Professors Edwin J. Elton, Martin J. Gruber, and Joel C. Rentzler, published in the April 1987 *American Association of Individual Investors Journal,* found that the average annual return for all public commodity funds in existence from July 1979 through June 1985 was *minus* 4.35%.

COMMON STOCKS. Over the long run, common stock has always outperformed safer investments. But do you have time to wait? If so, a periodic investment in two or three carefully selected no-load mutual funds (or closed-end funds selling at a discount) is probably your best bet.

Common stock used to represent ownership in a company. Alone, your few shares might not count for much, but along with tens of thousands of other shareholders, you owned the company. Management worked for you. In practical terms, however—witness countless examples over the last several years (a number of them beautifully documented by Benjamin J. Stein in *Barron's*)—management has arrogated control to itself. Its first interest is its own interest.

You and your fellow shareholders could sue your employees (the management) for thumbing their noses at you, but it's not a threat that worries them much—they are protected by liability insurance purchased at your expense.

CONDOS that were selling in Aspen for $240,000 in 1980 were selling for $160,000 in 1986. Condos that were selling in Houston for $70,000 in 1986 were selling for $35,000 in 1987. The lesson here may be: Don't buy condos in places everyone thinks prices can only go up forever (wasn't Houston supposed to be the most populous city in the country by the year 2000?). Bought right, however, a condo can be both a rent-yielding inflation hedge and your own personal time-share. After you retire, if it's in a state like Florida, it can become your own little tax haven as well. (Did you know Miami has the cleanest air of any major city in the country?)

Before buying a condo, be sure to have a good accountant go over the annual statement of the condo association and perhaps the minutes of the last few board meetings. Some condos are "troubled." Because not all the units sell, less is collected in common charges than is needed to maintain the building properly. That can lead some owners not to pay assessments out of protest, which can lead to even worse maintenance—and so it spirals until a hurricane comes along and exposes the developer for the corner-cutting inspector-bribing lowlife that he was (did you read *Condominium*?).

CONVERTIBLE BONDS and convertible preferred stocks yield almost as much as regular bonds and preferreds, in most cases, but may be converted into shares of the underlying common stock. If the stock runs up wildly, the bond will climb, too.

You can convert the bonds any time you want but ordinarily would not, because they almost always trade at a premium to their conversion value. The bond might be convertible into 40 shares of a $20 stock, which puts its conversion value at $800. But because it yields more in interest than the stock yields in dividends, and because the bond has preference over the stock if the company should go bankrupt, the bond might be trading at $850 or $1000 or even more. You *could* convert it into $800 worth of stock (if you were an idiot), but you would be better off selling it in the open market instead.

Convertibles, and the no-load mutual funds that invest in them, are a way to spread funds over two or three prongs at once. If we have deflation, and the underlying companies don't go broke, the high interest you've locked in will look great. If we have prosperity and stocks rise, your convertibles will share in at least some of the appreciation. If we have mild inflation, your convertibles may not fare too badly, either. After all, stocks used to be an inflation hedge—and over the long run probably still are.

CO-OPS are like condos, only less liquid. With a co-op you don't buy an apartment, you buy shares in the cooperative association that owns the building and lease the apartment from the association. The association has the right to disapprove any sale of your shares without explanation. It may be obvious that the members of the board nixed your buyer because he was handicapped or she was Oriental or he was Jewish or she was spread-eagled nude across 17 pages of *Penthouse;* but so long as they don't acknowledge it, they can't be touched by civil rights statutes.

COUNTRY FUNDS. The U.S. stock market is not the only game in town. Sometimes other markets offer better values. "Country" mutual funds are a convenient way to diversify your holdings over more than just U.S. securities. These closed-end funds (see page 195), traded on the New York or American stock exchanges, include the Mexico Fund, the France Fund, the Germany Fund, the Korea Fund, the Italy Fund, the Scandinavia Fund, and the First Australia Fund. But beware. In buying shares, you are betting on several things: that the country's stock market will rise, or at least not fall; that the country's currency will rise, or at least not fall; that the discount of the fund will narrow, or at least not widen; and that the clowns managing the fund will do a reasonably good job choosing the foreign stocks to invest in.

Not all these things have to go right for you to make money. The French market could fall 5%, but if francs gained 10% relative to the dollar, shares in the France Fund would probably rise. And vice versa.

The Korea Fund, in the summer of 1987, seemed no bargain. Up from $14 a share in October 1985 to $85 a year and a half later, it sold at a huge premium to net asset value. You were buying $1 worth of Korean stocks—themselves up dramatically over the same time period—for $2.25.

Rather than bet on a single country, you may prefer one of the many global mutual funds. They try to decide for you which countries offer the best values at any given time.

See also: Global Funds; Closed-End Funds; No-Load Funds.

COVERED CALLS. Say you own 100 shares of Johnson & Johnson, which is trading at 90. You think that at 90 the stock is awfully high; but you think, too, that it's a great company. You really wouldn't want to sell it and have to pay capital gains tax on your enormous profit (you bought the shares in 1983 at 28), so you do the opposite of buying a call on Johnson & Johnson—you sell a call. You give some nameless, faceless buyer the right to buy your 100 shares at, say, 95 any time between now and the third Thursday in October. In return, you receive $287.50, less a commission to your broker. This is called "writing a covered call." Should J&J rise above 95 and the call you sold be exercised, you're covered—you have the stock sitting right in your account, waiting to be sent off to its new owner. (The truly self-destructive sell "naked" calls.)

You figure: Hey. I get any appreciation in the stock up to $95; I get the dividend; and, to light a fire under my rate of return, I get this $287.50. In fact, I get it maybe four times a year, writing 90-day options each time—an extra $1000 or so a year (after commissions) on my $9000 of J&J stock. That adds 11.1% a year to my return.

Writing covered calls is perceived as the conservative way to play the options game, on the intuitively appealing notion that if option buyers lose money, it must be option sellers who make it. But that notion is wrong. It is options *brokers* who make money. The problem with writing covered calls is that you retain virtually all the risk while eliminating all chance of a really exciting gain. What if J&J drops off a cliff and you're still holding it? What good's a lousy $287.50 if the value of your shares drops from $9000 to $5750? Or what if J&J shoots from $90 a share to $135 in a month? You make the first five points of profit but give up everything from $95 to $135—$4000 on a 100-share option—all in return for that lousy $287.50 (less commission, less taxes).

Like most low-risk systems, writing covered calls works well under ordinary circumstances but kills you at the extremes.

See also: Naked Options.

CREDIT UNIONS often offer better deals than banks—and, if you're not already a credit union member, there may be one you can join.

Did you know Eastern Airlines Ionosphere Club members are currently eligible to join Eastern's giant (federally insured) credit union? In mid-1987 it was charging 7.9% for a 36-month car loan, versus 9.9% from a typical bank; 9% with 1.5 points for a 30-year fixed rate mortgage versus 10% and 2.5 points from a bank. Its $18-a-year MasterCard charged about 4% less than most, and its interest-bearing checking required no minimum balance. It even offers members a toll-free line to provide car shoppers with factory invoice prices on new cars and blue book prices on used cars, to help assure they're getting a good deal. For information, write the Eastern Credit Union (Box 028532, Miami, FL 33102) and then, should you want to join, call Eastern to join the Ionosphere Club first (cost: $105—but membership apparently need not be renewed to remain a member of the credit union).

DEBENTURES. Bonds you have to take out and clean every night. They are backed by the general credit of the issuer rather than any specific assets.

DIAMONDS are great if you're fleeing somewhere on foot. Otherwise, they're all but indistinguishable from fake diamonds (so you may as well save a fortune, if it's the dazzle you're after) and more difficult to appraise and sell than gold (so you may as well buy gold, if you want a disaster hedge).

DUAL-PURPOSE FUNDS. These are closed-end mutual funds with a twist. They are issued with two classes of stock, income shares and capital shares, and with a specific duration, after which the game ends and everybody goes home. If you buy the income shares, you get all the dividends from the fund's investments and, in 10 or 12 years, when the fund is liquidated, you get your original investment back (assuming it's there to give back). If you buy the capital shares, you get no dividends but all appreciation of the fund, if any, above its original value. In the meantime, both classes of shares trade freely in the market, in case you want to get out early.

At the very least, it's a great marketing concept. Here were all these neglected stocks growing too slowly to attract much attention as growth stocks and yielding too little to attract much attention for income accounts—and so, arguably, selling for less than they really should have. Now comes the dual fund to buy stocks like this, effectively doubling the yield for those who buy the income shares (but forfeit any appreciation) and doubling the capital gains potential for those who buy the capital shares (but forfeit all dividends); so suddenly there's something attractive here for everybody, including the mutual fund sponsor and its sales force, who between them may take 8.5% off the top for selling the deal and then something each year for managing it.

If it sounds complicated, it's not. Just picture that you and a friend pooled $45 each to buy one $90 share of Ford. Instead of your splitting Ford's $3 dividend equally—a paltry 3.3%—you, for your $45, would get the whole thing. That would be a somewhat less paltry 6.7% on your money (and the dividend could rise). Ten years from now, you and your friend agree, you will sell the stock and split the first $90 of the proceeds to get your money back. But everything above that he'll get to keep. Different strokes for different folks. If Ford is $200 a share in 10 years, he'll get his $45 back plus $110 more.

Once these dual-purpose funds are sold to the public, both classes of shares trade publicly. The capital shares are often listed as trading at a substantial discount to their net asset value, but that doesn't necessarily make them a bargain. You've got to wait for liquidation of the fund before that value is actually paid out.

Americus Trust units work the same way, only with single stocks. AT&T was the first to be split into "prime" and "score" components (the former for conservative investors willing to give up most of the potential price appreciation; the latter for swingers happy to give up dividends in hope of scoring a big gain). That was in 1983. Since then prime and score Americus Trust units have begun trading on two dozen other issues. Ask your broker.

See: Closed-End Funds.

FANNIE MAES. See: Ginnie Maes.

FARMLAND, unless you're a farmer, is an investment that violates two basic principles of personal finance: "Never invest in anything you know nothing about" and "Never try to run a business from a thousand miles away." Farmland that supports a farmer may not be sufficiently bountiful also to support a farm manager (to look after that farmer) and the mortgage you took out to purchase the land in the first place.

An awful lot of marginal farmland was sold in the early eighties to New Yorkers eager to depreciate the pivot irrigation systems the land required and even more eager to deduct the interest on the loans they took to make the purchase. Then they found that revenue from the farmland failed to meet their interest payments, and that land in need of irrigation was not much sought after in a grain glut.

You can now buy that same farmland from them, or from whoever foreclosed on it, for a fraction of the price. See chapter 12.

FRANCHISES account for more than 300,000 successful businesses in the United States, but also for what's been estimated to be as much as $500 million a year in losses. Before you invest your life savings in one of the 2000-plus franchise opportunities available, ranging from hemorrhoid clinics to auto repair, ask yourself some questions. Have you the energy to work 60 or 80 hours a week? Can you stomach detailed regulations governing the conduct of your business? Have you the capital to tide you over if profitability takes longer to achieve than the franchiser says it will? Are the guidance and brand name and advertising support and special recipes or equipment worth what the franchiser is charging—or could you set up a successful tanning salon without the help or expense of the franchiser?

Then ask the franchiser some questions. Better still, request a list of all its franchisees and call several at random to find out, in detail, what to expect. Don't settle for a few carefully selected success stories. Ascertain what proportion of the franchiser's revenues derives from selling franchises (something you won't be doing) and what proportion from selling its product or service (something that you will). Find out just what kind of training and support you can expect. Check with the Better Business Bureau, state agencies, and the Federal Trade Commission to see what kinds of complaints, if any, have been lodged.

"In short," concludes *Forbes*'s Ellen Paris, "the franchise business is like any other. Think of it as easy money, and you'll probably lose yours." But do your homework and work like crazy, and you could do very nicely.

FREDDIE MACS. See: Ginnie Maes.

FREQUENT-FLIER MILES. I once earned two free trips on Pan Am by flying just 9,050 actual miles but accumulating 41,082 "bonus" miles. So I'm hardly one who's down on frequent-flier programs because he neglected to sign up at the outset. No, I was in there flapping my greedy little wings from the start.

But just how much is a frequent-flier mile worth?

There are a lot of ways to figure this, but very roughly, 50,000 miles equals two round-trip tickets to Hawaii. Two round trips to Hawaii—again very roughly—equal $1000. (You could spend a lot more, but if it were your money, you wouldn't.) So what we're talking here—$1000 for 50,000 miles—is two cents a mile.

Or less. If you accept Eastern's offer of a lifetime membership in its Ionosphere Club for 100,000 miles (there being some question whether your lifetime or the airline's is the limiting factor), you are trading 100,000 miles for a $775 membership—less than a cent a mile.

As a rough rule of thumb, each mile is worth a penny or two.

For tax purposes, frequent-flier awards are considered discounts from the price of the tickets used to earn them. If you buy nine tickets and get the tenth free, that's no more "income" than is the fourth bar of soap you get free with the first three. But if your *employer* buys the tickets and you get the free soap, you're supposed to declare its value as income and pay tax on it.

So far, the government has had the great good grace not to bother with this, any more than it attempts to tax the value of personal phone calls made by employees at work or other modest perks of modern life. And rightly so. Here you and your companion were about to take a weekend up at the lake—travel cost: $18—but since you've got these free first-class tickets, you go to

San Diego instead. You *never* would have gone there for the weekend on your own $2240 (the cost of the trip in first class). So are the tickets really worth $2240? And how would you tax a first-class upgrade—an award that theoretically turns a $299 seat into a $900 seat, but that actually buys you just a couple of free drinks, some legroom, and hors d'oeuvres?

Hard as it is to assign a cash value to frequent-flier miles, a handful of companies have. If you'd like to sell your miles—or fly first class for half price—check the ads you may find in the *Wall Street Journal* classifieds—but beware. The airlines threaten loss of all your benefits if you sell your awards, and may not honor tickets they believe were sold in violation of their rules.

Many airlines do allow you to transfer (though not to sell) your awards. But you have to do it *before* you accept the award. Once your name is on the coupon, it's nontransferable.

Arguably a genteel form of commercial bribery (I'll give you a free trip if you get your employer to buy from me, even though he could get a better price elsewhere), these programs weaken price competition. But while they're around, it's foolish not to sign up for them . . . and equally foolish to waste much time or money in pursuit of an extra 1000 frequent flier miles, worth $10 or $20. I should know. I do it all the time.

FUTURES. See: Commodities.

GEMS. This one I love. Remember the rockhound who paid $10 for a stone at a show in Tucson that turned out to be the world's largest star sapphire? Is that a great story or what!

Worldwide news coverage notwithstanding, it wasn't a sapphire after all.

"According to several gem experts," reports *The Washington Post,* "the stone bought for $10 by Texan Roy Whetstine and appraised by one dealer at $2.28 million is nothing more than a rock. John Sampson White, curator of the National Gem and Mineral Collection at the Smithsonian Institution, told the *Los Angeles Times* that the stone was not the world's largest star sapphire but 'an insignificant stone.'

" 'The unusual and peculiar thing is that none of the people in any of the national press ever questioned its value,' said Cosmo Altobelli, appraisal committee chairman for the American Gem Society."

And to think I was just about to offer two million six.

GINNIE MAES are Government National Mortgage Association (GNMA) bonds and the subject of much hoopla in magazine and TV advertising. "High yields, government guaranteed." What's not clear to many people is that it's not the high yields that are government guaranteed, only the mortgages that underlie them.

Say you take out a home mortgage at 10% interest for 30 years. Without your even knowing, your bank may quickly sell it—and the others it wrote this week—to the Government National Mortgage Association. Your bank gets to keep the points it charged to make the loan; plus it will get a small service fee for collecting your monthly payments and funneling them to Ginnie Mae. But otherwise, it's been reimbursed by Ginnie Mae for that $100,000 check it wrote you and can lend the money all over again to somebody else. It's passed the loan off to Ginnie Mae.

Well, Ginnie Mae doesn't want to hold it, either. Instead, it throws your mortgage into a pool with hundreds or thousands of similar ones—perhaps $100 million worth this week (it's only Tuesday)—and sells them to investors. An insurance company might take $5 million, a pension fund might take $10 million, a mutual fund that specializes in Ginnie Maes might take $1 million—and so on.

A few hours later the pool is sold, and Ginnie Mae has its $100 million back, available to buy more mortgages. As for the $100 million it just sold, Ginnie Mae guarantees that all the interest and principal due on the mortgages will be paid to the investors (even if you personally fall a month behind on your loan). For this guarantee, and for funneling the money to the investors, it takes its own little sliver.

Once they've been packaged and sold to the public, Ginnie Maes trade like any other security. You can buy a piece of a Ginnie Mae pool through your broker (minimum: $25,000 face value). Or you can buy Ginnie Maes through Ginnie Mae mutual funds or unit trusts and, for what's usually a stiff fee, leave the selection and record keeping to someone else.

But before you do, understand that Ginnie Maes (and their cousins Fannie Maes and Freddie Macs) are tricky. Unlike normal bonds, they have no set maturity date. A little principal is paid back every month, as people pay down their mortgages; then every once in a while a big chunk of principal gets paid back when someone pays *off* his mortgage.

One consequence is that each monthly check you get is a blend of interest, which is taxable, and a return of your investment, which is not. That makes for checks in differing amounts each month and complicated record keeping.

Another consequence is that unsophisticated investors see a $312.34 monthly check and think of it all as a return on their investment—a high yield. Actually, some portion of it each month will be a return *of* their investment, not "yield" at all—no matter what some of the ads say.

If you buy into a pool of 30-year mortgages that were written at 13.5%, you have to assume, if mortgages are currently being written at 10%, that most of your investment will be paid back quickly, as homeowners refinance these loans. What's more, the price you have to pay to buy into such a pool will reflect today's lower interest rates. You won't be getting 13.5% interest on your money, any more than you'd get 15% by buying a 15% 30-year treasury bond that was issued in 1982. Such a bond will sell far above its $1000 maturity value because it pays $150 a year interest at a time when newly issued bonds might be paying only $80. The difference is that with a treasury bond, when you pay more than its $1000 face value, you know the $150 annual payments will last through the year 2012. With a participation in a Ginnie Mae pool, there's no telling how long the interest payments will keep up.

Two overall points may be helpful. The first is that, because of this extra complication and uncertainty, Ginnie Maes may often yield—truly—1% or so more than similarly safe investments of roughly equal (albeit more precise) maturity. So don't rule them out.

But at the same time, the extra complication gives the marketers of Ginnie Mae funds, and brokers, a fertile field for—let's just call it "unintentional misrepresentation." It also makes for wide spreads if you go to buy, or particularly to sell, Ginnie Maes directly. Better to buy only if you plan to hold on and not sell.

Invest in Ginnie Maes only if you understand how they work and what you're getting; only if you can avoid significant sales and management fees; and only if, after subtracting the local income tax you'll have to pay, the interest they yield is better than you could get from treasuries (which are local tax free).

GLOBAL FUNDS invest in securities anywhere, including the United States, as opposed to "international" funds that invest anywhere except the United States. See also: Country Funds.

GOLD. Considering how little there *is* of it—they say all that's ever been mined would fit in a cube the height of the Washington Monument—there are an awful lot of different ways to *bet* on it: bullion, coins (the American Eagle, the Canadian Maple Leaf, Krugerrands), rare coins, Rolex watches, mining stocks (South African or North American; speculative or producing), mining stock mutual funds, stocks in companies with lots of gold in inventory (jewelry retailers, Handy & Harmon), options on gold stocks, gold futures—even options on gold futures.

Unless you're skilled at grading mint states (when it comes to coin grading, "shiny" just begins to scratch the surface), I'd be ever so careful buying gold coins for much above their actual melt-down value. Instead, you may want to get your gold for as close to market price as possible (the smallest-possible spread) with the lowest-possible carrying cost (have you checked out the price of safe deposit boxes lately?) and the greatest ease of sale (you really don't want to have to get the stuff assayed). To that end, many investors now choose gold certificates—representing gold they never actually see—issued by banks like Citicorp and Security Pacific and brokerage firms like Shearson American Express and E. F. Hutton. It doesn't jingle when you unlock the vault to count it, and biting it just chews up the certificates—but if you've got to buy the sterile stuff in the first place, this may be the most practical way to do it. Unless, that is, the banks collapse and the captain of the boat taking you to Argentina, where you'll be safe, truly expected 100 ounces of *gold* for his trouble, not some E. F. Hutton certificate.

See also: Rare Coins; Silver; pages 117–119.

HIGH TECH. The paradox of high-tech investments is that they are probably the most important that can be made and in some ways the most spectacularly exciting (which would you rather fund: a new chain of doughnut shops or a cure for cankers?), but—unless you're an accomplished techie yourself, and perhaps even then—they're a tough way to make money. Ordinarily, the excitement of high-tech investments is already discounted in their price. Only if you are exceptionally good at foretelling the technological future have you much of a shot at guessing which bio-tech company selling at 200 times earnings will be the one that someday justifies that multiple and more. If you are a laser engineer, you may see an opportunity to invest in one of your company's customers or suppliers—or even to invest $5000 in a colleague's start-up idea. But civilians are probably best off leaving the high-tech-investment decisions to their no-load mutual fund managers.

HOUSES. Cozier than a bar of gold, a home is a good inflation hedge. And inflation or no, if you buy it with a 15-year mortgage, it's a good form of forced savings. But buy a home only if you want one. Strictly as investments, there are alternatives that are far more liquid and less trouble.

See also: Real Estate.

INDEX FUNDS. Most Wall Street pros (and most amateurs) generally do a little worse than the Standard & Poor's 500 average. This has been shown repeatedly, and derives from the fact that their performance is dragged down by transaction costs—commissions and spreads. If it were not for these, the average money manager—since he and his colleagues pretty much *are* the market—would do about average. Instead, though they're typically paid six-figure salaries (one of the costs that hurts their performance), they do a little worse than average. So why not just *buy* the average? Index funds are mutual funds designed to do just that. They simply buy all the stocks that make up the average (or else a representative sample) and then sit pat. They incur no further transaction costs.

The best such fund may be Vanguard Index Trust (800-662-7447), which charges no sales fee and barely more than a quarter of 1% annual management fee to mirror the Standard & Poor's 500 index. Rushmore's no-load Stock Market Index Plus (800-343-3355) charges almost three times Vanguard's management fee—.75% a year—but tries to improve its performance by buying index options. In 1986, it beat the S&P 100 by two percentage points, even after subtracting its management fee. But there's no assurance that in some other year the options trading might not hurt rather than help.

This a very simple concept but profound: just by investing all the money you have earmarked for the stock market in the Vanguard Index Trust, you will generally do about as well as or better than most bank trust departments, mutual fund managers, and private investors—with far less effort.

INDEX FUTURES are a way to gamble on the direction of the market as a whole. The most popular racetrack is the Chicago Mercantile Exchange, because that's where the various S&P 500 contracts run. They've got names like "the June contract" and "the July contract." Other, less popular index futures race elsewhere, such as the Kansas City Exchange, home to the Value Line Index futures contract. Sooner or later, you will lose your money.

See also: Commodities.

INDEX OPTIONS are a way to bet on index futures without risking more than you bet. The most popular option is the OEX (its symbol), traded on the CBOE (the Chicago Board Options Exchange), which is just like a call on a stock, only this stock is called the S&P 100 (the Standard & Poor's 100 index).

I refuse to try to make any of this comprehensible (your broker can send you pamphlets and brochures, if you insist), because the only people who make money with options in the long run are the people who send you the pamphlets and brochures.

INSIDE INFORMATION. I know *nothing*.

IPOs (initial public offerings) are new issues—stock in private companies whose owners have decided to sell shares to the public. Sometimes they do this to raise funds for future growth; sometimes they do it just to cash in; sometimes it's a combination of both. Whatever their reason, once the money is raised they immediately resume acting as if they owned the whole thing. But that's another story.

In bear markets, IPOs are few and far between. When the market's frothy, just about anything can go public, with customers clamoring to buy simply because they've seen other recent new issues rise.

Imagine, then, the frenzy over a new issue like Genentech, the biotech firm, which actually warrants excitement. Genentech went public at 35 but shot to 89 in the first few hours of trading. Have you ever wondered who actually gets the stock at 35? Or who gets Home Shopping Network—that hit 42 the first day—at the offering price of 18? One thing's for sure: you and I don't.

Getting stock at the offering price of a hot new issue is about as close as you can come to a no-risk way to get rich quick. You buy the stock at 18, sell it hours later at 42. There's no risk because the underwriters will almost never let a new issue go down significantly in the first few days of trading, by which time you're long gone.

So who gets these hot deals? Are they rationed out, a little for everybody? Is it the way Studio 54 used to be, where all the hopefuls would crowd outside on tiptoes, begging to be let in? (Steve! Pick me! Pick me, Steve!) No—but you're getting warmer. (Every so often a limo would pull up and someone would just waltz right in.)

The president of a medium-sized public company made $250,000 in the past year, he told me, "with stocks I didn't even know I'd bought." Sensing a story (don't ask me how I know these things, it just becomes second nature), I switched on my mental tape recorder, put up my hand as if to say, "Hold it right there," and asked him, "How?"

"How," he smiled, thinking I was pretending to be an Indian.

"No. How did you make all that money?"

"Oh," he said. "Well, you know we throw a lot of business Wall Street's way, in underwriting and pension fund management, and sometimes they'll call to tell me I've bought a stock. I don't ask them to do it; I guess it's their way of showing appreciation."

The stocks they've bought him are hot new issues; and by the time they've called him, they've already sold him out at a profit. If the stock should fail to rise as expected, they don't call him— they give the stock to one of the guys on tiptoes outside Studio 54.

The National Association of Securities Dealers (NASD), set up by an act of Congress as a self-regulatory body, has some rules about this. Stock in a hot deal may not be allocated to employees of the brokerage firm selling the shares or their relatives, nor to people generally who could be in a position to throw business the firm's way. So if a mutual fund were a big client of the un-derwriting firm, it could get shares, but the fund manager herself, or her husband, should not. Neither should the fellow with whom I was exchanging Navajo greetings.

By and large, the stock will be apportioned to the firm's best brokers to apportion to their best clients. The rich get richer. And sometimes the rules get bent.

Ordinarily, it is the new issues you can't get that you should buy, and the new issues your broker is trying to sell you that you should avoid.

JUNK BONDS. Any bond that yields a lot more than the going rate—because it's risky—is considered a junk bond. On the one hand, it may pay 13% or 14% when IBM bonds yield 9%. On the other hand, it may default. Some bonds start out solid but, as the fortunes of their issuers decline, turn into junk. (Bethlehem Steel was once the bluest of chips.) Other bonds are born junk, like the bonds issued by fledgling airline People Express. This is a fairly recent development, largely credited to Drexel Burnham's Mike Milken. Early on, Milken made a simple discovery: most bonds —even junky ones—don't default. What's more, the ones that do default may eventually result in less than total loss. So if you buy a diversified basket of bonds yielding 5% more than quality issues and 3 out of 100 of them go bust—well, you're still doing better than you would have had you bought a basket of 100 quality issues. Of course, if *half* your junk bonds defaulted one year, it would be a different story. The default rate on junk bonds was over 3% in 1986—a good year for the economy. What might it be in a really bad year?

KRUGERRANDS. One-ounce South African gold coins. See: Gold.

LBOs are leveraged buyouts. There you are working for IBM in the typewriter ribbon division, if they have one, and you are getting *really fed up* with some of the ways they do things. What's more, you think the company could be a heck of a lot more profitable if its assets were reorganized and if they got rid of 20,000 or 30,000 of their salesmen. So you go to a bank and borrow $50 billion to supplement your own $19,000 in life savings and offer $300 for each IBM share—$80 in cash and your personal IOU for the remaining $220.

IBM shareholders, impressed by your credentials and eager for the $300 a share, sell you 100% of the company. You immediately loot IBM's cash hoard to pay down some of your debt; and sell off its European, Asian, and South American operations to pay off some more. You sell IBM office buildings to a consortium of Canadian investors and simultaneously lease them back. After all this, you are the nearly debt-free owner of a substantially streamlined IBM, and you issue a memo telling people they can wear jeans and chew gum. (Actually, at the price Japanese securities are commanding as I write, it might be enough merely to spin off IBM Asia to eager Japanese stock-market investors. The rest of IBM you'd then have for free.)

For further instructions on leveraged buyouts, contact former

Treasury Secretary Bill Simon or the firm of Kohlberg Kravis Roberts & Co.

LIFE INSURANCE. See: Whole Life Insurance.

LIMITED PARTNERSHIPS. You and I are called limited partners because our risk is limited. We can only lose all we invest. The general partner, who actually runs the business, often invests little or nothing himself, but it would be he, not you, who would be named in a lawsuit over something the partnership did.

Limited partnerships are passé. Although they're still formed all the time, today's well-dressed executive invests in master limited partnerships.

See: Master Limited Partnerships.

LLOYD'S OF LONDON is not a company, but rather a confederation of 30,000 wealthy individuals worldwide. They are the silent partners whose collective tens of billions stand behind the insurance policies that Lloyd's several hundred syndicates write. If you have $150,000 in liquid assets and reasonably good table manners, you can join one or more of these syndicates. Yes, you put your entire fortune at risk by doing so—you really do. But Lloyd's members are only occasionally called upon to cover losses, let alone in amounts large enough to really hurt (though it happens). In most years, the premiums and investment income Lloyd's collects more than cover the losses it pays out. What's more, you can buy insurance—from Lloyd's, naturally—to protect you from oversize losses. The beauty of Lloyd's membership is that by merely pledging securities that continue to earn interest for you, you stand to earn an extra $20,000 or $30,000 a year (or more, depending on the size of your participation). If you think you might be interested, contact Lloyd's U.S. attorneys for more information—LeBoeuf Lamb Leidy & MacRae, 520 Madison Avenue, New York 10022.

The insurance business is cyclical, so the best time to join Lloyd's is when all the big insurers are hemorrhaging. By the time your application is approved, and you've flown to London to be formally sworn in, the market will already have begun to tighten—premiums will have begun to rise—and you will catch the good years of the cycle.

LOANS TO FRIENDS AND RELATIVES. "It is better to give than to lend," said British war correspondent Philip Gibbs, "and it costs about the same."

A better solution may be to offer to guarantee a bank loan. You are still on the hook if he or she defaults, but in the meantime the bank sends the nasty letters. What's more, the fear of a bad credit rating might actually do more to get the loan repaid than the fear of losing your friendship.

MASTER LIMITED PARTNERSHIPS, like regular limited partnerships, pass all profits through to the partners without first having to pay corporate income tax. But unlike regular limited partnerships—which typically have just a few dozen or at most a few hundred investors locked in to the partnership with no easy way out—*master* limited partnerships smell just like stocks. There are no minimum purchases, no suitability requirements, no partnership agreements to sign and notarize and—best of all—no barriers to bailing out at a moment's notice. Many trade on the New York Stock Exchange.

MLPs smell so much like stocks, in fact, that Congress or the IRS may decide that's more or less what they are and subject their profits to corporate taxation. In the meantime, however, everyone from Burger King to Mesa Petroleum to the Denver Nuggets has been spinning off to their shareholders profitable operations that would otherwise be double-taxed; and investors have been eagerly buying them for their hefty yields. An added incentive has been the hope that those yields will be classified as "passive income" (as opposed to "portfolio" income, like interest or dividends) and thus be available to sop up passive losses from prior years' tax shelters.

However this issue is decided, don't buy shares in a master limited partnership primarily for tax reasons. And don't be lured by high yields until you've ascertained what they represent. Are they your share in profits that will likely grow over the years? Or are they just a return of your own money, in disguise? An MLP that "yields" 14% a year isn't much of an investment if it's merely pumping out a seven-year oil supply but developing no new reserves. After seven years, you'd have gotten your money back, but there'd be nothing left. Your shares would be worthless. Far from earning 14% on your money, you'd have earned *no* return.

Many MLPs are offered to the public at yields in excess of actual profits. If earnings don't soon catch up, the advertised yield is bound to fall.

MINIWAREHOUSE PARTNERSHIPS build and operate self-storage facilities that are rented to individuals and small companies for whatever's outgrown their garage. As businesses, these inexpensive, low-maintenance structures often end up returning 8% or more on the cash put up to build them—a return that can grow with inflation (if there is inflation) as monthly storage rates rise.

But the warehouses warehouse more than junk. They also "warehouse" land. Typically, sites are chosen that, while only marginally desirable now, may in 10 years be worth much more. In the meantime, instead of sitting on raw land with no return, you and your fellow limited partners might earn 6% or 8% or 10% on your money, partially sheltered from taxes by depreciation. (Or, if a competitor opens up down the street, you might not.)

The late Gordon McLendon made a fortune on much the same principle, just in a different medium. Best known for his exploits in the early days of radio, his largest asset by the 1980s was a chain of several dozen drive-in movie theaters—no big deal until you realized they were in once-remote places that, over time, had come to be surrounded by skyscrapers. He claimed to have sold one of them in 1984 for $40 million.

I know of no drive-in-movie partnerships, but the three largest miniwarehouse syndicators are Shurgard Capital Group (999 Third Avenue, Seattle, WA 98104; 800-231-3955), Public Storage (Box 25050, Glendale, CA 91201; 800-421-2856), and Balcor/ Colonial (4849 Golf Road, Skokie, IL 60077; 800-422-5267). All are eager for your money, in chunks as small as $5000. All have been offering relatively conservative investments without a lot of leverage (but without much liquidity, either). All three charge 13% or more in sales and administrative fees up front and an annual fee for supervision, and then take a chunk of the profits, if there are any.

MONEY MARKET FUNDS are like checking accounts that pay interest. They're not federally insured but generally invest in short-term obligations of the federal government and large banks and corporations, so they're quite safe in all but the most dire circumstances.

Unless you're talking about parking a great deal of money, and leaving it parked for a long time, the operative word should be "convenience." Stick with your bank's money market account or with a money market fund tied to your brokerage account. (If you're in a high tax bracket, you may be interested in tax-free funds that operate like money market funds by investing in short-term tax-free bonds.) More important than searching for an extra half percent in interest is deciding what portion of your funds should be safe and liquid in a money market fund at all.

MORTGAGES. The first amazing thing to know is that when you take one out on your home, you are the mortgag*or,* not the mortgagee. The second amazing thing to know is that you can own mortgages as well as owe them. This happens when you sell your home to someone who persuades you to provide some of the financing. But if someone comes to you desperate for $20,000, nothing prevents you from lending it to him for a couple of years, at 14%, say, secured by his house, instead of to the U.S. Treasury at 7% (which is in effect what you do when you buy treasury bonds). Or lend it to him at three points over prime or at one-tenth your IQ (to be retested annually by a recognized testing service), or any which way you please. (Naturally, you'd want the advice of a competent attorney in drawing up the papers and looking into your state's usury laws, but that should be a closing cost—perhaps $200 or $300—you get the lender to pay.) This is more trouble than lending money to the U.S. Treasury, but more rewarding and not necessarily much more risky.

MOVIE DEALS. More than $1 billion was raised in limited partnerships from 1982 through 1986, much of it in $5000 chunks, to finance packages of Hollywood movies. This is less risky than backing a Broadway show. In most deals, investors are guaranteed to get their money back—eventually. But few sophisticated investors participate because the potential for profit is so modest. It's fun to be able to tell your date you have a piece of the movie you're watching; but after your broker takes 8.5% for selling the deal, and a further 15% or 20% in fees are taken off the top—not to mention all the costs and profit participations involved in actually making and distributing the movie—even a blockbuster partnership like the one whose 16 releases included *The Color of Money, Ruthless People,* and *Down and Out in Beverly Hills* can be expected to grow your money at little more than 15% a year, while others (even the one that included *Ghostbusters*) produce little or no return. There are many worse ways to have fun with your money, but better ways to invest it.

MUNICIPAL BONDS are issued by local governments. The interest they pay—with certain recent exceptions—is free of federal income tax and, for residents of that locality, free of local income tax as well. To chapter 5's New Yorker in the 59.7% tax bracket, an 8% New York City bond *really pays* 8%. An 8% certificate of deposit pays little more than 3%, after tax.

Four things you must always check when buying a municipal bond:

1. The creditworthiness of the issuer. Especially for long-term bonds, you probably want to stick with highly rated credits; and in any event, to be safe, spread your bets over a few different issuers (or buy shares in a municipal bond fund).
2. The call protection. Almost all municipals, even if they're issued for 30 years, are callable after 10—or sooner, under certain conditions. Particularly if you're buying the bonds above par, but even if you're not, you should have a clear understanding of when they may be called—and of the fact that, if interest rates drop, they will be.
3. The tax status. The new tax law divides municipals into

three types. First, and still the great preponderance, are those that are tax free. You want those. Second, and quite new to the scene, are those that are not (because, though issued by a local government, they are meant largely to assist some private enterprise). Forget about them. Third, and also new, are those that are tax free but count as a preference item in calculating the alternative minimum tax (see the footnote on page 193). If, as is likely, that's a tax you don't have to worry about (ask your accountant if you're not sure), then the extra yield these "AMT" municipals must offer to attract buyers is all gravy.

4. Price. You've got to—*got to*—shop around because, knowing that you won't, the bond departments of many brokerage firms will lull you to sleep with a modest commission and then run a knife through your heart with the spread. And you'll never even know it happened. (See chapter 8.)

To get the best price and a lot of good specialized advice, if you deal in quantities of $25,000 or more (and if you don't you should probably be in a municipal bond fund, if you're in municipal bonds at all), call Gabriele, Hueglin & Cashman (800-422-7435) and Lebenthal & Co. (800-221-5822), both in New York but with accounts throughout the country, and compare their offerings with your broker's. If you live in a high-income-tax state, it would also be a good idea to contact a local broker who specializes in the bonds of your state.

It's obviously most convenient to sell a bond to the broker in whose electronic vault it sits; but recently, on $500,000 face value of New York State zero coupon bonds, one well-known firm was offering $27,685, while Gabriele, Hueglin offered $29,750.

Think how much time you spend agonizing over whether to pay $199 for something out of the Sharper Image catalog you *know* you could get cheaper (and you know you don't need), and then try to spend half as much time, anyway, shopping around to buy, or sell, municipal bonds.

Note: You may not deduct interest incurred borrowing to buy

tax-free bonds. If you own any, the IRS will look harder than ever at any portfolio-interest deductions you claim.

MUTUAL FUNDS. Good idea. See: No-Load Funds; also Closed-End Funds; Index Funds.

NAKED OPTIONS. Here you sell someone the right to buy 100 shares of Johnson & Johnson stock from you at $95 each, say, figuring that between now and the time the option expires there's no way on God's earth J&J stock could ever reach $95, let alone anything higher. This is important, because you don't *own* 100 shares of Johnson & Johnson. You've "gone naked." (If you sold the option against shares you did own, your position would be "covered.") Let's say you were paid $287.50 (less your broker's share) for promising to sell Johnson & Johnson shares at $95. If the stock stays below 95—drops to 12, even—you simply keep the $287.50. If the stock rises to 100, you will be forced to make good on your promise. You will have to buy 100 shares of J&J at $100 each in the open market ($10,000) and then turn right around and sell them, as you promised, at $95 ($9500). This isn't so bad—you lost $500 on the stock but made $287.50 on the option (all of this before taking into account the brokerage commissions you'd have to pay along the way)—but what if Johnson & Johnson rose not just to 100 but, say, to 135?

The only sensible way to write naked calls—if there is a sensible way, and in truth there is not—is to do so on the solemn vow to buy those calls back at a modest loss as soon as the underlying stock begins to cross the price at which you're committed to sell it. But you won't do that. You will dig your heels in deeper when the stock hits 100 and, far from taking a modest loss, sell a few more calls. What goes up must come down, and all that. But people who dig in their heels frequently wind up digging their own graves behind them, heelful by heelful, as, in this hypothetical example, Johnson & Johnson climbs higher and higher.

Selling naked calls has all the disadvantages of regular short selling (except that you're not saddled with having to pay divi-

dends on the stock you've shorted)—namely, you can lose a fortune—and none of the advantages. If Johnson & Johnson does
fall precipitously, all you stand to gain is the same lousy $287.50
(less commissions) you were paid in the first place.

(You can also sell puts. Unlike a call, which gives someone the
right to buy a stock at a given price, a put gives him the right to
sell it to you at that price. You would sell a put if, say, Johnson &
Johnson were 90 and you were hoping to buy it at 80. By selling
someone the right to sell Johnson & Johnson to you at 80, you'd
pick up a little extra change. If the stock stayed above 80, you'd
keep that change. If it dipped below 80, you'd still keep it—but
have to fork over $80 for each share you had agreed to buy.)

NEW ISSUES. See: IPOs.

NO-LOAD FUNDS. Whether it's stocks or bonds you're after,
high risk or low risk, tax free or taxable, U.S. or international,
here's the way to get professional management, diversification,
and economies of scale at minimal cost. A mutual fund pools
your modest savings with those of others and invests the resulting
millions according to broad guidelines disclosed in its prospectus.

No-load funds are mutual funds that charge no sales commission (or "load") or back-end redemption fee. Study after study has
shown that they perform just as well, on average, as load funds,
which typically charge an 8.5% sales commission. Yet against all
reason, 70% of all mutual fund sales are of load funds. Merrill
Lynch alone reportedly collected more than $600 million in mu-
tual fund commissions in 1986.

True, some load funds do spectacularly well—but so do some
no-loads. True, too, some no-loads perform miserably—but so
do some load funds. Count yourself among the smart 30% and
this simple advice will save you $850 on every $10,000 you invest.

The first thing to do in choosing among the thousands of mutual funds is to rule out all the load funds and all the funds that

charge more than 1% a year in assorted advisory, administrative, and marketing ("12b-1") fees. That narrows the field considerably.*

The next thing to do is eliminate specialized funds that invest just in gold or in specific sectors of the economy (publishing or automotive products or technology), unless you believe you can guess better than a good broader-based mutual fund manager could which of these areas are most attractive at any given time. (It's likely you can guess as well, but can you guess better?)

Eliminate, too, funds that don't match your objectives. There's no point buying a tax-exempt bond fund if you're looking for long-term growth. There's no point buying an aggressive growth fund if you're looking to take only moderate risk.

And then examine the track records of those that are left. Many funds do brilliantly in rising markets but abysmally in falling markets because they take lots of risk. If you think you can call the major turning points in the market, you will want to buy them just as, after a few years' abysmal performance, they are about to shine. But this is not easy. In any event, beware buying a fund just because it's "hot." This year's big winner is frequently next year's big loser.

What you want, ideally, are funds that do a little better than most when the market as a whole is rising—and a little less badly when it's falling. There's no guarantee that they'll be able to do this in the future, but if they've managed to do it for 8 or 10 years in the past, you may have a leg up.

You can find such funds by perusing the special mutual fund surveys that *Forbes, Barron's, Money,* and others publish periodically and/or with the help of the *Handbook for No-Load Fund*

---

*A new reason to avoid funds with high advisory fees is that these are no longer deductible (although other fund expenses may be). Your fund may pay you 6% in dividends or interest (your share of what it earned), but it will report to the IRS that it paid you, say, 6.5% (your share of what it earned before deducting its advisory fee). You have to pay tax on such "phantom income." True, you also get to take that advisory fee as a miscellaneous deduction—but only if you itemize and, even then, only to the extent the sum of all your miscellaneous deductions exceeds 2% of your adjusted gross income.

Investors (Box 283, Hastings-on-Hudson, New York 10706—$25 including postage and handling).

Short of that, here are what may turn out to be several among dozens or even hundreds of decent choices for growth over the next decade. Really, the important thing isn't to choose the very best fund, which is possible only with hindsight anyway. It's to choose good performers (hard enough) *and then to invest in them,* month after month, year after year. It's not so much where you put your money as that you put it somewhere, rather than spend it, in the first place. Don't delay. If you can afford to put some money to work in the market for the long term but have yet to do so, choose two or three funds (and perhaps a closed-end fund or two) and begin investing—and determine to *keep* investing—*now.* If it appears to you the market is high as you read this (it certainly appears high as I write this!), start small—but start.

Vanguard Index Fund (Box 2600, Valley Forge, PA 19496—800-662-7447)—after all, *most* mutual funds will do a little worse than average (see page 213).

Mutual Shares and *Mutual Qualified Income* (26 Broadway, New York, NY 10004—800-344-4515).

Evergreen Fund and *Evergreen Total Return* (550 Mamaroneck Ave., Harrison, NY 10528—800-635-0003).

Fidelity Equity Income (82 Devonshire St., Boston, MA 02109—800-544-6666), which has begun charging a "low load" since I first began recommending it ten years ago, but which has also climbed more than 600% since then (as have Mutual Shares and Evergreen), so it's hard to strike it from the list.

Partners Fund (342 Madison Ave., New York, NY 10173—800-367-0776).

Twentieth Century Select (Box 200, Kansas City, MO 64112—800-345-2021).

Be sure to see also: Closed-End Funds.

OIL. You can invest in drilling partnerships, but the odds are lousy. Far better to buy shares in oil companies that may be selling for a fraction of the value of the oil and gas they've already found ("proven reserves"). There are no sales fees to pay or tax-time complications, and you can sell your shares (or borrow against them) on a minute's notice. Better still, why not let your mutual fund managers decide which oil stocks to buy and whether to be buying them at all?

OIL-LEASE LOTTERIES. The Interior Department holds bi-monthly drawings for the right to drill on federal lands. In a given lottery, as many as 500 or 600 parcels ranging from 40 to 10,000 acres may be up for grabs, and you have just as good a chance of grabbing one as Exxon. When you do win, Exxon rushes over and begs you to sell your lease for a million dollars. You waver and then say, "Okay."

That's the way it's sometimes portrayed, except that few of the leases are worth much, and the few that might be worth $50,000 or more attract hundreds or thousands of applicants, so your chances of winning are slim.

Enter any number of outfits eager to help you outwit the system. For a fat fee, often doubling the $75-per-parcel official application fee, they promise to identify leases that, though likely to be valuable, are also likely to be overlooked by most players. They'll handle the paperwork for you, they'll make all the decisions—all you have to decide is how many thousands of dollars you want to send them to wager on your behalf.

Save your money. But if you're interested in gambling this way on your own, write for the Interior Department's free brochure (Bureau of Land Management, Room 5600, Washington, DC 20240)—and be sure your phone number is listed, in case Exxon needs to reach you. Note that if you actually do win a lease, you must then pay the government $1 per acre per year to hold on to it—and that to dampen the carnival atmosphere, the Interior Department in 1984 began requiring the first year's rent along with your $75 application fee. It's refundable if you don't win (and you almost surely won't); but just having to come up with it has cut the number of applications. In 1982 there were 819,000 applications for 3160 parcels in Wyoming (the most active state); in 1986 there were "just" 194,000 applications for 2309 parcels. Of course, the drop in oil prices may have had something to do with it, too. The bad news, then, is that you can no longer apply for a lease with just $75; you have to deposit the first year's rent with your application. The good news is that with fewer people applying for each parcel, your odds of winning improve.

OPTION TENDER BONDS are long-term bonds with an escape clause. Every so often, according to a preset schedule, the issuer gets to change the interest rate—and you get the option of accepting that rate or cashing in your bond (tendering it) at par ($1000). They yield less than a true long-term bond, because of this escape clause, but a bit more than similar short-term bonds, because if you don't escape you spare the issuer the trouble of selling new bonds.

Interesting—but unless you're a professional bond manager who buys in million-dollar chunks, probably not worth the complication.

OPTIONS are great if you want to maximize your profit on inside information before they cart you off to jail or if you've got this perfectly legal hunch you can't resist playing. You've seen the new Commodore computer at a trade show, and you're just sure it will catch on. Instead of buying Commodore stock at $6 and doubling your money if it goes to $12, you buy out-of-the-money calls for 12.5 cents that give you the right to buy Commodore shares any time up until May for $10 a share. If Commodore does climb from 6 to 10 by May (how many stocks jump 66% in a few months?), you lose everything. (What good is the right to buy a stock at 10 that anybody else can buy at 10, too?) But if Commodore hits *12*, you exercise your right to buy it at 10 and immediately sell it for 12, making nearly $2 a share after commissions on each 12.5-cent investment. Instead of doubling your money, you sixteentuple it.

The problem is that, in those rare instances where you may actually succeed, you will inevitably be drawn to risk your winnings on another hunch, and another. Yet it is precisely those stocks on which options trade that are the ones a great many experts follow and in which you are unlikely to see something most of them have missed—let alone with sufficient frequency to overcome the handicap of the huge transaction costs that go with the game.

The key thing to remember about investing in options is that you are not investing at all, you are gambling. Over the long run, you will lose your money. Yes, $300 may "control" 100 shares of IBM—$15,000 worth of stock—giving you the right to buy it (if you've bought a call) or sell it (if you've bought a put) at a set price (the option's "strike price") up until a set date (the option's "expiration date"). But over the long run, you will get eaten alive by the commissions and spreads involved with each trade. Buy and sell that $300 call (well, it's $312.50 plus a $30 commission if you're buying, $287.50 less a $30 commission if you're selling), and before you say "Boo!" you're down $85—25%. It's a slot machine that takes $100 bills.

The other way to use options is to *reduce* risk. You wake up in the middle of the night with a premonition that the market will collapse. But rather than sell all your multiplicitous holdings, incurring transaction costs and taxes, you simply "sell the market short" by buying some market index puts. If the market goes down, your traditional holdings lose value, but your puts rise and shine.

Ordinarily, your puts will expire worthless because the market does not decline after all. Or it declines, but then recovers before you choose to take your profit. Or it declines, but by not enough to make your puts worth anything.

Hedging with options is a perfectly valid form of insurance. But like any insurance product, the odds in the long run are with the insurer.

See also: Covered Calls.

ORIGINAL-ISSUE-DISCOUNT BONDS are like zero coupon bonds (see page 252), only designed to make the accounting even more confusing. Instead of issuing them at $1000 a bond, like all the other red-blooded American bonds, these are issued at a discount. They pay interest like regular bonds but also have built-in long-term appreciation, like a zero coupon bond, as the value of the bond rises from its original issue price to its eventual $1000 value at maturity. Lest you treat that appreciation as a capital gain, the IRS requires that you pay tax on each year's imputed appreciation as if it were interest. If you should sell the bond before it's redeemed, the difference between what you actually got for it and the imputed price to which it should then have risen becomes your capital gain or loss. Fortunately, tax-sheltered accounts are spared having to worry about this.

PALs. The old tax shelters used lots of debt and depreciation to create losses that the 1986 Tax Act christened "passive activity losses" (PALs). Now the deductibility of those losses against ordinary income (like your salary) or portfolio income (like your dividends) is being rapidly phased out. To sop up the PALs that would otherwise go undeducted, syndicators have designed PIGs—passive income *generators*. These are real estate deals, among others, that use little or no debt. Instead, they buy properties for cash and distribute the operating income among the limited partners. With no mortgage to pay, there's often an 8% or 10% return to distribute that can be sheltered with losses from leftover tax shelters.

The same folks who got rich selling PALs will now install lights for their tennis courts selling PIGs. Before you buy, examine any deal strictly on its economic merits. What assumptions underlie the promised high yields? Are earnings from the enterprise, whatever it is, enough to produce those yields? Or do they depend on inflation to make all the projections work out? What if inflation *doesn't* come roaring back?

Here's a $6.6 million deal offered in units of $100,000— $25,000 a year for four years. The money will be used to acquire long-term leases to operate three parking garages in Manhattan. It projects "returns over nine years of 365% . . . *passive income* that may be used to offset other shelter losses." Of the $6.6 million investors put up, $885,000 immediately goes for sales commissions and legal fees and $530,000 immediately goes to the general partner to light his tennis court (total: 21%).

Thereafter, so long as the garages are able to raise their rates by 10% or 11% a year as projected (but expenses increase at under

5% a year), and so long as the garage leases can be sold after nine years for four times what was paid for them (never mind that they would now have nine fewer years to run), everything should work out as projected.

PENNY STOCKS, commonly defined as those selling for under $3 a share, fall into two broad categories: those initially issued for just pennies a share—a marketing ploy—and those that became penny stocks against their will.

The former are typically Canadian gold mining stocks and other ventures whose principal merit is that even a poor man can afford to buy 1000 shares and a dream. They are wildly speculative and burdened by back-breaking spreads. You are all but certain to lose money.

The latter are shares in real companies that have fallen close to or into the arms of bankruptcy, their once-lofty stocks commanding just pennies, or at most a few dollars, a share. These are highly speculative investments, but, often, not stupid ones. With Chrysler at 2¾ (presplit), all you could lose was 2¾. On the off chance it recovered, you could multiply your money 30-fold. The advantage of these stocks is that, unlike the others, no one is out promoting them. Quite the contrary—everyone is dumping on them. If Wall Street tends to overreact in both directions—and it does—these involuntary penny stocks may sometimes be the object of that overreaction.

Even so, you could lose a lot of money betting on the next Chrysler. The more conservative approach is to invest in a no-load fund like Mutual Shares (page 226) with a nose for value in the securities of fallen angels.

(It should be noted that a company worth $100 million could just as easily be divided into 1 million $100 shares or 500 million 20-cent shares. By itself, a low share price means nothing. Many British blue chips trade for just a dollar or two a share. In the United States, however, by convention, few healthy, well-regarded companies sell for less than $20, or certainly $10, a share; few tiny speculative companies sell for much over $10.)

PIGs—passive income generators—are investments designed to throw off income that can be matched against PALs—passive activity losses. See: PALs.

PREFERRED STOCKS pay a set dividend that will never rise —but will never fall, either, unless the issuing company gets a bad case of the mumps. They are like bonds that never mature.

The plain vanilla preferred stocks of healthy companies aren't very appealing because you're likely to be able to get nearly the same yield, free of local income tax, from long-term treasury bonds, which are safer, or from municipal bonds, which may be entirely tax free. You're also paying for a tax benefit you don't get: to corporations (but not individuals), preferred dividends are 80% tax free.

Preferred stocks in shaky companies may be more interesting. The yield is likely to be far more than you'd get on a safer investment, and corporate treasurers generally won't be competing with you to buy them—they'll stick with safer issues. You run the risk that the preferred dividend could be suspended; but no common stock dividends may be paid until the preferred dividend is restored—along with all the missed dividends that are in arrears, if it's a "cumulative preferred," as many are.

Of course, some companies go bankrupt, but even then your preferred stock may be worth something. It's in line after all the creditors and bondholders, but ahead of all the common shareholders. Given the market's talent for overreaction, you may find bargains among long-forgotten preferreds that have been dumped by discouraged shareholders.

It's probably best to leave all this to mutual fund managers equipped to analyze the securities in some detail. But if you are making your own investment selections, consider *convertible* preferreds. Like convertible bonds, they offer a degree of safety and high income along with the potential for price appreciation if things should go well. They're a conservative's way to play the market. Naturally, they are most appealing when the dividend is high and the "conversion premium" low. Who wants the right to convert a $50 share of preferred stock into six shares of a common stock currently selling for $4 each? What you want is a $50 preferred stock convertible into six shares of common stock worth $8 each. That way, the common stock need rise just a twitch for your preferred to get nudged up with it.

The last basic feature of preferreds to understand is that most, like bonds, are callable. The issuer has no *obligation* to redeem them (as a bond issuer does), but he often has the right to, at some specified price. The lower the shares are selling with relation to that price, the less likely they are to be called. Be wary of a preferred stock at 37 that can be called, come October, at 32. Even if it's not called, it's unlikely to go up much.

PREPAID TUITION PLANS, which go by a variety of names, are an increasingly popular way to make a cash payment now, while Jessica is still in Pampers, to avoid any further payments (except room and board and books) once she enrolls at Purdue. It's an appealing notion *if* you can find a plan that (a) guarantees that today's payment will cover tomorrow's cost, no matter how inflation may affect tuition; (b) is offered by an institution strong enough to honor that guarantee (colleges can go bust like any other institution—and will, if they make too many guarantees like this and the financial markets go against them); and (c) doesn't penalize you too heavily if your child should fail to gain admission or prefer to go somewhere else.

Such plans simplify your financial life ("Well, at least we have *that* out of the way") and provide an element of discipline many find helpful. Unlike a bond you could sell, or a savings account you could raid, there's no risk with one of these plans that the money will eventually be diverted to buy a sailboat.

There's also the government subsidy that underlies many of the plans: your savings may grow tax-deferred or even entirely tax free (the law is still unclear); and some states are considering subsidies of their own.

And there's this: If the plan you choose turns out, with hindsight, to have been a great bargain (because inflation zoomed and the college winds up taking a bath on its guarantee), well, you've obviously done well. And if the reverse proves true—the college actually winds up making a big profit on your money—that's not so terrible, either. The money has gone to a good cause. See: Charity.

PROGRAM TRADING is no alternative unless you have tens of millions of dollars, a large computer hooked up to some other large computers on the New York Stock Exchange floor, and a way to trade stocks with virtually no commission.

Program trading occurs when, for example, people have been bidding the price of S&P 500 futures contracts so high that somebody at Goldman Sachs says, "Hey, this is silly. The S&P 500 stands at 300 today, but people are paying huge premiums for the right to buy it at that price three months from now. Well then, I'll take that premium from them and, to lock in my profit, buy the S&P 500 at 300 today. I'll sell the futures contract and buy the actual shares it represents. Yes, it will cost me something to tie up my millions for those three months—but between the premium I'm being paid and the dividends I'll get, I'll have a guaranteed, can't-lose, locked-in profit."

I'm not saying guys at Goldman Sachs actually talk this way; I'm just trying to write it so I understand it.

So he turns on his computer and instructs it to do two things, very quickly, according to a program that was worked out long ago for just such a fortuitous occasion. First, the computer sells a zillion dollars' worth of S&P futures contracts to people willing to pay more than, mathematically, they're worth. Simultaneously, it buys a like amount of stock in the 500 companies that make up the index. This costs a zillion dollars, but Goldman can afford it. In 90 days, just as the futures contracts are expiring—at 350, say, because the speculators were right, the market really did zoom— Goldman will instruct its computer to buy back at 350 all the futures contracts it sold, for a whopping loss, while simultaneously selling all the stocks it bought, for an even more whopping gain.

If the market had plunged instead of soared, or if it had just treaded water, Goldman would still have had its can't-lose, locked-in, risk-free profit.

It works the same, only a bit more ominously, when the market is seized with fear and everyone is *selling* futures contracts, never mind how cheap. Big players may *buy* scads of undervalued futures contracts, while simultaneously selling a zillion dollars' worth of the actual stocks. Again a profit is locked in, no matter what the market does; but the pressure of all this selling could actually drive the market down—and thus increase the prevailing hysteria. At that point (the doomsayers would tell you), more short selling of the S&P 500 futures contract would take place, as computerized "portfolio insurance" programs kicked in, creating an even better opportunity for Goldman and others to execute mammoth programmed trades. Down, down spirals the market until it hits zero and bounces, lamely, like an English squash ball.

Everyone's pretty sure this will never happen, which is one of the few reasons it actually could.

PUBLICLY TRADED FUNDS. See: Closed-End Funds.

PUT-OPTION BONDS are a more general form of option tender bonds described on page 228.

PUTS. See: Options.

QUALITY is always good, but especially so when people get nervous. As in "a flight to quality." Quality is different from value, which is actually more to be desired. Lots of risky, low-quality investments may offer good value if you can afford the risk (was stock in the bankrupt Chicago-Milwaukee Railroad a quality investment at $11 a share in 1980? No, but neither was it to be sniffed at when it hit $78 the following year). The problem with quality is that it's rarely underpriced, particularly when everyone is fleeing to it. It may be better to flee to cash or to pick up quality stocks and bonds when there's no great concern over quality, so you don't have to pay much extra to get it.

RARE COINS. The Rothschilds started out this way—"old coins, rare coins, wonders of an ancient kingdom," they sang to their customers (at least in the Broadway re-creation)—but it is significant to note that they made their money dealing in them, not buying and holding them as investments. During inflationary times, you can make a great deal of money doing that—but you have to know how to buy them. With rare coins, it's not just the rarity that matters, it's the condition. A tiny nick in a proof Barber Half Dollar can cut its $5000 value by more than half.

Coin dealer James L. Halperin knows about this stuff. If you want to, too, write Heritage Rare Coin Galleries for *The NCI Grading Guide* (311 Market St., Dallas 75202—$29.95) or ask for a free copy of its *Numismatic Journal* (normally $5) and its cautionary pamphlet, *Important Information About Buying Coins,* which, naturally—these guys *are* coin dealers—is not cautionary enough.

At one coin show in November 1979, Halperin bought a 1913-S $10 gold piece from a dealer for $15,000, just after another major dealer had turned it down. *Later that same show,* he sold it to yet another dealer for $65,000. This is obviously an extreme; but if dealers themselves can have such varying views of a coin's value, what hope is there for the casual investor? Months later, at the very peak of the coin market, in April 1980, the same coin, which had passed through two more dealers' hands, finally landed in the safe of a private individual at a price of around $100,000. Seven years later, it would fetch about $35,000.

If you're not expert at judging the fully struck coin from the only nearly fully struck coin, watch out. If you're relying on an expert who stands to profit from your business, be equally wary. But even if you get what you pay for, the spreads are enormous —typically 25% to 50%.

(A new wrinkle is the Professional Coin Grading Service of Irvine, California, which has imposed something of a standard on the 200,000-odd rare coins it has so far graded, photographed, and then sealed in plastic. With some of the uncertainty removed, the market for these PCGS-graded coins is more efficient and prices are more reliably quoted and compared, so the spread has shrunk to "only" 10% or 20%.)

Coins are great to collect but dumb to invest in. "In the long run," says Halperin, "the collectors always seem to do better than the investors." They know what they're doing and *are* in it for the long run.

RAW LAND. Will Rogers's favorite investment. Just be sure to buy it in the path of a not-yet-announced highway. Or consider a participation in a miniwarehouse partnership.

See: Timberland.

REAL ESTATE. Funny, but most of the wealthy stockbrokers I know have most of their assets in real estate.

It comes in a million forms, ranging from your own home to shares in a company whose business is land development or even a company that may ostensibly be in some other business, but whose principal asset, purchased a century ago, is a city block in downtown Boston.

The preferred means of buying real estate in the first half of the decade, at least on cable TV, was with "no money down." All you needed was the cash for the tapes and seminars being offered by the no-money-down proponents. "Over 200 of our graduates now own more than $1 million of real estate each, using our methods," the promotional literature will say—never mentioning that they also owe more than $1 million in mortgages, the payments on which, in many cases, they are unable to meet.

REITs, or real estate investment trusts, are essentially high-yield, closed-end mutual funds that invest in real estate. The cash they receive in rent (if they're equity REITs, which own properties) or mortgage payments (if they're mortgage REITs, which finance them) is passed directly through to the shareholders and thus escapes corporate taxation. REITs were the bubble of the mid-seventies, as inflation caught builders and lenders by surprise.

I can't think of an easy way to evaluate the underlying values and prospects of a REIT (rhymes with beet), and so would either leave this to my no-load mutual fund manager or else wait until I read about one or two considered bargains by someone I trust, like *Forbes*.

RENTAL PROPERTIES. Unless the property you buy is occupied by a strong commercial tenant—Sears would be good—on a long-term, "triple-net" lease (meaning the tenant's responsible for the taxes, insurance, and all the expenses of operating and maintaining the property), you have to assume that owning income-producing property will be a part-time or full-time job. Never underestimate the cost of roof repair, drain and gutter unclogging, or the amount of damage that can be done by a small pet.

RESEARCH AND DEVELOPMENT DEALS have lost most of their appeal now that losses can't readily be written off against income, and profits, if they're achieved, aren't accorded favored treatment as long-term capital gains. But whatever the tax advantages or lack thereof, there's something awfully satisfying, at least to a nonscientist, in financing research and development.

The billions of dollars' worth of these deals Wall Street put together in the early to middle eighties took the form of limited partnerships aimed at well-heeled investors willing to put up a minimum (typically) of $25,000 to $150,000.

See: Chapter 11.

SAVINGS ACCOUNTS. See: Bank Accounts; Cash; Certificates of Deposit.

SAVINGS BONDS. See: U.S. Savings Bonds.

SCRIPOPHILY. A great hobby for stamp collectors with eye strain, scripophily is the collection of otherwise-worthless stock and bond certificates.

"In 1979," reported *US News & World Report,* "New Hampshire antique-stock dealer George LaBarre paid $100 apiece for 89 Standard Oil of Ohio certificates issued around 1880. He sold the documents, which were signed by company president J. D. Rockefeller and secretary Henry M. Flagler, for $275 apiece. In June 1986, a similarly signed certificate sold for $3,500."

Check Grandma's attic—though most old stock certificates, not signed by legendary figures, go for just a few dollars.

Write for a copy of the latest LaBarre catalog (Box 746, Hollis,

NH 03049) and/or R. M. Smythe's auction catalog and quarterly journal, *Friends of Financial History* (24 Broadway, New York 10004).

SECTOR FUNDS. Fidelity pioneered these and now has one for just about any group of stocks you can think of. If you somehow know that gold stocks or computer stocks or life insurance stocks are going to be hot, you can buy them as a group, with the specific stocks selected by Fidelity's experts in each field. Naturally, the best time to buy into one of the sector funds is when its group is in the doghouse. Each dog generally has his day. Fidelity even lets you short these funds, so that if you felt the run-up in broadcasting stocks was overdone, you could short them as a group. Just how you are to know which groups are headed which way, I'm not quite sure, but if you're willing to pay a 2% load to jump into the sector fund pool, and $10 each time you switch your money from one of the 35 funds to another, and 1% when you finally decide to get out, Fidelity is there to serve you (800-544-6666 or 617-523-1919). Vanguard (800-662-7447 or 215-648-6000) and Financial Strategic Portfolios (800-525-8085 or 303-779-1233) charge less to play but have smaller pools.

SELLING SHORT. You see a stock that's ridiculously overvalued and you sell it. If you don't own it, you sell it anyway. That's called selling short. Your broker will arrange for you to borrow the shares from someone who does own it (and then from someone else, if the first lender needs it back) and you can ordinarily take as long as you want to return it. The broker doesn't mind: in addition to his commission, he holds the cash you get for selling the stock and earns interest on it.

If the stock you're short goes down, you can buy it back for less than you sold it for, return it to its rightful owner, and keep the profit. (You will, however, have to pay tax on the gain, which is considered a short-term gain even if you'd been short the stock 12 years. Right now, that's academic; but one day, the difference between short-term and long-term gains will reappear.)

If the stock you're short pays a dividend, you won't get it—you'll pay it. Your broker will transfer it from your account to the account of the fellow from whom you borrowed it (who almost surely doesn't know it's been lent).

If the stock you're short goes up, you've got a problem. If it goes up a lot, you've got a big problem. Your broker will demand more collateral to be sure you'll be able to cover your short (buy the stock back and return it). If it keeps going up, you could run out of collateral or—which generally happens first—nerve. You throw in the towel, buy the stock back for triple what you were paid for it, and eat a big loss. Now, it's *really* ridiculously overvalued.

Sooner or later it will fall, but a lot of fortunes have been lost between sooner and later.

If you want to short a stock, try to buy puts instead. Your loss will be limited to the cost of the puts. You'll sleep better. (See: Options.) If puts don't trade on the stock you have in mind, make a note to short it only if it spurts up even higher in a huge gap— maybe 8 points in one day—on news reports of a "short squeeze." *That* may actually be the top and the time to short the stock—except, of course, that's precisely when most brokerage firms won't be able to handle the trade. "Sorry," they'll say. "We can't find anyone to lend the stock."

Most pros offer this advice: don't short a stock, no matter how overvalued, on the way up. Wait until the stock "breaks" and has begun to fall.

SILVER. Buy silver only if you have china and crystal of like caliber. Otherwise, stick to stainless steel.

In the original 1978 edition of *The Only Investment Guide You'll Ever Need,* I pooh-poohed gold as an investment for all but the very wealthy (for whom a small cache could serve as insurance). Although this advice looked a little dumb for a while as gold tripled, I still believe it to be basically sound.

In the 1983 revision to that book, I substituted for the gold a small cache of silver, noting that at a historically wide price ratio of 40 to 1, whatever gold did, silver was likely to do better. Well, now the gold/silver ratio stands at 60 to 1. Even so, I reiterate my view—not on the theory that my view has any merit (I think that's been proven), but on the theory that unless silver is found to be carcinogenic, I must eventually, at least briefly, be right.

SINGLE PREMIUM DEFERRED ANNUITIES. See: Annuities.

SINGLE PREMIUM LIFE INSURANCE is like an annuity that includes just enough life insurance to qualify for more favorable tax treatment. If you invest $20,000 in an annuity, it grows tax-deferred until you withdraw the money, like an IRA. If you invest $20,000 in a single premium life insurance contract (a one-time thing; there are no further premiums to pay), some of your money goes to pay for life insurance, but the rest accumulates cash value that, under current law, you can borrow without ever having to repay. It's like an IRA you don't have to wait until 59½ to withdraw from, and on which you *never* have to pay tax, so long as your withdrawals are in the form of policy loans.

Need some money for tuition or a new car? You can't borrow from your IRA, but you can borrow, at virtually no cost, from a single premium life insurance contract.

Just when Congress will lower the ax, and whether it will chop retroactively, is anyone's guess. If it does, choosing to tax such policy loans as withdrawals, you may decide you'd rather invest your money elsewhere. But once you buy such a policy, you're all but forced to keep it. There are surrender charges for dropping it in the early years; and all the interest the policy has earned becomes immediately taxable. So you're locked in to the insurer for the long pull, while the insurer, in most cases, is locked in to the high interest rate it enticed you with for only a year or two. If the general level of interest rates falls, so will the yield on your policy.* If the general

---

*If it falls far enough and you've borrowed virtually all the principal from the policy, you may be forced to pay more into it to keep up the life insurance benefits—not so much because you care about those benefits, though you might, as to assure the investment's tax-favored status as a life insurance policy. (This could also happen if the insurer's mortality experience proves worse than expected, and it raises its rates.)

level of interest rates rises, the insurer may or may not pass on all the benefit to you.

Call USAA Life (800-531-8000) for information by mail or, if you'd prefer to be taken to lunch (the cost of which will naturally be reflected in the price), contact a Northwestern Mutual agent. Hundreds of other companies also offer single premium life, many of them doubtless very good. But you can't interview them all, and comparing what they have to offer is all but impossible. Too much depends on how well they'll invest your money, how tightly they'll control their expenses, and how fairly they'll apportion their investment results between you, their locked-in customer, and new groups of policyholders they're trying to attract.

I suggest these two companies because USAA, dealing by mail, traditionally keeps its expenses low and policyholder values high; and because the Northwestern Mutual has traditionally done a good job investing its policyholders' money. Also, being mutuals, they don't have to decide how to divvy up earnings between policyholders and stockholders—the policyholders *are* the stockholders.

STAMPS. Philately will get you nowhere.

STAPLES. Buying toothpaste and tuna fish in bulk when they're on sale is a way to stretch $1000 to buy $1400 of the very same goods you'd have bought in the course of a year anyway.

STOCKS. See: Common Stocks; Preferred Stocks.

STRATEGIC METALS. Germanium, chromium, indium, magnesium, tantalum, molybdenum—all the things you need to make a really good ball bearing or fight a modern war. There is no practical way to speculate in these metals, other than perhaps to buy stock in a few of the mining companies that produce them. The buying of actual metals, with warehouse receipts proving that somewhere in London sits your ton of cobalt, is nuts-o. Between the spreads and storage charges, not to mention the cost of tying up all that money in something that pays no interest or dividends and might or might not actually be in that warehouse, you haven't got a prayer.

If you're a Saudi prince or a South African mining magnate, this might be something clever to do. But for the rest of us, if and when there develops a reasonably convenient way to speculate in these things, it will be because the prices have been making headlines and going out of sight—just the time not to buy.

STRIPS. These are zero coupon bonds, formed by "stripping" a big treasury bond issue into a lot of little zero coupon bond issues —one for each promised semiannual interest payment and one more for the principal amount to be repaid at maturity (page 114). STRIPS stands for "separate trading of registered interest and principal of securities." They are very much like CATS (Salomon's "certificates of accrual on treasury securities") and TIGRs ("treasury investment growth receipts").

See: Zero Coupon Bonds.

TAX CERTIFICATES. Now this is interesting. Every municipality has its own rules, so you'll have to check it out yourself, but here's how it works in Miami. Property taxes are due March 31 of each year. If they still haven't been paid by June 1, the county says, "Well, gee. We're owed this $2654.91, and we want it." Rather than take the guy's house away, it creates a "tax certificate," in this case for $2654.91, and during the first few days in June auctions it off—and thousands of others like it. You go to the auction with cash or a cashier's check and bid on the right to pay the delinquent taxes. You don't bid dollars, you bid interest rates—namely, the lowest rate you'd be willing to accept. The bidding for each tax certificate starts at 18% and goes down from there. Let's say you bid 16.24% and win. That means you must pay Dade County, then and there, the $2654.91 that was delinquent. But it also means that the delinquent property owner must pay *you* the $2654.91 plus interest within two years if he doesn't want to lose his house. (Don't worry; you never have to meet him. He pays it off down at the tax collector's office, which pays you.) He can pay sooner if he wants, but you are guaranteed a minimum of six months' interest even if he redeems the certificate the next day. Thus, for anywhere from six months to two years you'll be earning 16.24% annual interest.

Not surprisingly, some investors go to these public auctions year after year and earn far more than they could from a savings account.

You must research the rules thoroughly for your particular area (talk to people down at the property tax department, to real estate agents, mortgage lenders, a local real estate attorney, and to the sharp little old lady sitting next to you at the auction), but in Dade County, anyway, here are the negatives. The first is that you have to attend a boring auction for hours on end, until you've spent all the money you intended to—which is the second negative. You can't just buy one neat $50,000 chunk (although a single year's delinquent taxes on some commercial properties may be that large and larger); you have to deal in these odd little increments—and then keep track of them as they're paid off. The third negative is that the term of the investment is uncertain—six months to two years—and that, in the meantime, the certificates are illiquid (although you can endorse them over to others or pledge them as collateral).

Other than that, the risks are not bad. One is that the year you finally decide to try this, so many other people will have caught on that, instead of yielding the 16% you were hoping for, the bidding will go too low to be of interest and you'll have wasted your time. The second risk is that you'll snag a portfolio of 16% tax certificates at a time when two-year treasury bonds are yielding just 7%—but that something awful will happen that sends interest rates to the moon, and you'll be stuck earning "just" 16% while everybody else gets 40%.

The final risk is that you won't get paid back. After all, if the property owner couldn't pay his taxes when they were due, who's to say he'll be able to pay them—plus interest—two years later? In Miami, at least, this is the kind of "risk" auction attendees dream of. Because if your certificate is not redeemed, you get the property free and clear—wiping out all other claims against it. There are very few properties not worth more than two years' property taxes; most are worth 40 or 50 times the tax. This is why tax certificates—in Miami, at least—are almost always paid off within two years. If the property owner himself doesn't redeem the certificate, the bank holding his mortgage will, to protect its investment.

Check the twists and risks in your area carefully—the game isn't always this attractive or clear-cut. But for someone willing to do a little research, and with the time to acquire and keep track of a portfolio of little gems, this could be a rewarding exercise.

TIMBERLAND. Money doesn't grow on trees, but trees grow and can be sold for money. Until passage of the new tax law, that revenue was treated as a long-term capital gain. Now, it's treated as ordinary income—and the expenses you incur cultivating and maintaining the land prior to harvesting may not be deductible against other income as it used to be.

Even so, for the (very) patient investor who loves the outdoors, 100 or 1000 acres in the Southeast, at perhaps $200 an acre in mid-1987, down from $450 at the peak in 1979, could make sense. The land may gradually become more valuable, the timber itself may become more valuable (especially at the rate we seem to be poisoning forests), and in the meantime, it just keeps growing without having to be fed, lassoed, or harvested except when you choose to.

An intelligent investment of this sort would take a lot of homework. You might wish to contact the trust departments of a couple of southern banks for their counsel and for possible management of your land. But remember, kids: only you can prevent forest fires—and if you don't, you're out of luck. You can't buy fire insurance on timberland.

TREASURY BILLS, NOTES, AND BONDS. Safer than airbags, these are obligations of the U.S. government issued for up to a year (bills), 2 years to 10 years (notes), or 30 years (bonds). When you hear talk of "the long bond" yielding such and such a rate, that is the interest rate you can currently get by buying the U.S. Treasury's latest 30-year bond—the bond that has the longest maturity. Each time the treasury issues a few hundred million dollars in new 30-year bonds, *that* bond becomes "the long bond."

Treasury securities are not subject to local income tax (which helps a lot in a place like New York or Minnesota) but *are* subject to federal income tax. The one twist here is that treasury bills (but not notes or bonds) are issued at a discount (you'd pay $9500, say, for the minimum purchase of 10) and redeemed at par ($10,000). It's the evaporation of that discount that represents your interest. So if you buy the bills early in the year and they don't mature until just after the start of next year, there's no tax to pay on the interest until April 15 of the *following* year. People get awfully excited over this slight tax-deferral opportunity. Yet it's just when the tax deferral is most alluring—because interest rates are high, and having an extra year's use of the tax obligation seems most valuable—that you should perhaps consider locking in a high interest rate not for a few months or a year, with a T-bill, but for several years—or 30—with a treasury note or bond.

If you do buy a 30-year bond, that doesn't mean you have to hold it for 30 years. You can sell it any time just by calling your broker. But what you'll get, six years from now, say, depends on the general level of interest rates at the time. Say you paid $1000 for a bond that yields $80 a year—8%—but in the meantime rates have shot up, so that nobody wants to buy a bond that pays just 8%. To sell it, you'll have to let them have it at a price low enough—perhaps $850 instead of the $1000 you paid—so that the $80 a year it pays *is* attractive. (Your $150 loss is deductible.) On the other hand, rates might have fallen over the years. In that case, someone might eagerly pay you $1100 for your bond. That $100 profit is a taxable gain (subject to local as well as federal tax).

Treasury securities are safe and liquid. There's a very narrow spread involved in buying and selling them. And unlike most other bonds, they're not callable. If they say they'll pay interest until 1995 or 2003 or whenever, they really will.

As for short-term money, unless you're talking about lots of it, it's probably easier just to put it into a savings account or money market fund than to buy 90-day treasury bills and "roll them over" every three months. Except on really large transactions, your bank or broker is likely to charge $25 or $50 each time, which cuts deeply into whatever interest rate and tax advantage there may be buying them. (To save the service charge, you can buy your bills directly from a Federal Reserve Bank—call or write the one nearest you or in Washington for instructions and forms.)

Take a look at the "Treasury Bonds, Notes, and Bills" listing in *The Wall Street Journal* to see what treasuries of different maturities are yielding (once your eyes focus, you'll find this in the right-hand column). Note that prices of treasury bonds and notes (but not bills, which are in a separate section below) are quoted in a strange way. A quote of 98.10 does not mean the bond is selling for 98.10 cents on the dollar, as you'd expect— $981.00 for a $1000 bond. Rather, treasury bonds trade in "32nds," and the number after the decimal point—which you'll notice is never higher than 31—is the number of 32nds. Thus, a treasury bond quoted at 98.10 is selling for "ninety-eight and ten thirty-seconds percent" of its $1000 par value. Reason enough, it's always seemed to me, to steer clear of treasuries. (Actually, you can all but ignore the prices and the 32nds. Just tell your broker how much you want to invest and ask what rate of interest you can get on bonds of various maturities. Chances are he or she won't want to talk about 32nds, either. Just be sure you understand the difference between "current yield" and "yield to maturity." See: Bonds.)

UNIT TRUSTS are mutual funds that buy a fixed basket of securities at the outset—typically, municipal bonds—and then just hold on. You pay a 4% sales charge to invest and then over the years receive your proportionate share of the interest and principal those bonds pay and repay.

For your 4% you get diversification. You may also sell your shares back to the sponsor at any time for their then-current market value. The sponsor doesn't mind—that just means he gets to sell them to the next guy at a second 4% mark-up. Because of that mark-up, these trusts are aggressively marketed. But you should buy no-load bond funds instead. Only if you're planning to hold the trust a long time might you come out better by paying the 4% up front but avoiding the annual management fee of a no-load fund.

But I doubt it. In the first place, how likely is it, really, that you'll sit with this investment for 10 years? (What if it specializes in Massachusetts municipals, which are not subject to Massachusetts income tax, but you one day move to California? What if you want to use the money to start a business or buy a house?) Second, why pay 4% in sales fees when you can pay that same 4%, over a period of years, for active management? There's always the chance—admittedly, slim—that management of a bond fund may actually be worth something.

And there's one other problem. If you're in the unit trust business, you want to attract buyers by offering an eye-catching yield. Might you not be tempted to secure such a yield by loading up your trust with low-quality (and therefore high-yielding) securities? By the time anything goes wrong, if it ever does, you'll very likely be long gone.

Or maybe not. Less than a year after Minneapolis-based Miller & Schroeder issued a municipal bond unit trust in March 1986, *Forbes* reports, the 9.84% tax-free return it was sold with had fallen into alarming disrepair. Despite a generally favorable economy, 19% of the bonds in the portfolio were either in default or in serious trouble.

U.S. SAVINGS BONDS. Not just for babies anymore, but of particular interest to small savers. Their guaranteed minimum yield, currently 6% if you hold them five years, makes them something of a deflation hedge; their link to 85% of the five-year treasury rate makes them a modest inflation hedge, should interest rates rise; and they have two tax advantages. First, they're free of local income tax. Second, they offer a choice. You can pay federal income tax as interest is accrued each year (good if you or the baby are in a low tax bracket) or defer it all until the bonds are finally cashed in. What's more, you can generally renew maturing bonds to keep deferring the tax—and then trade them in for series HH bonds, deferring it yet another 10 years.

Savings bonds cost half their face value, so you can buy one for as little as $25—half the $50 that will be paid when the bond is redeemed in 12 years. You don't have to wait 12 years to redeem it (although you do have to wait 5 years to get the full rate of interest), and you may get more for it than $50 if interest rates have risen in the meantime. Check your local bank for details; or if you have a question it can't answer, contact the Bureau of Public Debt, Parkersburg, WV 26106-1328 (phone: 304-420-6112).

With all the talk of "HH" and "EE," you might assume there are dozens of different kinds of U.S. savings bonds. Actually, there are just these two—EE and HH, and HH bonds can only be acquired in exchange for EE bonds. Unlike EE bonds, HH bonds pay semiannual interest that is subject to federal (but not local) income tax. But it's only when you cash in the bonds themselves that all the untaxed EE interest you accumulated is finally subject to tax.

UNIVERSAL LIFE INSURANCE is a form of whole life that separates the insurance and savings elements and lets you decide, within limits, how much to pay in premiums each year. Don't blindly accept the interest rates at which the ads say your cash value will compound; they may actually be lower if the insurance component of the policy is higher than it should be or if an annual administrative fee is charged but not figured into calculation of the yield. Also, beware high yields that rest in part on high-yielding junk bonds and high yields that are high now but can quickly fall.

See also: Whole Life; Single Premium Life.

VARIABLE LIFE INSURANCE is universal life with the added twist that the cash build-up, and sometimes the death benefit, of your policy varies with the success or failure of the insurer's investments in the stock market. Buy term insurance and invest the difference in mutual funds of your own choosing—either in a regular, taxable account or (if you don't mind trading liquidity for tax deferral) under the umbrella of an IRA or other retirement plan.

VULTURE FUNDS. "Swift as an eagle," the nine-year-olds at Ethical Culture School in Manhattan used to cheer, "sharp as a vulture. Hooray, hoorah for Ethical Culture." Sure, and then they grew up to be real estate syndicators. A vulture fund is a real estate limited partnership specializing in distressed properties in terribly overbuilt places like Houston, Denver, and Oklahoma City (and Phoenix and Tampa and...). Even when you add in the sales fees and other transaction costs, you'll do well if these properties recover fast enough. If they don't, some other vulture will come along and eat you for lunch. Among the companies offering such funds in mid-1987 were Angeles Corp. in Los Angeles (800-421-4374), August Financial Corp. in Long Beach (800-821-3332), and Integrated Resources in New York (800-221-2627).

WARRANTS are options. But unlike the options that have their own page or two of prices in *The Wall Street Journal* each morning—short-term puts and calls created by bookies for clients who want to place bets—warrants are calls created and sold to the public by the underlying companies themselves, often with several years, not just several months, to run. This doesn't vest them with any moral superiority; typically, they're thrown in as a speculative kicker to help sell an issue of new shares to the public. With warrants, as with options, you're not buying a stake in some company; you're making a bet its stock will go up.

WHOLE LIFE INSURANCE is term insurance plus a relatively low-yielding but tax-deferred savings plan. If you hold the policy until death, the interest your cash value accrues is never subjected to income tax, only to estate tax. And under current law, you can without penalty or taxation borrow it from the policy (though the deductibility of interest on such loans is being phased out unless you can prove you used the borrowed funds to make investments). You never have to pay the loan back; it's simply subtracted from the death benefit your heirs receive.

Whole life forces you to save by penalizing you heavily if you drop the policy in the first few years. One big minus is that despite good intentions, many people do wind up dropping the policies and suffering that penalty. Only if you really do keep a whole life plan in force for 10 or 20 years may the interest it pays on your savings become moderately competitive. Even then, a bout of inflation can ravage its value. Buy term insurance and invest the difference.

See also: Single Premium Life; Universal Life; Variable Life; Chapter 4.

WINE, I know nothing about. (*Whine* is another matter.) Wasn't it I, after all, who bought a case of Beaujolais—and put it away to age? It was a big deal when James Bond unmasked his foe on that railroad dining car by observing him order red wine with fish, but believe me, aging Beaujolais is by far the bigger faux pas. The only thing I know for sure is that for the price of a single bottle of red wine at a restaurant you can buy a case of something that, stored properly, could one day impress the heck out of the bowling league. Oh, yes; avoid screw-off caps.

See also: *Liquid Assets: How to Develop an Enjoyable and Profitable Wine Portfolio* by William Sokolin (Macmillan, 1987).

WORLD BANK BONDS. Who wants to lend to the U.S. Treasury when he can have the whole world in his debt? Actually, though triple-A rated, World Bank bonds are perceived as riskier than treasury bonds and so pay a higher yield. The only problems are, first, that they could conceivably *be* riskier, but, more to the point, they are subject to local income tax. In many states, therefore, outside of a tax-sheltered account, the extra interest they pay goes straight to taxes. (You'll find current yields on the same page as treasuries in *The Wall Street Journal*.)

WRITING OPTIONS. See: Covered Calls.

X-DIVIDEND STOCKS. If you see a stock marked with an x in the newspaper, it means it's too late to buy it if you want to get its most recently announced quarterly dividend. See page 152.

YOUR CAREER. If you're young, this is your biggest asset— your future earning power. Protect it with disability insurance and computer skills or a second language or a course in better communications skills or even a health club membership (if you use it) could prove far more valuable than 100 shares of stock.

YOUR OWN BUSINESS. This is what America—and getting rich—are all about. With rare exceptions, people don't get rich speculating in the financial markets. They get rich by scraping together enough to open their own business and then working fourteen hours a day, six or seven days a week for five or ten years to make it succeed. The risks and difficulties should never be minimized—this is not for everyone!—but there are 14 *million* small businesses in America, so neither is it exactly an impossible dream.

One of many upbeat books you can read to get you going is Sandi Wilson's *Be the Boss: Start and Run Your Own Business* (Avon Books, $3.95).

ZERO COUPON BONDS pay no interest and so don't cost very much. Their sole value comes from the promise that at maturity, years from now, they will be redeemed for $1000. Even so, the "imputed" interest at which they're geared to grow is taxed, so they're poorly suited for all but tax-sheltered accounts (for which they can be very handy) or as gifts to zero-bracket taxpayers (children under 14 may currently receive up to $500 in investment income annually free of federal income tax). They're also subject to spreads of up to 10% or more, so shop around as best you can, both buying and selling, and *don't* buy if you aren't planning to hold on for a long time.

With a zero, you're spared the trouble of reinvesting semiannual interest payments—a nuisance if they're small. And the bond is geared, by virtue of its eventual ascent to $1000 at maturity, to compound at a certain rate—say, 9%. With a normal 9% bond you're assured of 9% interest on the bond—but what kind of interest will you earn on *that?*

Fine point: Just because a zero sells for a fraction of its $1000 par value, don't assume it can't be called. Some zeros are callable according to an "accretion schedule" set forth in their prospectuses when they're first sold. Be careful about buying callable zeros for more than their then-current call price.

ZERO COUPON CONVERTIBLES. When priced attractively, these can be good for your retirement fund. You're assured they will appreciate to their full $1000 par value at maturity (assuming the issuer doesn't go broke); but if the common stock into which they're convertible appreciates faster, so will your bond.

Convertible zeros, like regular zeros, shouldn't be bought for regular taxable accounts, because they pay no interest in cash but are taxed as if they did.

They're most attractive when selling at just a slight premium to their conversion value. Seagram's zero coupon convertible sells for just $360 at this writing, yet is convertible into 4.61 Seagram common shares worth $353. You pay a $7 premium for the guarantee that even if Seagram's stock goes into the tank, you'll get $1000 for your bond in March 2006—a modest 5.5% compounded rate of return. You get the additional privilege of being able to redeem the Seagram bond each year at a price that starts low but gradually rises to par.

Ask your broker for a list of zero convertibles, their conversion ratios (how many shares of stock you're entitled to per bond), call features, and redemption options. In addition to Seagram, a handful of other companies have issued these bonds—Merrill Lynch, Waste Management, Beverly Enterprises, Staley Continental, National Medical Enterprises, Trinity Industries, G. Heileman Brewing, and Lomas & Nettleton. One broker specializing in this area is Edward J. Lovellette at Plenge, Thomas & Co. in Phoenix.

But remember: if the underlying stock is already trading at lofty levels, there may not be much appreciation potential for your bond (buy *low,* sell high); and if the issuer goes broke, the guaranteed redemption feature of the bonds may be honored only in part, if at all.

AFTERWORD

Let's sum up. Spend less than you earn. Buy low, sell high. Cut your own hair with one of those Brookstone doohickies. Diversify. Stick with no-load and closed-end mutual funds, and run the other way when someone you don't know calls out of the blue to make you rich. If you went to college together and he has a grandmother, run faster.

What have I left out?

The main thing, I think, is that you can—and must—take responsibility for your own affairs. It's fine to get help—I hope this book has provided some—but ultimately it's your money and your future. The more you pay others to take it over for you, the less you may be left with. (This is even more true now that financial and tax advisory fees are deductible only to the extent they, and your other miscellaneous deductions, exceed 2% of your adjusted gross income.)

"'Your purpose,'" a well-known San Francisco financial planner was quoted in *The Wall Street Journal* as having told a group of fellow financial planners, "'is to get up before [potential clients] and confuse them. And step two is to create a dependency.'" (Step three, in many cases, is to start selling them things.)

If you earn six figures and need a good financial planner to sit you down and help you work through the sorts of overall planning we did in chapter 2 (you did do it, didn't you?) and to help you wriggle out of the tax shelter mess you got into before the tax law changed — swell. There are loads of competent financial planners to help you make sense of your finances. But until you internalize the plan, whether you worked it out with a 79-cent legal pad or a $2500 financial planner, it won't mean anything. You've got to make it *your* plan, and you're not likely to if you simply rely on someone else once a year to work it out for you.

Buying fancy exercise equipment is fine, but it's not enough. You've got to *pedal*.

Acknowledgments

This book is my own fault. Even so, I'm tremendously fortunate to have had over the years the support of scores of extraordinary people I can only begin to thank. Among the very most important to me: Clay Felker and Sheldon Zalaznick; Joni Evans; Jesse Kornbluth, Marie Brenner, Scot Haller, and Jane Berentson; Murph and Nancy Levin, John Kraus, Peter Burns, the Zofnass clan, the Shutzers, the Bortzes, Ken Smilen, Laura Sloate, and Matt Nikitas; Rob Fleder, Jim Morgan, and John Rezek; Walter Anderson and David Currier; John Hawkins and Jerry Rubin (not that Jerry Rubin, the real Jerry Rubin); David Hollander, Arthur Lubow, Tom Moore, Bill Stern, Stan Watson, and Don Trivette; Mom and Steve. Warm thanks to them all and, with specific reference to this book, to Fred Hills, Dick Wagner, Bill Krems, and George Potter. If only I'd ever been able to make them a little *money*.

Index

261

ABOUT THE AUTHOR

Andrew Tobias is a graduate of Harvard College, where he ran the student business conglomerate, and Harvard Business School. In addition to writing best-selling books, he is a popular speaker, a contributor to several national magazines, and the author of *Managing Your Money*, the leading computer software in the field of personal finance.